Georgia
Entertains

Built in 1871 to replace an older structure destroyed in the Civil War, the famous lighthouse at St. Simons is now the home of the Coastal Georgia Historical Society. Drawing courtesy of the Coastal Georgia Historical Society, by artist Barbara Mueller

Georgia Entertains

Margaret Wayt DeBolt

with

Emma Rylander Law *and* Carter Olive

RUTLEDGE HILL PRESS
Nashville, Tennessee

Published in Nashville, Tennessee, by Rutledge Hill Press, 513 Third Avenue South, Nashville, Tennessee 37210.

Previous edition of *Georgia Entertains* published by Donning Company / Publishers, Norfolk, Virginia, as *Georgia Sampler Cookbook* in 1983.

Library of Congress Cataloging-in-Publication Data

DeBolt, Margaret Wayt, 1930-
  Georgia entertains / Margaret Wayt DeBolt with Carter Olive and Emma Rylander Law.
  p. cm.
  Rev. ed. of: Georgia sampler cookbook. ©1983.
  Includes index.
  ISBN 0-934395-74-8
  1. Cookery—Georgia. 2. Cookery, American—Southern style.
I. Olive, Carter. II. Law, Emma Rylander III. DeBolt, Margaret
Wayt, 1930-   Georgia sample cookbook. IV. Title.
TX715.D3143   1988   88-6721
641.5—dc19   CIP

1 2 3 4 5 6 7 8 — 93 92 91 90 89 88

Manufactured in the United States of America

For the good cooks of Georgia,
past and present,
and for all who have
graciously shared treasured recipes.

A Way of Life in Georgia

We try to maintain a way of life in Georgia, as well as saving and restoring our buildings, because we feel that some things from the past are worth keeping.

—Dr. Tucker Bryson, Washington

Southern "Receipts"

This book is so full of good dishes to sample
I hope you will follow an old boy's example
And have a few hardy, brave souls in for dinner
Whose object is just to get loaded—not thinner
Then cook them a meal while nobody is looking
Of fattening, unreconstructed home cooking . . .
Serve sherry and port—toast the South's ancient glories
I'll pour the corn whiskey—and tell a few stories
Let's cherish the good things while we still possess them
and end with the toast "To the Ladies, God bless them!"

—Johnny Mercer, From Savannah Kitchens

Contents

The Sidney Lanier Cottage, 935 High Street, Macon, was the birthplace of one of Georgia's most beloved poets in 1842. Lanier, best known for his "The Marshes of Glynn" and "Song of the Chattahoochee," died in 1881. His former home is now open to the public and is the headquarters of the Middle Georgia Historical Society.

"Out of the hills of Habersham,
Down the valleys of Hall,
I hurry amain to reach the plain,
Run the rapid and leap the fall . . ."
—Song of the Chattahooche

"Vanishing, swerving, evermore curving again into sight,
Softly the sand-beach wavers away to a dim gray looping of light,
And what if behind me to westward the walls of the woods stand high?
The world lies east: how ample, the marsh and the sea and the sky!"
—The Marshes of Glynn

Lanier was supposedly inspired to write his most famous poem while a guest at the home of his brother-in-law, Henry C. Day, of Brunswick.

Georgia Entertains

"Southern cooking." The very words conjure a happy association of warmth and hospitality as well as a distinctive regional cuisine. One sees in memory the cool, pleasant dining room of the Savannah townhouse, with its antique sideboard of family silver and old china, its polished table set for the noon meal with shad or gumbo. One thinks of hearty plantation breakfasts, oyster roasts on a brisk spring evening, tailgate picnics on campus, election barbecues, debutante parties, and the colorful buffet of the holiday open house.

The phrase recalls the food which made Dixie and Georgia famous: chicken, fried or spicy in a rice dish; hearty, thick soups on a chill day; the homey scent of warm bread; vegetables from the garden; the first ripe fruits of another lazy summer. One remembers the checkered tablecloth at the church homecoming; the fun of picnics and potluck suppers and swapping special recipes afterward; the prize-winning relishes, July's jewels under glass, at the country fair.

The famed foods of the state have grown out of its history and geographical variety, from the north Georgia mountains and rolling middle Georgia hills, to the tidal Low Country: game, farm produce, peanuts, peaches, watermelon, seafood. Recipes trace its British heritage, with influences from the native Indians, Austrians, Huguenots, and later ethnic immigrations.

Because the New South is a cosmopolitan area, blending hope with heritage, the legacy is a rich one. Our first book, *Savannah Sampler,* included many traditional favorites. This book is, by request, a continuation of that collection, along with many later contributions from friends. Again we have added a literal taste of the past in the hints and "receipts" of old Georgia cookbooks: "Restoration Receipts," one Savannah reader calls them.

We are grateful to all those who shared their memories and expertise. Witty, capable Emma Rylander Law, food consultant for our first *Sampler,* contributed many more of her personal favorites collected during her long professional career, and was working on this volume at the time she left us. Ably assisting with recipe selection and testing in her place has been our mutual friend Carter Olive, food-wise chef and former owner with his wife Barbara of Carter's restaurant in Savannah's historic district.

As with our first volume, the work has been an act of love for the state we all call home.

—Margaret Wayt DeBolt

Georgia's Early Cuisine

The early history of Georgia, the last English colony, is made more colorful by accounts of the foods which the courageous settlers enjoyed. It is known that the good ship Ann, on which founder James Edward Oglethorpe and his band of 130 men, women, and children reached the New World from England, carried beef, pork, molasses, flour, and rum among other provisions.

James Oglethorpe ordered a day of thanksgiving in Beaufort, South Carolina "out of his own purse" for the colonists, to celebrate their safe arrival there before continuing on to what is now Savannah. The menu consisted of "four fat hogs, eight turkeys, many fowl, English beef and other provisions, and a hogs' head each of punch and beer, and a large quantity of wine. . . . Everything was conducted in the most agreeable manner; no one got drunk, neither was there the least disorder among the crowd."

According to Armstrong State College history professor Dr. John Duncan, after the English reached Savannah the Yamacraw Indian Chief Tomochichi and his wife served the guests "roast, boiled pork, buffalo, beef, fowl, pancakes, and tea." On another occasion, Senawky, the chief's wife, gave the Reverend John Wesley milk and honey.

When Wesley, then a young Anglican clergyman, left Savannah in 1736, his friend Margaret Burnside gave him as a parting gift a small loaf of gingerbread and a pint of rum.

One early account speaks of the garden in which Oglethorpe planted "diverse sorts of seeds. . . . thyme, with other pot herbs, and several sorts of fruit trees," as well as "sage, leaks, skellions, cellery, liquorice, etc."

When Trustees Garden, the first public agricultural experimental garden in America, was established on what is now East Broad Street, it was planted with "oranges, olives, white mulberries, figs, peaches and many curious herbs," as well as grape vines.

In December 1734 Robert Parker wrote the Georgia trustees in London of his celebration of the holiday:

> Being Christmas Eve, my people desired leave to go out this morning to provide themselves a dinner, tho we have good Beeff, Porke, Cheese Flower ec. They are now come home and have brought 3½ Couple of Ducks 1 pair of Doves one Turkey and a fine Buck together with a fine young pig.
> . . . We are not altogether destitute of provisions when we have time to seeke, for if especially Turkeys Venison ducks and in plenty but very shy.

Although rum was prohibited in the early days of the colony along with slavery, Parker enjoyed his dinner with "Best Beer," ordering twenty hogsheads to be sent by "freight cheepe."

A Few Suggestions For Using This Book

Taste is a personal matter. Check each dish in progress with your own preferences in mind; later you may want to experiment with other additions. Part of the fun of reading cookbooks, even if one does not wish to try a certain recipe at present, is getting new ideas for food methods and combinations. We have tried at times to include these, along with our own comments about an accompanying menu: this, again, is only a suggestion.

All oven recipes should be carefully tried the first time in accordance with the peculiarities of your own stove and the directions adjusted accordingly, as oven temperatures at a certain setting do vary from stove to stove.

To us, the word "gourmet" has become so overused as to be meaningless. A simple dish or meal may certainly be so described if it is expertly prepared and served. Today's trend is toward simpler menus, less use of prepared foods and mixes, and more knowledge of good diet and nutrition. We have tried to reflect this in our selections.

Above all, have fun in the kitchen! Enjoy cooking for the creative and deeply satisfying pastime which it can be. Confidence grows with success. The greatest pleasure of all is adapting recipes to the tastes of family and friends, and enjoying the warmth and fellowship which accompanies a well-prepared and graciously served meal.

Graves Barn, built about 1899 in Sparta.
—Drawing by Sterling Everett

Acknowledgments

From Savannah Kitchens, Savannah.

Society As I Have Found It by Ward McAllister. New York: Cassell Publishing Co., 1890.

Family cookbook of Sophie Meldrim Shonnard, courtesy of Mrs. Shonnard, Savannah.

Favorite Recipes From Savannah Homes, Savannah, 1904.

Colonial Kitchens of Washington-Wilkes by the Iris Garden Club, Washington.

The Mint Julep by Richard Barksdale Harwell. Savannah: Beehive Press, 1975. Used by permission.

Some Good Things to Eat by Emma Rylander Lane. Clayton, Ala., 1898.

Bryan family cookbook, used by permission of the present owner, Talley Kirkland, Savannah.

Family cookbook of Lucinda Williams (Mrs. Peter), used by permission of Miss Katherine Kirkwood Scott, Milledgeville.

House-Keeping in the Sunny South by Mrs. E. R. Tennant, Atlanta, 1885. Courtesy of Mrs. Rita Trotz, Savannah.

Hints from Southern Epicures, Savannah, circa 1890. Courtesy of Mrs. Rita Trotz, Savannah.

Ye Olde Time Salzburger Cook Book, courtesy of Mrs. Amy LeBey, curator Salzburger Museum, Savannah.

Blessed Sacrament Parrish Cookbook, Savannah.

Holiday Cooking in This Old House by Orral Ann Moss, Beaufort, S.C., circa 1978. Used by permission.

St. Paul's Cookbook, Savannah, courtesy of Anne Seyle (Mrs. Charles).

Centennial Receipt Book: Juliette Gordon Low, Hostess and Homemaker by the Girl Scouts of the U.S.A., 1960. Used by permission of the Juliette Gordon Low Girl Scout National Center, Savannah.

Some Choice Receipts from Savannah Homemakers, Savannah, 1904, courtesy of Savannah Public Library.

The Pirates' House Cook Book by Frances McGrath, Savannah, 1964. Used by permission of Herb Traub.

The College President's Wife Entertains by Perrin Eidson, Atlanta, 1976.

Lew Davis hints and recipes courtesy of Ethan Allen Inc., Savannah.

Family cookbook of Mary Howell Scott, Milledgeville, circa 1918.

Bethesda: America's Oldest Home for Boys by Dr. John Duncan, courtesy of the Bethesda Alumni Association, Savannah.

The White House Cook-Book by Mrs. F. L. Gillette and Hugo Zieman, 1887. Courtesy of Mrs. Betty W. Rauers.

The Geechee Cook Book, Savannah.

Woman's Day Encyclopedia of Cookery. New York: Fawcett Publications, 1966.

Heavenly Herbs by Lane Furneaux. Dallas: Ladybug Press. Used by permission of Mrs. Furneaux, Emma R. Law's cousin.

How Girls Can Help Their Country: A Handbook for Girl Scouts by W. J. Hoxie, 1913, copyright by Juliette Gordon Low. Used by permission of the Juliette Gordon Low Girl Scout National Center, Savannah.

Johann Martin Bolzius Answers a Questionnaire on Carolina and Georgia by the Georgia Salzburger Society. Courtesy of Mrs. Amy LeBey, curator, Salzburger Museum, Ebeneezer.

Georgia Peanut Commission

Georgia Peach Commission, Atlanta, Ga.

    Patchwork Pantry, Rutledge, Ga.

    Favorite Recipes, Eatonton, Ga., 1950.

    More Gems From Many Kitchens, Garden Club of Georgia, 1971.

Sharing Southern Secrets Cook Book, Macon, 1948

200 Years of Cooking In Georgia, Macon, 1976

Coastal Cooking With Georgia Products, Georgia Extension Service.

Brown's Crossing Cookbook, Milledgeville, Ga., 1985.

Congregational Meeting House Book Book, White Bluff, Savannah, 1976.

Georgia
Entertains

Appetizers

Peanut Puffs

Yield: about 30

½ cup water
¼ cup butter or vegetable oil
¼ teaspoon salt
½ cup unsifted flour
2 eggs
1 cup chopped peanuts
Oil for frying
Salt to taste

Bring water, butter, and salt to a full rolling boil in a 1-quart saucepan. Reduce heat and quickly stir in flour, mixing vigorously with a wooden spoon until mixture leaves the sides of the pan and forms a soft ball. Remove from heat and beat in eggs one at a time, beating well after each addition, until mixture is very smooth. (You could use an electric mixer on low for this.) Stir in peanuts; mix well.

Drop dough into hot fat (370 degrees F.) by teaspoons. Keep small, as they will puff up. Don't crowd them. Fry until golden brown. Remove and drain on paper towels. Salt as desired before serving warm.

—Emma R. Law

Parmesan Pecans

Yield: 2 cups

2 tablespoons butter
½ teaspoon onion salt
½ teaspoon prepared mustard
½ teaspoon Worcestershire
 sauce, or to taste
2 cups pecans, in halves and
 large pieces
⅓ cup grated Parmesan
 cheese

Heat butter in a medium skillet until melted. Stir in onion salt, mustard, and Worcestershire. Add pecans, tossing lightly to coat with seasoned butter. Stir over low heat 3 to 5 minutes to toast lightly. Remove from heat and sprinkle with cheese, tossing lightly as cheese melts. Turn out onto cookie sheet to cool.

Note: ½ teaspoon salt and ½ teaspoon dried grated onion may be used in place of the onion salt, if desired. Or experiment with other flavored salts, such as garlic.

Watermelon Sandwiches

Cut rounds of the meat (pink) from watermelon, about ¾ inch thick. Combine cream cheese with a little mayonnaise to make a spread. A dash of chives or Worcestershire sauce may be added, if desired. Spread filling between rounds and serve with a spring of parsley on top as an excellent first course!

—Helen Baker Torrey

Rum Pecans

Yield: 2 cups

2 teaspoons instant coffee
¼ cup sugar
¼ teaspoon ground allspice
2 cups pecan halves
2 tablespoons dark rum
⅛ teaspoon salt

Combine all ingredients in a one-quart saucepan. Bring to a boil over medium heat. Cook three minutes, stirring constantly. Spread over waxed paper and separate nuts as they cool.

Buffet Beef

When offering the ever-popular sliced roast beef at a buffet, it is best accompanied by thinly sliced rye bread and butter, Dijon-type mustard, and sour cream flavored with horseradish so the guests may help themselves.

Ardsley Park Marinated Mushrooms

Yield: 4 to 6 servings

1 pound fresh button
   mushrooms
Water and salt as needed
¼ cup wine vinegar
⅔ cup vegetable oil
½ teaspoon garlic powder
1 teaspoon onion flakes
1 teaspoon sugar
1 tablespoon lemon juice
1 teaspoon oregano or
   tarragon
1 teaspoon salt
⅛ teaspoon pepper
2 tablespoons dried parsley
   flakes

Wash and cap mushrooms, saving stems and very small ones for other use. Place in boiling salted water to cover and boil one minute after water boils again. Drain. Prepare marinade from remaining ingredients. Pour over caps, cover, and chill for a minimum of 24 hours. Drain and serve cold.

Peppier Pepper

In all recipes calling for black pepper, and for table use, freshly ground will give a better flavor.

Blue Cheese-Mushrooms

Yield: about 20

1 pound mushrooms
¼ cup green onion slices
2 tablespoons butter
1 4-ounce package crumbled
blue cheese
1 3-ounce package cream
cheese

Remove stems from mushrooms. Set caps aside and chop stems finely. Sauté stems and onions in butter. Combine with remaining ingredients and mix well. Fill mushroom caps. Place on rack of broiler pan and broil 2 to 3 minutes, or until golden brown. Serve hot.

Cheese-Stuffed Mushrooms

For a very fast and easy hors d'oeuvre, wash and dry fresh large mushrooms. Take off stems and reserve for other use, leaving just the caps. Fill hollows with Boursin herb cheese, at room temperature, or other soft mild-flavored cheese or cheese spread, such as cheese-pimento. Cover and chill until time to serve, but remove from refrigerator 30 minutes before serving time.

Emma's Chicken Liver Paté

Yield: 12 or more servings

1½ pounds chicken livers
1 tablespoon grated onion
2 tablespoons minced parsley
¼ teaspoon pepper
⅓ cup chopped pistachio
nuts or blanched almonds
½ teaspoon dried oregano
¾ teaspoon dried basil
1½ teaspoons anchovy paste
6 strips bacon, crisply-
cooked and minced
3 tablespoons melted butter
3 tablespoons pale dry
cocktail sherry or Scotch
whiskey

Simmer liver until tender. Drain. Mash well or put in blender a minute or two. Crush spices as finely as possible. Blend all ingredients together and pack into a mold or serving dish. Cover with plastic wrap and chill. This makes a nice cocktail spread with party rye bread.

—Emma R. Law

General Robert Taylor built this handsome Greek Revival home in 1839, but its most famous occupant was Henry W. Grady, (1850—1889,) editor and orator who coined the phrase "The New South." The Prince Avenue house is now the headquarters of the Junior League of Athens.

Grady described the house as "an old Southern home with its lofty pillars, and its white pigeons fluttering down through the golden air."

Serving Hint

In estimating how much food to prepare for a party, remember that the more different kinds of food available, the more each dish will serve—like a Chinese banquet.

Shrimp Paste

Pick and pound the shrimp in a mortar, with a spoonful of fresh butter to the quart of shrimp. Add mace and red pepper. Put into a jar, pour more melted butter over the top, and cover. This will keep but a few days.

—Family cookbook of Sophie Meldrim Shonnard, Savannah

Soused Shrimp

Yield: 8 servings

6 medium onions
6 lemons
1 cup white vinegar
½ cup water
4 teaspoons salt
2 teaspoons sugar
1 teaspoon dry mustard
½ teaspoon ginger
1 teaspoon whole black
  pepper
1 bay leaf
¼ teaspoon hot sauce
1 cup vegetable oil
3 pounds shrimp, cleaned
  and deveined

Slice onions thinly and set aside. Squeeze ½ cup lemon juice; slice remaining lemons thinly and set aside.

Combine next 9 ingredients in a saucepan and bring to a boil. Lower heat and simmer for 5 minutes. Cool, strain and add lemon juice and oil.

Cook cleaned, deveined shrimp just until pink. Drain and set aside.

Layer shrimp, onions, and lemon slices in a large crockery or glass bowl. Pour marinade over and refrigerate at least overnight, covered.

Serve shrimp with onions and lemon peel along with party rye or pumpernickel bread.

—Gail Hart

Tybee Shrimp Dip

Yield: 4 servings

2 tablespoons prepared
  horseradish
¾ cup ketchup
3 tablespoons chili sauce
2 tablespoons lemon juice
½ teaspoon salt, or to taste

Mix well. Serve as a dip for shrimp, or pour over individual portions in a shrimp cocktail and garnish with parsley.

Potted Shrimp

Yield: 6 to 8 servings

1 pound fresh shrimp, peeled
  and deveined
1 teaspoon salt
Water as needed
⅛ teaspoon red pepper
1 large garlic clove, coarsely
  chopped
1 onion, quartered
Celery tops to taste
Herb bouquet of parsley,
  crumbled dried thyme, and
  bay leaf
½ cup (1 stick) butter, at
  room temperature
¼ teaspoon mace
¼ teaspoon nutmeg
Dash hot sauce
1 teaspoon lemon juice
1 tablespoon dry sherry
Salt and pepper, to taste
Parsley (optional)

Place shrimp in boiling salted water, to cover, in a 4-quart saucepan to which pepper, garlic, onion, celery tops, and herb bouquet have already been added. Cover. Three minutes after water boils again and shrimp are pink, drain and cool. Chop finely, almost to a paste.

Cream butter with seasonings and add shrimp. Taste and add more salt and pepper if desired. Place in a covered container and refrigerate until ready to use: this is best done several hours before serving. Serve with cocktail bread and crackers, as a spread.

Super Shrimp Dip

Yield: 4 cups

8 ounces cream cheese, at
  room temperature
8 ounces sour cream
2 tablespoons steak sauce
2 tablespoons lemon juice
2 tablespoons chili sauce
1 teaspoon salt, or to taste
Dash hot sauce
1 teaspoon Worcestershire
  sauce
2 pounds cooked shrimp,
  shelled, deveined, and
  finely chopped

Combine all ingredients except shrimp in a large bowl. Gently fold in shrimp, and place in serving dish. Cover and refrigerate until well chilled. Serve with crackers or sliced cocktail bread.

—June Bland

Oyster Cocktails

For each glass of chilled oysters, allow 1 tablespoon vinegar, 1 tablespoon ketchup, 1 tablespoon Worcestershire sauce, ½ teaspoon lemon juice or to taste, 1 teaspoon horseradish, and a few drops of Tabasco sauce.

—Mrs. T. M. Cunningham,
Favorite Recipes From Savannah Homes, 1904

Crab Spread for Celery

Yield: about 1½ cups

1 8-ounce package cream
  cheese, at room
  temperature
1 6½-ounce can white crab
  meat, drained
⅛ teaspoon salt, or to taste
Dash red pepper
Celery

Combine first four ingredients. Wash and dry celery and cut into desired lengths. Stuff with spread and refrigerate covered until ready to serve.

Celery with Brandied Cheese

Yield: about 1 cup

¼ pound blue cheese, at
  room temperature
½ cup (1 stick) butter, at
  room temperature
2 tablespoons brandy
1 teaspoon Worcestershire
  sauce
Celery

Combine first four ingredients. Cut celery into bite-size serving pieces. Fill celery with mixture and wrap or foil. Chill until just before serving.

For Juicier Meatballs

For juicier meatballs, always brown and drain before combining with sauce. At this point, they could be frozen and then used later.

—Carter Olive

Cranberry Meatballs

Yield: about 60

2 pounds lean ground beef
1 cup bread crumbs
⅓ cup dried parsley flakes
2 eggs
2 tablespoons Worcestershire
*   sauce*
½ teaspoon pepper
½ teaspoon garlic powder
⅓ cup ketchup or tomato
*   sauce*
2 tablespoons minced onion

Sauce:
1 16-ounce can jellied
*   cranberry sauce*
1 12-ounce bottle (1½ cups)
*   chili sauce*
2 tablespoons brown sugar
1 tablespoon lemon juice

In a large bowl, combine beef, bread crumbs, parsley flakes, eggs, sauce, pepper, garlic, ketchup or tomato sauce, and onion. Blend well. Form into balls about 1¼ inches in diameter. Arrange in a large skillet and brown on all sides in a little vegetable oil, repeating process until all are browned. Or, if desired, place in an oven pan on a rack. Preheat oven to 350 degrees F. and bake for about 30 minutes, or until brown.

Meanwhile, in a large saucepan combine cranberry sauce, chili sauce, brown sugar, and lemon juice. Cook over moderate heat, stirring occasionally, until mixture is smooth and cranberry sauce is melted. Add drained meatballs and simmer to combine flavors, about 10 minutes. Serve warm.

Note: If you prefer, drained warm meatballs and sauce could be served separately, for dipping.

For extra nutrition, wheat germ or whole-wheat cereal crumbs could be used in the meatball recipe in place of bread crumbs.

Benne-Cheese Crisps

Yield: about 3½ dozen

½ cup (1 stick) butter, at
*   room temperature*
1 3-ounce package cream
*   cheese, at room*
*   temperature*
1 egg, well beaten
1 teaspoon imitation rum
*   extract*
1 cup sifted flour
2 teaspoons baking powder
¾ teaspoon salt
1 teaspoon paprika
⅛ teaspoon cayenne pepper
⅓ cup toasted benne seed, or
*   to taste (see page 10)*

Cream butter and cheese together well. Beat in egg and extract and set aside. Sift together dry ingredients. Blend into first mixture. Fold in benne seed.

Preheat oven to 375 degrees F. Drop dough by teaspoons, about an inch apart, on lightly greased cookie sheets. Bake for about 10 minutes, or until golden. Do not overbrown. Cool on racks. Store in airtight container.

Benne Seed

Benne seed, called sesame seed in the North, is a special southern ingredient which was first brought to Dixie by the slaves and planted for good luck around their homes. It was the black cooks who first made benne seed cakes and candy in the plantation kitchens. They also pounded the tiny seed into a paste, which was eaten on hominy. The good fortune said to be carried by the seed is still there—in its flavor.

Benne seeds, toasted, add a special flavor to fried chicken, cooked green beans, and baked potatoes when sprinkled on their sour cream topping.

Toasted Benne Seed

When a Southern recipe calls for toasted benne seeds, this refers to placing the seeds in a shallow baking pan in a preheated 350 degrees F. oven for about 10 to 15 minutes. Stir several times for uniform coloring, and again before using.

Cook seed to a golden color only; do not brown. Seed need not be toasted if used in a dough which will bake, unless the golden color and more distinctive flavor is desired. Some cooks like to keep a jar of browned seed in the refrigerator, ready to use.

Small amounts of benne seed may also be toasted in a skillet. Stir constantly while cooking over low heat until lightly browned.

Georgia Peanut-Cheese Ball

Yield: 1 12-ounce ball

1 8-ounce package cream
  cheese, at room
  temperature
½ cup peanut butter
½ teaspoon Worcestershire
  sauce
2 tablespoons finely chopped
  parsley
Chopped peanuts as needed

Combine cheese and peanut butter until smooth. Stir in sauce and parsley. Roll in a ball; wrap in plastic and chill. Before serving, roll in peanuts. Serve with whole wheat crackers.

This award-winning photograph by Rick Vanderpool of Athens has become the symbol of the Brown's Crossing Craftsmen Fair. Since 1969, the event has been held the third weekend in October nine miles west of Milledgeville in what was once a thriving farm community.

Shrimp-Cheese Spread

Yield: about 1½ cups

*4 ounces cream
   cheese at room
   temperature
2 tablespoons tomato juice
½ teaspoon lemon juice
1 tablespoon minced parsley
1 cup ground or finely
   minced shrimp
   (4½-ounce can)
Tabasco sauce to taste*

Combine and serve with crackers or cocktail bread.

Cheese and Date Nibbles

Rich, unusual, and very delicious!

Yield: about 50

*¾ cup grated Cheddar
  cheese, at room
  temperature*
*1 cup (2 sticks) butter, at
  room temperature*
⅛ teaspoon cayenne pepper
2 cups sifted flour
1 pound pitted dates
Pecan halves

Preheat oven to 400 degrees F. Blend cheese, butter, and pepper; work in flour. Roll dough to about ¼ inch thick. Cut in circles about 2¼ inches in diameter. (Use a cookie cutter this size if you have one.)

Place a date at one side of each circle of dough. Place a pecan half beside each date. Fold pastry over and close by pressing sides with tines of fork. Place on lightly greased cookie sheet. Bake for about 12 to 14 minutes; do not brown very much.

—Emma R. Law

Ham-Sherry Cheese Dip

Yield: 2 cups

*3 ounces cream cheese, at
  room temperature*
1 4½-ounce can deviled ham
¼ cup dry sherry
*1 cup small-curd cottage
  cheese*
Few drops hot sauce
½ teaspoon salt
*¼ cup finely chopped green
  onion or fresh parsley*

Blend cream cheese and ham until smooth. Add remaining ingredients and place in serving bowl. Chill covered. Serve with crackers, potato chips, or fresh sliced vegetables.

Dip In A Bread Bowl

Cut a thin slice from the top of a round or oval loaf of rye bread. Hollow out the inside, saving the bread removed to use as bread crumbs or in stuffing. If desired, "sawtooth" the top crust with a sharp knife as you would a watermelon. Fill with your favorite party dip, with extra thinly sliced pieces of party rye on a bread board beside it.

Athens Beer Cheese

Yield: about 6 cups

1 pound sharp Cheddar
  cheese, grated, at room
  temperature
1 pound mild Cheddar
  cheese, grated, at room
  temperature
1 6-ounce can tomato paste
1 teaspoon garlic salt
1 tablespoon onion flakes
1 tablespoon Worcestershire
  sauce
1½ cups beer

Combine ingredients; chill covered. Serve with crackers.

Rosy Pecan-Edam Bowl

Yield: 10 servings

8 ounces Edam cheese, at
  room temperature
⅓ cup beer
2 tablespoons butter, at room
  temperature
2 teaspoons Worcestershire
  sauce
⅛ teaspoon hot sauce
½ cup finely chopped pecans

Cut a two- or three-inch slice from the top of the cheese to allow you to scoop out contents. Do not remove red coating from cheese. Scoop out cheese, leaving ¼-inch shell for bowl. Shred or chop scooped-out cheese. Gradually blend with remaining ingredients, using an electric mixture at low speed if you wish, until mixture is smooth. If necessary, add a little more beer. Stuff shell with cheese mixture, saving remaining part for refills. Refrigerate covered for at least several hours before serving, removing from refrigerator 30 minutes before serving.

Note: This also makes a nice hostess gift at holiday time with the red-coated top slice replaced and wrapped with plastic wrap and a ribbon.

Cognac-Cheese Ball

Yield: about 2½ cups

1 8-ounce package cream cheese
8 ounces soft Cheddar cheese, at room temperature
4 ounces blue cheese, crumbled
1 tablespoon cognac
½ teaspoon paprika
½ cup finely grated or minced pecans

Blend cheeses well. Mix in cognac and paprika. Cover and refrigerate until firm enough to mold in a ball. Roll in nuts. Cover and refrigerate until needed. Leave at room temperature 20 to 30 minutes before serving. Accompany with seedless grapes and crackers.

Note: Brandy or bourbon may be used instead of cognac.

Founder's Memorial Garden, University of Georgia Campus, Athens, a joint project of the Garden Club of Georgia and the University's Department of Landscape Architecture. The garden is located at the restored antebellum Lumpkin House, state headquarters of the Garden Club of Georgia, and honors the founders of America's first garden club, the Ladies' Garden Club of Athens, organized in 1891. Courtesy of the Garden Club of Georgia.

Brie With Almonds

For a fast and delicious hot cheese dish, place a whole Brie cheese in a small casserole and sprinkle with slivered almonds. Bake until hot, about 20 to 25 minutes, in a 350 degrees F. oven and serve with crackers.

Mrs. Charlton's Cheese Straws

An updated version of a very old Savannah recipe.

Yield: about 2½ dozen

½ cup (1 stick) butter, at
*   room temperature*
1 cup grated Cheddar cheese
½ teaspoon dry mustard
⅛ teaspoon salt
1 cup flour
3 teaspoons cold water

Mix butter with cheese and seasonings. Add flour and water. Form into a dough. (If desired at this point, chill in waxed paper for easier handling.) Roll out about ¼ inch thick on floured surface, adding a little more flour to the dough if necessary. Cut into strips about ½-by-4 inches, with a pastry wheel if you have one. Score edges with a fork if desired.

Preheat oven to 400 degrees F. Bake on a greased cookie sheet for about 8 to 10 minutes. Do not brown.

Note: For a sharper taste, ½ teaspoon red pepper may be substituted for the dry mustard.

For a distinctive flavor, untoasted benne seeds may also be sprinkled on cheese straws before baking.

Cheese-Olive Bites

Another nice version of the popular cheese straws recipe is to make up a cheese dough, rolled flat according to directions, and then to lay large, drained stuffed green olives on it. Cut a square of dough around each and close it up, covering olive and pinching dough closed. Bake on greased sheets about 10 to 12 minutes in a preheated 400 degrees F. oven. (Do not brown.) Serve hot.

If desired, olive bites may be made ahead of time and placed on a cookie sheet, then placed in the freezer. When they are thoroughly frozen, transfer to plastic bags or freezer containers and keep until needed. May be baked frozen in a preheated 400 degrees F. oven on greased sheets for 15 minutes.

The 1888 Mary Willis Library in Washington was founded by Dr. Francis T. Willis in memory of his daughter. Georgia's first privately endowed free public library, it is known for its Tiffany glass and Victorian architecture.

A Land of Plenty

Hampton Plantation has plenty of milk, cream and butter; turkeys, fowls, kids, pigs, geese and mutton; fish of course, in abundance. Figs, peaches and melons, oranges and pomegranates are available, and the house affords Madeira wine, brandy, and porter [sic].

—Aaron Burr writing from St. Simons Island,
August 1804, to his daughter Theodosia

Beverages

Colony Punch

Yield: about 1 gallon

*1 quart canned cranberry
 juice cocktail*
*4 tablespoons lemon juice
 (or juice of two lemons)*
*1 quart unsweetened
 pineapple juice*
*1 12-ounce can frozen
 orange juice concentrate,
 thawed in the refrigerator
 and undiluted*
½ cup peach brandy
2 quarts ginger ale

Combine ingredients in a chilled punch bowl in order given. This is also nice at Christmas because of the color. You could add a bit more brandy for adult groups.

Note: In order not to have the punch diluted by melting ice cubes, and to add more color, freeze a three-ring mold of canned red Hawaiian Punch with a few mint leaves, and add this to the punch bowl before serving.

—Elaine Hussey, Colony Book Shop

Block Mold

A half-gallon milk carton, washed and dried, may also be used as a punch mold to keep the beverage cold without diluting it. First, pour in 2 cups of limeade and freeze. (If necessary, cut off top of carton and cover with plastic wrap or foil.) After limeade has frozen, add a second 2-cup layer with a pre-chilled cherry drink. Repeat with orange drink, or any other color and fruit combinations you like. Allow 2 to 4 hours for each layer to freeze. When ready to serve, peel away carton and float ice in punch bowl.

17

Columbus Punch

A fruity, non-alcoholic punch that young people like, with the blocks of sherbet taking the place of an ice ring.

Yield: 35 5-ounce servings

1 12-ounce can orange juice concentrate
1 12-ounce can lemonade or limeade concentrate
2 quarts chilled apple juice
2 quarts chilled ginger ale
1 half-gallon block of lemon, lime, or orange sherbet

Combine concentrates and juice in chilled punch bowl. Stir in ginger ale. Add blocks of sherbet and serve.

Note: Rather plain cookies that do not compete with the flavor of the punch may be served.

For a less sweet drink, substitute club soda or bitter lemon for one bottle of ginger ale.

Frosty Punch Bowl

Beat one egg white with 1 tablespoon water. Brush a 1½ inch band around the top outside of the bowl. Sprinkle waxed paper with sugar. Roll the edge of the bowl in this. Stand at room temperature 20 minutes, then repeat. Set in a cool place overnight (or for several hours) before using.

Frosted Glasses, Frosty Drink

At least an hour or more before serving time, rub the rims of wine or champagne glasses with a little citrus fruit juice, and then dip lightly in confectioners' sugar. Chill in the freezer until frosted; serve with cold drinks.

Frozen Color

When making an ice ring, sliced oranges, lemons, and maraschino cherries may be added for extra color.

Mint Sweetener

In place of one cup sugar or honey in the punch bowl, substitute 1 10-ounce glass mint jelly, heated to a liquid.

One tablespoon mint jelly per cup is also a nice addition to hot tea.

Percolator Punch

Here's the easy way to serve a hot spiced drink to a crowd, with no reheating, or straining spices.

Yield: 30 5-ounce servings

½ gallon apple cider
1 46-ounce can pineapple juice
1 6-ounce can frozen orange juice, thawed in refrigerator
1 6-ounce can frozen lemonade or limeade, thawed in refrigerator
1 quart water
1 quart apricot nectar
½ cup sugar (optional)
2 teaspoons whole allspice
2 teaspoons whole cloves
4 cinnamon sticks, broken into several pieces each

Combine juices and water in the percolator. Place sugar, (if used) and spices in basket. Allow to perk through cycle and serve hot.

Note: Fruit juice combinations may be varied, such as cranberry juice (with additional sugar if desired) at Christmas, and spices to taste.

Harvest Cooler

A refreshing non-alcoholic drink that consists of equal parts apple juice and soda water or ginger ale mixed and served over ice in a tall glass, with a little lemon juice and sugar added if desired.

Lemon Cubes

When serving iced tea, it will have more flavor if lemonade is frozen in cubes and used in the glass rather than plain ice cubes which dilute the drink.

A Dash of Lemon

A little lemon juice adds more flavor to bottled colas, especially the diet ones.

One tablespoon lemon juice added to one cup fresh milk will give you a glass of buttermilk.

The Early Salzburgers

The inhabitants who have the ability cook a healthy beer for themselves out of syrup, Indian corn, and hops, or the tops of the white or water firs, which is very cheap. Strong barley beer comes from New York, at times also from England. . . . It is cheaper by the barrel. In these lands, little beer is drunk. People from various nations rather adopt the ways of the English, who make a brew out of water, sugar cane brandy, and sugar, called rum.

Those who can do so also add juice of Seville or bitter oranges which comes from the West Indies, also grown frequently towards the south in this and the neighboring colony (Florida), and are very cheap. They also make a drink out of water, wine and sugar. None agrees with me so well as the described cheap house beer, which is rather similar to the Löbeginer beer.

—Salzburger pastor Johann Martin Bolzius, 1751,
writing about life in Ebenezer on the Savannah River, where
he helped establish a Lutheran colony of Austrians in 1734

Corn Beer

Boil a quart of corn until the grains crack. Put into a jug, and pour in two gallons of boiling water. Add a quart of molasses, a handful of dried apples, and a tablespoon of sugar. It will be ready for use in 2 or 3 days.

—Mrs. Alice Rhoda Gnann Ferrel (Mrs. Lloyd)
Ye Olde Time Salzburger Cook Book, Savannah

Beer Punch

Champagne tastes, beer budget? This light, refreshing summer drink is said to taste like the former—or like Aunt Mary's dandelion wine! The recipe is thought to have come to the American South from the Caribbean.

Yield: 12 servings

12 lemons
2 limes
2 cups sugar
2 cups water
1 cup grapefruit juice
*2 12-ounce bottles any light
  beer*
Lemon slices for garnish
Mint or cloves as needed

Squeeze lemons and limes, straining juice and saving the rinds. Set aside.

Mix sugar with water in a large saucepan. Bring to a boiling point, stirring to dissolve sugar. Add fruit rinds. Cover, and let stand 5 to 10 minutes. Remove rinds and discard. Cool syrup. Add fruit juices and pour over ice in a chilled bowl just before serving. (An ice ring is good here.) Add beer. Garnish with lemon slices and fresh mint, or cloves stuck through the lemon slices.

A State Marker to a Brewery

Large pieces of tabby, a colonial building material made of sand, lime, oyster shells and water, and a state highway marker on Horton Road near du Bignon Creek at Jekyll Island, are all that now mark the site of Georgia's first brewery, operational in the 1730s. According to the sign, "Crops of barley, rye and hops, planted and raised in the fields of Major William Horton of Oglethorpe's Regiment, were used in making beer for the soldiers at nearby Fort Frederica on St. Simons Island. . . . The remains of Horton's tabby house stand northeast of the brewery."

Currant Shrub

The currants should be very ripe. Squeeze them; to each quart, add one pound of sugar. Put the currants and sugar in a kettle. Boil ten minutes, skimming well. When cold, allow one gill (½ cup) brandy to each quart of juice. Bottle and seal. It improves with age.

—Captain H. C. Buckner, *House-Keeping in the Sunny South*
Atlanta, 1885

Bill's Wedding Punch

Yield: 1 gallon

2 fifths champagne
1 32-ounce bottle 7-Up
1 fifth dry white wine, such
   as Rhine or Chablis
1 46-ounce bottle white
   grape juice

Combine in a chilled punch bowl with ice ring and serve.

—Dr. W. A. Wayt

Teetotaler's Punch

Yield: 1⅓ gallons

2 32-ounce bottles 7-Up
1 46-ounce can red
   Hawaiian Punch
1 46-ounce can white
   Hawaiian Punch

Combine in chilled punch bowl and serve.

—Dr. W. A. Wayt

Georgia Peach Punch

Yield: 30 servings

2 quarts peeled, sliced
   peaches, puréed
1 fifth Rhine wine
½ cup lemon or lime juice
1 cup pineapple juice
1 cup orange juice
1 quart ginger ale
1 quart champagne

Mix peaches with wine and fruit juices and chill for several hours. Then mix with ginger ale and champagne in a chilled punch bowl, with an ice ring made of sliced seasonal fruits and white grape juice.

Note: For a non-alcoholic punch, chill peaches in white grape juice rather than wine and substitute an extra bottle of ginger ale for the champagne.

Peach Daiquiris

Yield: 2 servings

1 large peach, peeled, seeded,
   and coarsely chopped
1 teaspoon sugar
1 ounce lime or lemon juice
3 ounces light rum
½ cup crushed ice

Mix all ingredients in blender for 10 to 20 seconds. Serve at once.

To Mull Wine

To every pint of wine, allow a large cup full of water, sugar, and spice to taste. Boil cloves, grated nutmeg and cinnamon in the water until the flavor is extracted. Then add the wine and sugar, bring to a boiling point, to serve.

—Bryan family cookbook, Savannah, circa 1885

Hot Spiced Wine

One 1853 family punch recipe says that the ideal party drink should contain one sour (such as lemon) in proportion to two sweet (sugar or honey), four strong (such as rum or bourbon), and eight weak (water or fruit juice). The following recipe, somewhat livelier, still has all four necessary ingredients:

Yield: 5½ cups

¼ cup sugar or honey
½ teaspoon ground cloves
½ teaspoon ground nutmeg
½ teaspoon lemon or orange peel
⅔ cup orange juice
1 cup water
1 26-ounce bottle Burgundy, rosé, or claret

Dissolve sugar or honey with spices in juice and water in a two-quart saucepan and mix well. Bring to a boil and then simmer for three minutes. Stir in the wine and heat, but do not boil. Keep warm until serving time. Serve in heated punch cups. If desired, a slice of orange or a small stick of cinnamon may be used for garnish.

Orange Cordial

Take the peel of five oranges, cut thin; with one gallon of whiskey, and five pounds of sugar. Remain standing three or four months. Strain, and bottle.

Hints From Southern Epicures, Savannah, 1890

Rees Park Bandstand in Americus, a center for community events from weddings to barbecues. Drawing by Anna Cheokas

Southern Hospitality

It was a feast day every day—no excess, you know, but wine bibbling for two hours, and a night cap after the lecture.

—William Makepeace Thackeray, while a guest at the home of Andrew Low in Savannah, 1853

Summer Wine Punch

Yield: 28 5-ounce servings

1 gallon Rhine wine, chilled
2 28-ounce bottles soda water, chilled
2 7-ounce bottles quinine water, chilled
1 12-ounce can pink lemonade, thawed in the refrigerator

Mix all ingredients together in a large chilled punch bowl with an ice ring, preferably of white grape juice and fresh fruits.

Coastal Rice Wine

This will make you tipsy!

Yield: nearly 4 gallons

2 medium oranges, sliced
6 pounds (13½ cups) sugar
2 pounds seedless raisins
3 pounds (7½ cups) rice
2 packages yeast
2 gallons lukewarm water

Mix all ingredients and place in a 4-gallon crock. Cover with a cloth. Stir with a wooden spoon once a day for 21 days. Filter or strain through a cloth; bottle as desired.

—Billie Love

Serving Wine

How many wine servings in a bottle? That depends on the type. A fifth (25 ounces) of table wine such as rosé, Chablis, or Burgundy serves 4 persons. With a champagne, a fifth serves 5 to 6. For dessert wines like sherry or port, a fifth serves 8.

Party Planning

When ordering liquor for a party, remember that there are 17 1½-ounce drinks to a fifth of liquor, or 200 drinks to a 12-bottle case. To be safe, allow three drinks per guest in your plans.

Muscadine Wine

Squeeze the pulp and juice in a pan. Let stand until it ferments. Strain off the juice, and let it stand 12 hours, taking off the froth as it rises. Then, to a gallon of juice, add three pounds brown sugar. Strain it into a cask or demijohn. Let it stand slightly corked for three months, then bottle it, and to each bottle put a small lump of loaf sugar.

—Family cookbook of Mrs. Lucinda Williams, Milledgeville, 1857

The Very Best Blackberry Wine

Wash the berries, and let them stand until they ferment. Strain them. Let the juice stand about 12 hours, and then skim off the froth. To one gallon of juice, add 3 pounds of sugar, and one quart of water. Let it stand again 12 hours, and skim and pour into jugs or bottles. Let stand open until the fermentation is entirely through, then stop up the vessel about two or three months. Then pour off, bottle, and seal tight.

—Family cookbook of Mrs. Lucinda Williams, Milledgeville, 1857

Mint Julep

The drink is very rarely of pure water; it is either a compound of brandy and water or of strong Madeira wine. It is customary to invite guests who call on a Gentleman at any period of the day and especially at mid-day, to refresh themselves with brandy and water, or with wine. It is a civilty [sic] established by society.

—Dr. William R. Waring of Savannah,
in a paper presented to the Georgia Medical Society,
1832, now at the Georgia Historical Society

Iced Brandy

Combine dessert and after dinner drinks by blending, for each guest, two scoops ice cream and one ounce brandy for 30 seconds. Serve immediately in champagne glasses.

One ounce Kahlua per guest, or ½ ounce cream de cacao, may be substituted for the brandy.

Hot Buttered Rum

Yield: 8 servings

2 tablespoons brown sugar
1 teaspoon whole allspice
1 teaspoon whole cloves
¼ teaspoon salt
½ teaspoon ground nutmeg
1 3-inch stick cinnamon
2 quarts cider, divided
1 cup dark rum, or to taste
Butter as needed

In a large saucepan, combine sugar, spices, and two cups cider. Bring to a boil. Reduce heat, cover, and simmer for 20 minutes. Strain to remove whole spices. Return cider to kettle along with remaining cider and rum. Heat, but do not boil. Place one teaspoon butter in each warmed mug, and fill with hot cider mixture. Serve hot.

Prune-Raisin Port or Sherry

Put five pounds each seeded raisins and prunes through a meat grinder. (Some also grind the seed, a few at a time.) Put all in a crock with five pounds granulated sugar, 1 yeast cake (or package), and 2½ gallons water. Stir, and let stand from three to six weeks. Strain by filtering through paper or cloth, and bottle.

—Family cookbook of Sophie Meldrim Shonnard, Savannah

Something For Everyone

When planning a party, remember to have at least one type of non-alcoholic drink available for those who wish it, preferably also a diet one. Above all, do not plan to serve only one alcoholic punch or drink, which poses an embarrassing dilemma for those who do not care for it. Rich hors d'oeuvres should be balanced with fruit and vegetable offerings for dieters. Coffee should always be available at the end of the party for those who would like a cup before starting home.

The Woodruff House on Coleman Hill in Macon was begun about 1836. It was later owned by one of the largest planters of cotton in the state, Joseph Bond. Occupied by both Confederate and Union forces during the Civil War, it was later host to Jefferson Davis during an 1887 Confederate reunion. Now owned by Mercer University, it has been renamed to honor Mercer benefactor George W. Woodruff.

Macon Sassafras Tea

Wash the sassafras roots, cut into two- or three-inch pieces, place in a deep pan, and cover with cold water. Boil 12 to 15 minutes. Strain and serve hot. Add sorghum molasses to sweeten if desired. The tea is a delicate pink, delicious as a cold drink.

Sassafras tea was once used as a blood purifier. It was also recommended for poor appetites.

It may be substituted for 1 cup liquid in making a plain cake. It also gives more flavor to some desserts and candies.

—Kathryn Stewart

Father Boland's Gaelic Coffee

With the South's large population of Irish descent, and Savannah's famous St. Patrick's Day Parade, Irish Coffee is a popular drink on March 17.

The first essential step is to heat your glass or cup with boiling water. Now, pour this out and fill to three-fourths with piping hot coffee. Add two teaspoons brown sugar, and stir vigorously. Add one jigger (minimum) good Irish liquor (Scotch may be substituted), and stir briskly.

Nearly top the glass to the brim, but leave a little room for the whipped cream. Now, take the whipped cream and pour it slowly over the back of a hot spoon so that it floats on top of the coffee. Sip coffee gently and soothingly through the whipped cream, and relax. When this one is consumed, you'll want another.

Note: Do *not* put a cherry on top of the whipped cream.

—Father J. Kevin Boland,
Blessed Sacrament Parish Cookbook, Savannah

Coffee Liqueur

Yield: 2 quarts

1 2-ounce jar instant coffee,
  or instant espresso coffee
4 cups sugar
2 cups boiling water
1 whole vanilla bean
1 pint brandy, bourbon or
  vodka

Combine coffee and sugar in boiling water. Stir until sugar is dissolved. Cool. Add vanilla and brandy, bourbon, or vodka. Store in a half-gallon jar, covered, in a dark place for one month before serving. Bottle as desired. Vanilla bean may be used again.

Note: After making one batch, you may wish to adjust sugar and water amounts to personal taste, or try with various flavored dessert instant coffees now available.

Coffee In A Bowl

An old Navy recipe, sometimes served on New Year's at brunch.

Yield: 12 servings

3 cups strong black coffee
3 cups vanilla or chocolate
  ice cream
3 cups light or dark rum or
  to taste

Blend ingredients well and serve cold in a chilled punch bowl or cups.

Note: Bourbon or blended whiskey may be used instead of rum.

Blender Coffee Whitener

Yield: 1 cup

*1½ cups non-fat dry milk
  powder
1 tablespoon sugar
1 teaspoon cornstarch*

Combine all ingredients in a blender or food processor and blend on high speed until mixture is fine powder. A blender makes the mixture much creamier and easier to dissolve than if mixed by hand.

Mocha Coffee

For extra flavor, add one teaspoon cocoa to coffee beans if grinding them at home.

—Carter Olive

Cinnamon Coffee

To make capuccino, the Italian after-dinner drink, pour coffee over whipped cream in demitasse cups. Add a dash of cinnamon. Serve with sugar if desired.

Coffee for a Crowd

One pound of ground coffee yields 60 cups of coffee. If using instant, use 3 tablespoons per quart water. If you want to use your percolator for the sake of convenience, allow water to boil well and then add instant coffee when it is on the "keep warm" cycle.

Half a pint of coffee cream should serve 25 people.

Mocha Coffee Mix

Yield: about 32 servings

To make a mocha coffee mix, combine ¼ cup unsweetened cocoa with a cup of instant coffee. For a single cup, add a small amount of cold water to 1 teaspoon coffee mixture and stir to make a paste. Then fill the cup with boiling water and stir. Add cream and sugar, if desired.

If more cocoa flavor is desired, mix 5 tablespoons instant coffee with ⅔ cup non-fat dry milk, 2 tablespoons unsweetened cocoa, and 6 tablespoons sugar. Use about 2 tablespoons for each cup, according to taste. Add boiling water. This makes about 15 servings.

Grandmother Lamar's Receipt for Syllabub

The popular nineteenth century southern drink syllabub was brought to the colonies by English settlers and is of pre-Elizabethan origin. This authentic Savannah recipe is from the family cookbook of Sophie Meldrim Shonnard, and was given her by Miss C. L. Woodbridge.

One pint of rich cream
One pint of milk
½ pint of sherry
¼ pound (about 2¼ cups) sugar

Mix all in a deep bowl, and churn with a syllabub churn. As it gets thick, take a tablespoon, and take the foam all off the top. Put it in a glass bowl in which you are going to serve it. Keep doing this until it is all whipped up. Then, carefully pour the liquor that won't whip up, at the edge of the glass bowl, under the whipped up cream. Put bowl in the ice box until ready to serve. This amount fills one large bowl, and a small one, so that you can serve more if needed, or use the next day.

Note: In place of the syllabub churn, a whisk, rotary, electric beater, or food processor (on high for about six minutes, so that cream is stiff but not curdled) may be used. Mixture should be stiff.

Strawberry Slush

Yield: 4 servings

2 cups sliced fresh or frozen strawberries
1½ cups cranberry juice cocktail
Club soda

Put berries and juice in blender or food processor and blend smooth. Put several ice cubes in a tall glass and half fill with berry mixture; fill to top with club soda. Stir, and serve immediately. May also be spiked with vodka!

—Brown's Crossing Cookbook

Superfine Sugar

For each cup desired, blend 1 cup sugar with 1 teaspoon cornstarch in the blender, until sugar is very fine. This is excellent in drinks because it dissolves quickly. It may also be used instead of confectioners' sugar in cooked recipes. However, the commercial product is better for use in uncooked icing recipes.

Spiked Buttermilk

Buttermilk spiked with wine or rum is said to have been the favorite drink of the Reverend Doctor William McWhir, principal of Sunbury Academy in Liberty County, Georgia and a friend and correspondent of President George Washington.

Midway Congregational Church, 1792, replacing an earlier structure burned by the British. Courtesy Liberty Country Historical Society

Soups

For Perfect Soup

A cupful of milk will counteract the effects of too much pepper in the soup.

If the soup has been made too salty, add a few peeled slices of raw potato, and cook five minutes longer. Then remove the potato, which should have absorbed much of the salt.

A teaspoon of brown sugar will also counteract the effects of too much salt in the soup.

—Family cookbook of Mary Howell Scott,
Milledgeville, circa 1918

Mock (Tomato) Bisque Soup

Yield: 10 cups

A quart can of tomatotes, three pints of milk, one large tablespoon of flour, butter the size of an egg, pepper and salt to taste, a scant teaspoonful of baking soda. Put the tomatoes on to stew, add the milk in a double kettle to boil, reserving one-half a cupful to mix with flour. Mix the flour smoothly with this cold milk, stir into the boiling milk, and cook 10 minutes.

To the tomatoes, add the soda, stew well, and rub through a strainer fine enough to keep back the seeds. Add the butter, salt, and pepper to the milk and then the tomatoes. Serve immediately.

—*Juliette Gordon Low Centennial Receipt Book*, Savannah, 1960

Brunswick Stew

Cook a 5 or 6 pound hen all to pieces, the day before, and pick apart, leaving out the fat, skin, and bones. The next day, put on early in a big stew pot with the skimmed chicken broth, 2 cans tomatoes, 8 cut-up white potatoes, 1 quart butter beans or 2 cans, 2 red peppers, cut-up, and one large well-browned pork chop. Also put in one bunch onions, about six, saving as many more and the corn for later, as onion flavor cooks out. Cook all slowly for several hours. Add the other bunch cut-up onions and about 9 ears of cut-up corn, or two cans, about ½ hour before serving. Season to taste with Worcestershire sauce and salt and pepper. It should be gummy and thick; the corn at the last will thicken it considerably.

If you have any left, it will be even better the next day. This serves any number, at least 12.

—Family cookbook of Sophie Meldrim Shonnard, Savannah

Cock-A-Leekie Soup

The historic origins of this soup are part of the South's Scotch-Irish heritage.

Yield: 6 to 8 servings

1 3-pound stewing chicken,
  cut up
4 cups water
½ cup finely chopped carrots
½ cup finely chopped celery
½ cup finely chopped onion
2 sprigs parsley or a handful
  of celery leaves
2 teaspoons salt
¼ teaspoon pepper
1 bay leaf
1½ cups (½ pound) sliced
  leeks
1 cup finely chopped potato
½ cup barley
2 cups light cream
Parsley for garnish

Simmer chicken in water with carrots, celery, onion, parsley, seasonings, and bay leaf, covered for about an hour, until chicken is tender. Remove from heat. When cool enough to handle, remove chicken from broth. Skin and remove meat from bones.

Chop meat into small pieces. Cool broth, skimming fat. Add leeks, potato, and barley and return to heat. Bring to a boil, reduce heat, and simmer covered about 20 minutes, or until potatoes and barley are tender. Blend in cream and chicken. Reheat, but do not boil. Serve with sprigs of parsley.

Note: This is even better done in two stages: first, cook the chicken and remove. Cool broth, covered, in refrigerator overnight, so you can remove all the fat from the top of the broth. The second day, chop chicken and continue as above.

Mary's Turkey Soup

Here are two uses for that leftover turkey carcass, one a clear soup and the other a hearty vegetable one.

Yield: about 6 servings

Cover turkey bones with water in a large kettle. Add salt, bay leaf, a handful of celery leaves, a carrot, and an onion, each coarsely chopped. Bring to a boil and simmer, covered, for about two hours. Strain, cool, and skim broth. Reserve any meat on the bones, chopping very fine and returning to soup. Skim any fat from broth. Season to taste. Add 1 tablespoon claret for each cup of broth, if desired. Heat, but do not boil. Serve hot.

Hearty Turkey Soup

Yield: about 6 servings

For a hearty vegetable soup, strain and skim broth as above. Discard bones, saving any bits of meat and chopping these fine before returning to soup kettle. Now add four potatoes, peeled and diced; one small onion, finely chopped; and three medium stalks of celery, finely chopped. Bring to a boil and simmer for about half an hour, or until vegetables are tender. Check seasoning, adding salt, pepper, garlic or onion salt, and Worcestershire sauce as desired. Serve hot, garnished with a little finely chopped fresh parsley.

Salzburger Drop Soup

Boil in enough water to make a thick, rich broth, the giblets and bony parts of one small hen. When the chicken is tender, remove from the broth, and add two or three beaten eggs seasoned with salt and pepper. Bring to a slow boil, and serve. A little nutmeg may be shaken into each bowl if desired.

—Pearl Rahn Gnann, *Ye Olde Time Salzburger Cook Book*, Savannah

Chicken-Okra Gumbo

The word gumbo, meaning the hearty meat, tomato, okra, and rice dish that is both a soup and a main course, comes from the African word for okra, its distinctive thickening ingredient.

Yield: 4 to 6 servings

1 3-pound frying chicken,
  cut into serving pieces
About ⅓ cup flour
Salt and pepper to taste
Red pepper to taste
Vegetable oil
1 cup chopped onion
1 cup chopped green pepper
1 28-ounce can tomatoes
2 pounds sliced okra
Chopped green onion and/or
  chopped fresh parsley

Coat chicken well with flour seasoned with salt, pepper, and red pepper by shaking in a large plastic bag. Brown over moderate heat in vegetable oil in a large skillet, turning to brown all sides. Remove from pan and add onion and green pepper to the oil, stirring well until limp but not browned. Add tomatoes, okra, and chicken pieces. Bring to a boil and simmer, covered, for about an hour, or until chicken and okra are tender. Serve over cooked rice, garnished with fresh green chopped onion and parsley.

Note: The gumbo mixture may also be frozen, adding meat and garnishes later as desired.

Beef or Seafood Okra Gumbos

For a beef gumbo, one or two pounds stewing beef, cut into bite-sized pieces and with as much visible fat removed as possible, may be browned in the vegetable oil before adding vegetables. Return to gumbo with the okra and tomatoes and simmer for about one hour, seasoning to taste with salt, pepper, 2 bay leaves, and 1 teaspoon or more Worcestershire sauce.

The traditional Creole way of making a gumbo began with a roux, or flour browned in vegetable oil, before adding other ingredients, but in these recipes okra is used alone as the thickening ingredient. Gumbo may be simmered until as thick as desired, but only add fresh shrimp during the last 15 minutes of cooking time for best results.

For a shrimp gumbo, cook vegetables as above for about 45 minutes, and then add 2 pounds shelled shrimp, cleaned and deveined, and cook for another 15 minutes before serving. For a seafood gumbo, several whole crab and some claw crabmeat, or one 6½-ounce can oysters and their liquid, may also be added with the shrimp if desired.

With seafood gumbos, 1 tablespoon lemon juice and 2 bay leaves, with ½ teaspoon hot pepper sauce may be added with the tomatoes and okra as desired.

The 1896 Gibbs Farm House and Barnyard at the Georgia Agrirama, Tifton, helps recreate the days of the 19th Century family farm.

Okra Soup

Use a 6-quart soup pan. Put a 5 to 10 cent soup bone into it, and cover with cold water to about ½ the pan. Let it boil well, and skim off fat from broth thoroughly. Meanwhile, cut up 1 quart of tender okra, 1 small onion, 4 ears tender corn, 2 green peppers and a handful of lima beans. Put this into the bouillon. When the okra has cooked up thick, add the tomatoes, 1 can, or 1 quart fresh tomatoes, rubbed through a colander to take the seeds. Add a pinch of dissolved baking soda to the tomatoes, and red or white pepper. At the very last, put in salt to taste.

—Mrs. H. R. Jackson, *Some Choice Receipts of Savannah Homemakers,* Savannah, 1904

Catfish Gumbo

Yield: 6 servings

1 pound skinned catfish
 fillets, fresh or frozen
 thawed
½ cup chopped celery
½ cup chopped green pepper
½ cup chopped onion
1 clove garlic, finely chopped
¼ cup melted fat or oil
2 beef bouillon cubes
2 cups boiling water
1 16-ounce can tomatoes
1 10-ounce package frozen
 okra, sliced, or 2 cups
 fresh
¼ teaspoon pepper
2 teaspoons salt
¼ teaspoon thyme
1 whole bay leaf
Dash liquid hot pepper sauce
1½ cups hot cooked rice

Cut fillets into 1-inch pieces: set aside. Cook celery, green pepper, onion and garlic in fat until tender. Dissolve bouillon in water. Add to vegetable mixture with tomatoes, okra, and seasonings. Cover and simmer for 30 minutes. Add fish. Cover and simmer for 15 minutes longer or until fish flakes easily when tested with a fork. Remove bay leaf. Place ¼ cup rice in each of six soup bowls. Fill with gumbo.

—Georgia Extension Service

Stock Pot

Keep a pot going all day, into which you can put any broken-up bones or scraps left over, to make a nourishing broth. Clean turnips, carrots and onions improve it. Before using it, let it get cold, so as to skim off the fat.

Barley, rice or tapioca may be added, and for flavoring add salt, pepper, chopped parsley, celery, a clove, or mace.

As Mr. Holding said, "The only method I know of for properly making your meat thoroughly indigestible, is to hurry a stew."

—"How Girls Can Help Their Country,"
Handbook for Girl Scouts by W. J. Hoxie, 1913

Coastal Bouillabaisse

Yield: 8 to 10 servings

*2 to 3 pounds firm-fleshed
fish*
Salt and pepper
1 cup chopped onion
*2 garlic cloves, finely
chopped or crushed*
1 cup chopped celery
¼ cup chopped parsley
⅓ cup chopped green pepper
*1 28-ounce can tomatoes, or
4 cups cooked tomatoes*
2 tablespoons lemon juice
*2 teaspoons Worcestershire
sauce*
2 tablespoons flour
Olive or vegetable oil
*1½ pounds shrimp, cleaned
and deveined*
*1 pound flaked cooked
crabmeat, cartilage
removed*

Bone fish and cut into serving-sized pieces. Season. Prepare fresh vegetables and mix thoroughly. Pour off some of the juice from the tomatoes and mix it with the lemon juice and sauce. Mix well. Add flour gradually to the tomato juice mixture, and make a thin paste.

Brush oil on the bottom and sides of a large, heavy pot, one with a tight-fitting lid. Place a layer of seasoned fish in the pot. Spoon over this the tomato-flour mixture. Place a layer of vegetables over this. Mash a few tomatoes and sprinkle over the vegetables.

Repeat layering until all ingredients are in the pot. Cover and cook over medium heat until tomato juice starts to boil; then reduce to low heat. Cook, covered, for 45 minutes to one hour, or until fish flakes easily with fork.

The shrimp and crabmeat should be added 10 minutes before serving the stew. Serve hot in large bowl.

A Very Delicious Crab Soup

Stew two large onions in a tablespoon of butter, a button of garlic stewed in a tablespoonful of sweet cream, 1 dozen large tomatoes scalded and strained through a sieve. Put the above in one quart water. Pick 1 dozen crabs, add fat of crabs and season with salt, cayenne and black pepper, marjoram, thyme, and parsley to taste; boil one hour slowly. When finished, add a glass of the best sherry wine and serve with sliced lemon.

—Mrs. C. Phillips, *Some Choice
Receipts of Savannah Homemakers*,
Savannah, 1904

Helen's Crab Meat Chowder

The word chowder comes from *la chaudiere*, the large French copper cooking utensil used to make the classic soup, and from the medieval word caldron.

Yield: 6 servings

1 chicken bouillon cube
¼ cup hot water
1 16-ounce can cream-style corn
2 cups milk
3 green onions with their tops, chopped
2 tablespoons flour
2 tablespoons butter or margarine
1 teaspoon salt, or to taste
⅛ teaspoon pepper
Dash cayenne pepper
1 6½-ounce can crab meat, or 1 cup or more fresh crab meat
Lemon wedges (optional)

Dissolve bouillon in hot water. Place corn, milk, onions, bouillon, and flour into blender container. Cover and run on high speed for 3 minutes, or until smooth. Empty into a saucepan and add butter and salt. Cook, stirring constantly until mixture thickens. Add pepper and cayenne. Flake crab meat, removing any bits of shell, and add to chowder. Heat through, but do not boil. Serve with lemon wedges.

—Helen DeCastro

Cabbage Soup

Yield: 8 servings

1 large cabbage (about 1½ pounds)
1 cup chopped onion
2 tablespoons butter
3 cups water
4 chicken bouillon cubes
¼ teaspoon pepper
1 teaspoon salt
2 tablespoons quick-cooking tapioca
3 cups milk
1 cup finely chopped cooked ham or bacon
1 teaspoon celery seed

Remove and set aside outer leaves of cabbage head and coarsely chop the rest (about 8 cups). Sauté cabbage with onion in the butter in a large saucepan, until cabbage is limp and wilted but not brown. Add the water, bouillon, and seasonings, and simmer for one hour. Dissolve the tapioca in the milk for five minutes, according to package directions. And tapioca and meat, and continue simmering for 15 minutes more, but do not boil. Serve hot, sprinkled with celery seed.

Crystal Chili

Here's the famous chili recipe of the Crystal Beer Parlor, a Savannah institution since 1933. The chili is thick, delicious, and uses no tomatoes or green peppers.

Yield: 4 8-ounce servings

1 cup chopped onion (about 2 medium onions)
2 tablespoons vegetable oil
1 pound lean ground chuck
2 teaspoons chili powder, or to taste
1 teaspoon cumin seed, or to taste
1⅓ cups beef stock (or 2 bouillon cubes and hot water)
1 16-ounce can kidney beans, or 2 cups cooked beans

Sauté onions in oil until soft, but not brown. Add ground chuck to onions, and brown meat. Drain excess fat, if any. Add remaining ingredients and stir together. Cover pan, bring to a boil, and simmer on low heat for at least two hours.

Cheddar Soup

Yield: 4 servings

⅓ cup butter
⅓ cup flour
4 cups milk
1 teaspoon salt
⅛ teaspoon pepper
½ teaspoon celery seed
1 cup shredded or grated
 Cheddar cheese
3 tablespoons minced parsley
2 tablespoons minced chives

Melt butter in a 2-quart saucepan over moderate heat. Add flour and stir until pale gold. Gradually stir in milk, salt, pepper, and celery seed. Continue to stir until slightly thickened. Lower heat and add cheese. Cover and barely simmer for about 7 minutes. Do not boil. Remove from heat and serve, garnished with parsley and chives.

Onion Variation

If desired, cook ½ finely chopped onion in the butter until tender, but not brown, before stirring in the flour and seasonings.

Apple-Onion Variation

Also, one may finely chop three green onions and one small peeled and cored apple (about one cup), and sauté them in the butter before adding the flour. Cook flour mixture about three minutes before adding the liquid. Garnish soup with a little grated nutmeg. (If a very smooth soup is desired, apple and onion may be puréed in the blender or through a sieve and returned to the soup after being browned.)

Benne Seed Topping

Toasted benne, or sesame seeds, are especially good as a topping for Cheddar Soup and many others.

—Emma R. Law

White Sauce Hint

White sauce will never be lumpy if you melt the butter and add flour, blending well; then remove it from the heat before adding the milk.

—Perrin Eidson

Cream Celery Soup

Pound a head of celery, and boil it in one pint of rich chicken broth for 20 minutes. Mix two tablespoons of flour with a little of the broth, and add this back to the boiling chicken broth and celery; also, half a pint of milk. Season with salt and pepper to taste. If too thick, add a little more cream or broth to suit the taste. Strain, and serve at once.

—*Rare Recipes from Washington-Wilkes,*
Washington, 1919

Corn Chowder

Yield: 8 servings

4 cups cubed potatoes
½ cup chopped onion
3 cups water
1½ teaspoons salt, divided
4 cups milk
1 teaspoon butter
1 tablespoon flour
⅛ teaspoon pepper
1 16-ounce can corn, whole
  kernel or cream-style

Cook potatoes and onions in water with 1 teaspoon salt until tender. Drain, saving liquid. Add liquid to milk. Melt butter in the bottom of soup kettle, and add flour, rest of salt, and pepper. Gradually add liquids, stirring continuously to thicken soup, and bring to a boil, but do not boil. Add corn and cooked vegetables. Heat well. Check seasonings. Serve hot.

Note: Chicken broth, if available, may be used in place of part or all of the 3 cups of water.

If fresh of frozen corn is used, it may also be added raw, and simmered in chowder until ready to serve.

Fresh Mushroom Soup

Yield: 6 1-cup servings

1 pound fresh mushrooms
6 tablespoons butter
2 cups chopped onions
½ teaspoon sugar
¼ cup flour
1 cup water
1¾ cups chicken broth
1 cup dry vermouth
2 teaspoons salt, or to taste
¼ teaspoon pepper, or to
  taste

Slice ⅓ of the mushrooms; finely chop the rest. Melt butter in a 2-quart saucepan. Add onions and sugar; sauté until golden. Add mushrooms and sauté for 5 minutes. Stir in flour until smooth. Cook two minutes over medium heat, stirring constantly. Pour in water gradually, stirring constantly, and continue to stir until smooth. Add remaining ingredients. Heat to boiling. Reduce heat and simmer, uncovered, for 10 minutes. Serve hot.

—Betty W. Rauers

Canned But Creative

You can make a fast crab stew by adding crab meat to cream of celery soup, along with a little sherry.

Sherry adds more flavor to any canned cream soup.

Perk up the flavor of cream of chicken soup with ½ teaspoon poultry seasoning and a little fresh or dry chopped parsley.

Add ¼ cup peanut butter to a can of tomato soup, and a third more milk than usual, for a peanutty soup.

Mustard and grated cheese, along with some diced parsley, will enhance cream of potato soup.

A little chili sauce, and some grated onion, will make a better Manhattan Clam Chowder.

Dilute vegetable soups with tomato juice and any water saved from cooking fresh vegetables.

Add a little apple juice to beef bouillon, and sprinkle grated cinnamon over the top.

Drawing by Margaret Berry

Chilled Peach Soup

Yield: 4 to 6 servings

*2 cups peeled and sliced
  fresh peaches*
2 tablespoons lemon juice
¼ cup honey, or to taste
2 cups dry white wine

Combine peaches with lemon juice and put through a strainer, or whip in the blender until puréed. Stir in honey and white wine, combining well, preferably with a wire whisk. Chill and serve cold in cream soup cups.

Note: If desired, a few peach slices, rubbed with lemon to keep the color, may be reserved and used for garnish, or added extra.

In place of the honey, ¼ cup melted fruit jelly, such as apple, peach, cherry or strawberry, may be used for the sweetener.

Potato Soup

Three potatoes, 1 pint milk, 1 teaspoonful chopped onion, 1 celery stalk, 1 teaspoonful salt, ½ teaspoon celery salt, ½ tablespoonful white pepper, ¼ tablespoonful cayenne pepper, ½ tablespoonful flour, 1 tablespoonful butter. Wash and pare the potatoes and let them soak in cold water half an hour. Put them into boiling water and cook until very soft. Cook the onion and celery with the milk in a double boiler. When the potatoes are soft, drain off the water and mash them. Add the boiling milk and seasoning. Put through a strainer and put on to boil again. Put the butter in a small saucepan, and when melted and bubbling, add the flour, and when well mixed, stir into the boiling soup. This flour thickening keeps the potato and milk from separating and gives a smoothness and consistency quite unlike the granular effect which is often noticed. If the soup be too thick, add more very hot milk.

—Mrs. Frank Miller, *Favorite Recipes From
Savannah Homes*, Savannah, 1904

To Make Croutons

To make croutons, butter a slice of evenly cut bread, and divide it into cubes ⅓ of an inch thick. Place these on a tin plate, and place in a moderate oven for 15 minutes. When done, they should be light brown, crisp, and brittle. Sprinkle on soup just before serving.

—Mrs. George W. Anderson,
Favorite Recipes From Savannah Homes, 1904

Cream of Sweet Potato Soup

The sweet potato is a truly native American vegetable, and was cultivated by the Indians before the arrival of the colonists. Although sweet potatoes and yams may be used interchangeably in most recipes, they are of different botanical families!

3 tablespoons butter or
margarine
1 cup finely chopped onion
2 medium carrots, finely
chopped
½ cup finely chopped green
pepper
2 cups chicken stock
2 tablespoons finely chopped
fresh parsley, or 1
teaspoon dried parsley
2 cups mashed cooked sweet
potatoes
2 cups milk
1 cup grated Cheddar cheese
2 teaspoons Worcestershire
sauce
½ teaspoon salt
⅛ teaspoon pepper
Nutmeg to taste

Melt butter or margarine in a large saucepan over medium heat. Add onion, carrots, and green pepper; stir until onion is limp, about 5 minutes. Stir in stock and parsley, and bring to a boil. Reduce heat to low; cover and simmer until vegetables are tender, about 15 minutes.

Stir in potatoes and milk and heat to simmering, stirring constantly. Add cheese and stir until melted. Stir in seasonings, except nutmeg; taste and adjust if more needed. Serve hot, with a little ground nutmeg on each bowl.

Note: This is also a good use for leftover mashed sweet potatoes; adjust seasonings to compensate for any already in potatoes.

Violet's Onion Soup

Use a chicken or turkey, or domestic or wild duck for your meat stock. Cook meat for a long time as for regular stock the day before; set overnight and skim fat. Take your onions, one large Spanish onion for four people, and slice. Put in a frying pan with butter, and just warm good for browning. Put in the soup, and simmer for an hour. Leave the onions in; don't strain. Put a round piece of toast ½ inch thick, with thick cheese, in the bottom of each plate. Serve with grated Parmesan cheese; not the bottled kind, but the lump grated.

—Family cookbook of Sophie Meldrim Shonnard, Savannah

Doughboy Dumplings

Yield: 4 servings

1 cup flour
½ teaspoon salt
2 teaspoons baking powder
2 tablespoons vegetable
 shortening or butter, at
 room temperature
½ cup milk

Sift the dry ingredients together and blend in shortening. Stir in milk. Blend only until flour is completely moistened. Drop by large serving-spoon-fuls onto any good simmering hot stew. Cover tightly and cook for 15 minutes without lifting lid.

Artichoke Soup

Yield: 6 to 8 servings

1 14-ounce can artichoke
 bottoms
3 10-ounce cans chicken
 broth
1 whole clove garlic
1 cup dry white wine
Salt and pepper to taste
Tabasco (optional)

Mash artichokes. Add broth and garlic. Bring to a boil. Pour in wine and heat just to boiling. Season as desired, adding Tabasco for a spicy taste. Remove garlic before serving.

—Fantasies Shop, Savannah

Oaklodg, a handsome 1873 residence in Tennille. Drawing by Sterling Everett

Yogurt-Cucumber Soup

Christopher Columbus planted the cucumber in Haiti, and Spanish explorers later brought it to the New World. Dieters are grateful, since the average cucumber has only about twenty-five calories.

Yield: 4 servings

2 medium cucumbers, peeled and sliced (about 3 cups)
1 cup water
¼ cup onion slices
¼ teaspoon salt, or to taste
⅛ teaspoon pepper
¼ cup flour
2 cups chicken broth, divided
¼ teaspoon ground cloves, or 1 bay leaf
1 cup plain yogurt, chilled
1 tablespoon finely chopped dill or chives

Combine cucumber slices with water, onion, salt, and pepper in a 2-quart saucepan. Cook, covered, until very soft. Put through a fine strainer or blend in electric blender until smooth. Set aside. Combine flour with ½ cup chicken broth in the same saucepan. Stir until smooth. Gradually stir in the remaining chicken broth and blend well. Add the purée and cloves or bay leaf. Stir the soup over low heat until it begins to simmer. Simmer for two minutes, but do not boil. Remove from heat and chill in a covered container.

When ready to serve, stir in the yogurt and dill or chives. Serve very cold in chilled bowls.

—Peggy Gunn

Mt. Kisco Wine Soup

Yield: 4 servings

4 cups red or white wine
1½ cups hot water
2 cups bread cubes
4 tablespoons butter
2 tablespoons grated lemon peel
4 egg yolks
2 tablespoons sugar

Pour the wine and hot water into a 2-quart saucepan. Cover, heat, and simmer 30 minutes, but do not boil.

Meanwhile, sauté 2 cups bread cubes in butter until well toasted. Add lemon peel, mix well, and set aside. Keep warm.

Beat egg yolks until foamy and add the sugar. Continue to beat until well blended. Stir in 1 cup of the warm wine mixture, and then gradually combine the two mixtures, stirring constantly. Cook together for one minute, but do not allow to boil. Serve warm over croutons in bouillon cups.

—Betty W. Rauers

Salads

Valdosta Asparagus Mold

Yield: 4 to 6 servings

¾ cup sugar
1¼ cups water, divided
¼ cup wine vinegar
2 envelopes unflavored gelatin
2 cups cooked asparagus, drained and cut into thirds
1 tablespoon lemon juice
1 cup chopped celery
¼ cup chopped stuffed green olives
¼ cup chopped onion or green onions
½ cup chopped pecans

Combine sugar, 1 cup water, and vinegar and bring to a boil in a small saucepan. Dissolve gelatin in ¼ cup water and add to boiled mixture. Mix well and cool. When partially set, add remaining ingredients. Chill until firm, and serve on lettuce with mayonnaise if desired.

Nell May's Chicken Aspic

Boil one roasting chicken, and cut up fine, as for salad. Blanch ⅓ pound shelled almonds, and cut into threes. Chop 1 bunch celery as for salad. Take one quart of the water the chicken was boiled in, and skim off all grease. Heat to boiling point, and remove from fire. Add Knox gelatine [*sic*] as directed and stir until dissolved. Add the juice of one lemon to this, salt and pepper, then chicken, nuts, and celery. Put in molds, and when cold, in the icebox overnight.

—Family cookbook of Sophie Meldrim Shonnard, Savannah

49

Jellied Cranberry Salad

Yield: 8 servings

*4 cups (1 pound) fresh
  cranberries*
1 cup sugar
1 envelope unflavored gelatin
½ cup apple juice
½ cup finely chopped celery
*½ cup finely chopped peeled
  apple*
⅓ cup chopped pecans

Wash cranberries; drain and remove stems. Chop coarsely. Add sugar. Set cranberry mixture aside about 15 minutes, stirring occasionally.

Sprinkle gelatin over apple juice in small saucepan, and soften 5 minutes. Place over low heat, stirring until gelatin is dissolved. Mix well and cool until partially set. Add gelatin mixture, celery, apples, and nuts to cranberries; mix well. Pour into 3⅓-cup mold. Refrigerate covered until firm, for 6 to 8 hours.

To unmold, run a small spatula around edge of mold. Invert on a serving plate; place a hot, damp dishcloth on bottom of mold. Shake to release. Repeat if necessary. Serve with mayonnaise if desired.

Shrimp Aspic

Cook one small can of tomato sauce with five times the amount of water, adding a small stalk of celery, half an onion, half a lemon, a large sprig of parsley, and salt and pepper to taste. Cook down until mixture measures about three cups, and strain. Add ½ cup cold water, in which two tablespoons gelatin has been dissolved. Add to this two cups of boiled peeled chopped shrimp, one cup of minced celery, and one cup of chopped peeled [hard-cooked] eggs. Pour all into a ring mold and put on ice. When set, turn out on a platter garnished with lettuce, and serve with a small bowl of chili sauce dressing (such as on p. 64) in the center.

Tomato Aspic

One can tomatoes, ½ lemon, 1 slice onion, 1 teaspoon salt, ½ teaspoon pepper, a few celery tops, 2 bay leaves, gelatine [*sic*] and cold water. Strain the tomatoes, after bringing them first to a boil. Put the juice in a small pan with the onion, bay leaves, celery, salt, and pepper. Bring again to a boiling point, and add the gelatine, mixed according to directions with cold water. Mix until it is dissolved, and add lemon juice. Strain. Put in molds on ice 4 hours. Serve on lettuce leaves with mayonnaise.

—Mrs. F. B. Screven, *Some Choice Receipts of
Savannah Homemakers*, Savannah, 1904

Drawing by Margaret Lanier, Guyton

Sour Cream Green Bean Salad

Yield: 8 to 10 servings

4 cups canned (or frozen, cooked) French Style green beans, drained
1 small onion, chopped fine
1 tablespoon sugar
1 tablespoon cider or white wine vinegar
½ cup sour cream
Salt and pepper to taste
Chopped pimento (optional)

Combine beans with onion. Blend remaining ingredients and pour over. Toss lightly. Refrigerate, covered, until time to serve. Good for potluck dinners.

—Jessie Schandolph

Burke County Cole Slaw

Yield: 4 servings

⅓ cup sour cream
⅓ cup mayonnaise
2 teaspoons lemon juice
½ teaspoon celery seed
1 teaspoon sugar
Salt to taste
Cayenne pepper to taste
3 cups shredded cabbage,
   white and/or red
½ cup shredded carrots
½ cup finely chopped green
   pepper

Blend first 7 ingredients together; cover and chill. Toss vegetables together; cover and chill. When ready to serve, toss both mixtures together.

—Emma R. Law

Wilmington Island Apple Slaw

Yield: 8 servings

4½ cups thinly sliced cored,
   unpeeled red apples (about
   1½ pounds)
3 cups finely shredded green
   cabbage
1 cup sour cream
3 tablespoons lemon juice
1 tablespoon sugar
¾ teaspoon salt
⅛ teaspoon pepper
1 tablespoon poppy seed

In a large bowl, lightly toss all the ingredients until well combined. Refrigerate at least one hour before serving. This is especially good with pork or barbecue.

—Gail Hart

Cold Slaugh Dressing

Mix one cup cream in the double boiler with the yolks of three eggs; ½ teaspoon mustard; 1 teaspoon salt; 3 tablespoons sugar; 3 tablespoons vinegar; dash cayenne pepper, and 1 teaspoon celery seeds. Cook over hot water until thick and smooth, stirring well. Cool and pour over thinly sliced cabbage. For best results, cabbage should be cut and placed in ice water for three hours to get crisp, then drained well before adding dressing.

—Family cookbook of Sophie Meldrim Shonnard, Savannah

Carrot-Citrus Salad

Yield: 4 to 6 servings

½ cup raisins or currants
2 tablespoons pineapple or
 orange juice
4 cups shredded carrots
1 cup drained crushed
 pineapple, or 1 cup
 mandarin orange slices
½ cup mayonnaise, or to
 taste

Place raisins or currants in a bowl and pour juice over. Set aside for about five minutes. Then add carrots and fruit, mix well, and toss with mayonnaise. Add more mayonnaise if desired.

Cucumbers in Yogurt

Yield: 4 to 6 servings

2 large cucumbers, chilled
1 cup plain yogurt
¼ teaspoon salt
⅛ teaspoon white pepper
¼ teaspoon finely grated dill
 weed
2 tablespoons grated onion

Wash and place cucumbers in refrigerator early in the day. An hour or so before serving, mix remaining ingredients and refrigerate, covered. About 15 minutes before serving, peel cucumbers and cut into thin slices. Mix with yogurt and refrigerate again. Serve on lettuce, sprinkled with parsley if desired.

Eggs with Louie Dressing

This recipe is easier than making deviled eggs, and the dressing is also good with other salads.

Yield: 4 servings

½ cup ketchup
½ cup mayonnaise
2 tablespoons sour cream
1 teaspoon lemon juice
⅛ teaspoon dried basil, or to
 taste
2 tablespoons dry red wine
Salt and pepper to taste
½ teaspoon onion powder
4 extra large eggs, (or 8
 small ones), hard-cooked
 and shelled

Combine dressing ingredients and blend well. Cut eggs vertically in half, and place on lettuce. Spoon dressing over eggs and sprinkle with chives, capers, or fresh parsley.

Old-Fashioned Wilted Lettuce Salad

Yield: 4 to 6 servings

6 cups salad greens
1 cup green onion slices, or
   fresh onion rings
2 slices lean bacon, cut into
   ½-inch pieces
1 egg, well-beaten
3 tablespoons vinegar
2 tablespoons sugar
¼ teaspoon salt

Wash and dry salad greens, and break into bite-sized pieces. Add onions. Set aside.

Sauté bacon bits in a small skillet until lightly brown. Remove and drain on paper towel, setting aside fat to cool in skillet. Combine egg, vinegar, sugar, and salt; gradually stir into cooled bacon fat in skillet. Return to very low heat and cook, stirring constantly, until thickened. Pour over greens. Add bacon and serve immediately.

—Gail Hart

Mushrooms with Shallots

Yield: 4 servings

½ pound fresh mushrooms
¼ cup minced shallots or
   young green onions
1 tablespoon Dijon-type
   mustard
3 tablespoons white wine
   vinegar
⅓ cup vegetable oil
Salt and pepper to taste
Salad greens for garnish
Parsley for garnish

Wash, drain, and dry mushrooms with paper towels. Cut into thin "umbrella" slices. Place in a bowl. Blend shallots, mustard, vinegar, oil, salt, and pepper. Pour over mushrooms. Cover and marinate for about 2 hours in the refrigerator. Drain if necessary and serve garnished with a few greens and parsley.

Columbia Pea Salad

Yield: 4 servings

2 cups cooked peas, drained
¼ cup chopped onions or
   green onions
¾ cup chopped celery
¼ cup chopped sweet red
   pepper
½ teaspoon celery seed
¼ teaspoon pepper
½ cup mayonnaise, or to
   taste

Combine ingredients in order given, and check flavors. Cover and chill for at least two hours before serving.

Pecan-Pepper Salad

Yield: 4 to 6 servings

4 ounces cream cheese, at room temperature
1 ounce crumbled blue cheese
⅓ cup pecans, coarsely chopped
¼ cup French dressing, or to taste
1 teaspoon Worcestershire sauce
Dash hot sauce
2 green peppers, tops and insides removed
Lettuce

Combine cheeses, nuts, and seasonings. Pack into green peppers, cover, and chill for several hours. Before serving, slice peppers crosswise into slices about ⅓ inch thick, with a very sharp knife. Serve on lettuce, with additional French dressing optional.

—Harry Harman, Valdosta

Emma's Hot Potato Salad

Yield: 4 servings

6 strips bacon, chopped
2 teaspoons flour
1 tablespoon sugar
½ teaspoon salt
¼ teaspoon pepper
¼ cup white wine vinegar
½ cup water
4 cups hot sliced cooked potatoes
½ cup chopped onions
¼ cup minced parsley

Fry bacon over moderate heat until crisp. Drain, reserving 2 teaspoons fat to return to skillet. Push bacon pieces to side and sprinkle in flour, sugar, salt, and pepper. Stir until smooth. Cook over low heat, stirring constantly, for a moment or so. Stir in vinegar and water. Continue cooking, stirring constantly, until mixture thickens slightly. Stir in potatoes, onions, and parsley. Serve hot.

Marinated Salad

For a quick vegetable salad, cooked and drained mixed vegetables, green beans, peas, or asparagus may be marinated with French or Italian dressing. Chopped celery, green pepper, onion, or sliced stuffed green olives may be added if desired. Drain and serve on lettuce or other greens, garnished with tomato, cucumber, or radish slices.

Buccaneer Shrimp Salad

Yield: 3 to 4 servings

*1 pound shrimp, boiled,
    shelled, deveined, and
    chopped*
⅓ cup chopped green pepper
1 cup chopped celery
*2 hard-cooked eggs, shelled
    and chopped*
*2 tablespoons sweet pickle
    relish or chopped sweet
    pickles*
*2 tablespoons grated onion
    (optional)*
½ cup mayonnaise
*1 tablespoon prepared
    mustard (optional)*
½ teaspoon salt, or to taste
⅛ teaspoon pepper
Lettuce
Paprika for garnish
Tomato slices for garnish
Olives for garnish (optional)

Combine first 6 ingredients. Combine mayonnaise with mustard and seasonings and stir into salad. Serve on lettuce, sprinkled with paprika. Garnish with tomato slices and olives as desired.

Herb Dressing

Yield: 1¾ cups

1 garlic clove, crushed
¼ teaspoon dry mustard
½ teaspoon paprika
¼ teaspoon black pepper
¼ teaspoon dried basil
1 cup olive or vegetable oil
*¼ cup tarragon vinegar or
    red wine vinegar*
⅛ cup Burgundy wine
*¼ cup parsley, finely
    chopped*

Combine ingredients well in order listed. Cover and chill, shaking well before serving over salad greens.

Note: This is especially good with a fresh mushroom and onion salad.

Georgia Shrimp Mousse

Yield: 12 servings

2 envelopes unflavored
  gelatin
½ cup cold water
8 ounces cream cheese, at
  room temperature
¾ cup chopped celery
¼ cup chopped green pepper
1 cup mayonnaise
1 tablespoon grated onion
2 cups cooked shrimp,
  shelled and deveined,
  finely chopped
2 tablespoons pimento, finely
  chopped (optional)
¾ teaspon salt
⅛ teaspoon pepper

Soften gelatin in cold water and dissolve over low heat. Fold into cheese in a mixing bowl and combine with other ingredients. Pour into oiled mold and chill until firm, covered. Serve with mild-flavored crackers.

Emma's Whipped Salad Dressing

Yield: about 1 cup

¼ cup sugar
⅛ teaspoon ground mace
1 tablespoon flour
⅓ cup orange juice
2 tablespoons lemon juice
½ cup heavy cream

Mix sugar, mace, and flour in a small saucepan. Stir in juices. Cook over moderate heat, stirring constantly, until mixture boils and thickens. Cool, stirring occasionally. Cover and refrigerate until needed. When ready to serve, whip cream and fold into chilled mixture, blending well. Serve with fruit salads.

—Emma R. Law

Salad Savings

To get the last bit of mayonnaise or salad dressing out of a jar, dribble a little wine vinegar into the jar, place the cap on tightly, and shake well.

For fruit salads, a little orange juice may be added instead of vinegar.

Andersonville's Pennington St. James log and fieldstone 1927 church is open daily to the public and has been the scene of many weddings. Drawing © by Patsy Payne Lewis, courtesy Andersonville Guild

Spinach Salad

Yield: 6 to 8 servings

Salad:
2 to 3 bunches fresh spinach
8 ounces drained canned
   bean sprouts, or handful
   of fresh bean sprouts
4 ounces water chestnuts,
   drained and sliced thin
2 cut-up hard-cooked eggs
8 slices bacon, fried crisp
   and crumbled
1 small onion, sliced thin

Wash spinach; drain. Remove stems. Toss in large bowl with other ingredients and add dressing.

Dressing:
1 cup salad oil
½ cup wine vinegar
½ cup sugar
⅓ cup catsup
Dash salt

Blend well and pour over greens, which should be chilled. Fresh mushrooms, sliced, may also be added.

—Kathleen Horst, *Macon*
Brown's Crossing Crookbook

Sliced Tomatoes and Cucumbers with Mint Dressing

Yield: 6 servings

⅓ cup red wine or tarragon
  vinegar
⅔ cup vegetable oil
¼ cup sugar
½ teaspoon salt
⅛ teaspoon pepper
½ cup chopped fresh mint
  leaves (use less if dried
  mint)
4 cucumbers
6 ripe tomatoes
Romaine lettuce

Combine first 6 ingredients and shake well. Peel and thinly slice cucumbers, and slice tomatoes thinly also. Arrange in a shallow dish, and pour dressing over. Cover and chill for several hours, spooning dressing over occasionally. To serve, drain and place on lettuce.

Augusta Turkey Salad

Yield: 3 to 4 servings

3 cups chopped cooked
  turkey or chicken
4 hard-cooked eggs, chopped
1½ cups chopped celery
1½ cups white grapes,
  halved
½ cup chopped pecans
1 cup mayonnaise, or to taste
1 teaspoon salt

Combine ingredients and check seasoning. Serve on lettuce or other greens.

Note: If desired, this also makes a good molded salad, combined with 2 envelopes unflavored gelatin, 1 cup hot turkey broth and 1 cup water, according to package directions. Chill until firm, and serve on greens.

—Geneva Hendrix

Waldorf Salad

Pare and core (just as ready to use), 4 large, tart apples, and cut in pieces. Add 1 quart celery, cut in ½ inch pieces, 1 teaspoon salt or to taste, 2 tablespoons tarragon vinegar, 1 teaspoon paprika; mix together, and stir in 1½ cups stiff mayonnaise dressing. Serve on lettuce leaves, or decorate with celery tops.

—Mrs. Thomas J. Charlton, *Some Choice Receipts of
Savannah Homemakers*, Savannah, 1904

Atlanta Buttermilk Dressing

Yield: 1½ cups

½ cup buttermilk
1 cup mayonnaise
¼ cup finely chopped onion
2 tablespoons finely chopped
    parsley
1 garlic clove, finely chopped
½ teaspoon paprika

Stir buttermilk into mayonnaise and blend well. Add other ingredients and blend. Cover and chill before serving.

Note: For a low-calorie dressing use low-calorie mayonnaise.

Celery Seed Dressing

Yield: 1¾ cups

1 teaspoon salt
1 teaspoon dry mustard
1 teaspoon paprika
1 teaspoon celery or poppy
    seed
½ cup corn syrup or honey
¼ to ⅓ cup vinegar, to taste
    (may be part lemon juice)
1 cup corn oil
1 tablespoon grated onion

Place all ingredients in a bowl and beat with a rotary beater until well blended and thickened. Place in a covered container and chill several hours. Shake before serving.

Note: For a variation, add ⅔ cup ketchup before blending.

Salad A L'Italienne

Pare and cut up a good size carrot and turnip and boil in separate salted waters for 10 minutes each; drain, and let them cool. Cut up separately two truffles, and six mushrooms; also the breast of a cooked chicken. Mix all with a sauce made of 1 teaspoon anchovy sauce, 1 tablespoon of vinegar, 2 tablespoons oil, ½ teaspoon salt, 1 saltspoon paprika, and a pinch of cayenne. Form into a mound, and serve with either a piece of cooked cauliflower, or Brussels sprouts, or asparagus tips, on top.

—Mrs. H. R. Jackson, *Some Choice Receipts of
Savannah Homemakers*, Savannah, 1904

Blue Cheese-Mustard Dressing

Yield: 1 cup

½ cup olive or vegetable oil
¼ cup wine vinegar
¼ cup crumbled blue cheese,
* at room temperature*
¼ teaspoon salt
⅛ teaspoon ground pepper
1½ teaspoon Dijon-type
* mustard, or to taste*
½ teaspoon sugar (optional)
1 teaspoon garlic powder

Combine ingredients and blend well. Cover and chill to allow flavors to blend. Serve on salad greens.

Emma's Egg-Free Mayonnaise

Yield: 1½ cups

⅓ cup chilled evaporated
* milk*
½ teaspoon salt
¼ teaspoon paprika
¾ teaspoon dry mustard
1 tablespoon lemon juice
⅛ teaspoon hot sauce
1 cup vegetable oil

Place all ingredients but the oil in a chilled bowl. Beat at high speed until double in volume. Gradually add oil, mixing in while beating on high speed, until all is absorbed. Refrigerate until needed, covered.

—Emma R. Law

Garlic Vinegar

To make a good flavored vinegar for salads, steep 1 large garlic clove, cut in quarters, or 2 small ones, halved, in a pint of vinegar for about 2 weeks before using.

Prepared Vinegar For Salads

To 2 gallons of good vinegar, add 1 pound of ginger, 1 of horseradish, 1 of mustard seed, and 1 ounce black pepper, 1 of mace, 1 of nutmeg, and garlic if desired. Put all into the vinegar and let it remain covered for a year, stirring frequently.

—Bryan family cookbook, Savannah, circa 1885

Fishermen's Wharf Salad Dressing

Yield: 2 cups

¾ cup chili sauce
1 cup mayonnaise
1 tablespoon grated onion
 (optional)
¼ cup pickle relish
1 teaspoon lemon juice
1 teaspoon Worcestershire
 sauce, or to taste
½ teaspoon horseradish

Combine ingredients and blend well. Serve with seafood salads.

Fruit Salad Dressing

Yield: 1½ cups

½ cup sugar
1 teaspoon dry mustard
1 teaspoon salt
½ teaspoon orange juice
3 tablespoons white wine
 vinegar
1 cup vegetable oil
¼ cup mayonnaise
1 tablespoon celery seed

Combine all ingredients except celery seed. Blend well with electric mixer or beater. Add seed and stir well. Chill. Shake well before serving.

Note: As in most salad dressings, seasoned salts such as celery salt may be used in place of the salt in this recipe.

Olive Salad Dressing

Yield: about 2 cups

1 cup mayonnaise
½ cup chopped stuffed green
 olives
2 tablespoons oil from olives
2 hard-cooked eggs, peeled
 and chopped
⅛ teaspoon paprika
½ teaspoon onion salt

Mix ingredients and serve on lettuce wedges or other green salad.

Peanut Butter Salad Dressing

Yield: 2 cups

½ cup peanut butter
1 3-ounce package cream cheese, at room temperature
2 tablespoons honey
1 tablespoon lemon juice
¾ cup pineapple or orange juice

Blend peanut butter and cheese. Gradually mix in honey and juices, stirring until well blended. Chill, covered, and serve over fruit salads.

Spicy Russian Dressing

Yield: 1½ cups

1 cup mayonnaise
¼ cup ketchup
2 tablespoons wine vinegar
2 tablespoons chopped chives or parsley
2 tablespoons chopped pimento
1 tablespoon prepared horseradish
½ teaspoon garlic salt or powder

Combine ingredients in order given; cover and chill well before serving.

Hayden Pearson's Salad Dressing

Yield: 1 cup

½ cup vegetable oil
¼ cup vinegar
¼ cup ketchup
¼ cup finely chopped onion
1 garlic clove, minced
1 teaspoon Worcestershire sauce
⅛ cup sugar
1 teaspoon salt

Combine ingredients well and shake in a bottle, or combine with blender. This is better after about 4 days in the refrigerator, to allow flavors to combine. It is also an excellent dip for cauliflower and other fresh vegetables.

—Sophie Meldrim Shonnard

Sour Cream Salad Dressing

Yield: 1 cup

1 cup sour cream
¼ cup confectioners' sugar
1 tablespoon lemon or lime juice
⅛ teaspoon salt
1 tablespoon poppy or celery seed

Combine ingredients and chill well, covered, before serving. Excellent on a fruit salad.

Sour Cream-Thousand Island Dressing

Yield: 1½ cups

⅓ cup chili sauce
3 tablespoons chopped green pepper
1 hard-cooked egg, finely chopped
1 tablespoon grated onion
½ teaspoon celery or onion salt
1 cup sour cream

Combine ingredients. Cover and chill.

Chili Sauce Dressing

Mix 6 tablespoons salad oil with ¼ teaspoon onion juice, 2 teaspoons vinegar, 1 teaspoon salt, ¼ teaspoon red pepper, dash of paprika, and 1 teaspoon sugar. Beat well, and add 2 teaspoons chili sauce, or to taste. Mix until smoothly blended.

You can also make a good sauce with 1 cup mayonnaise to ½ cup chili sauce.

—Family cookbook of Sophie Meldrim Shonnard, Savannah

Cohen Row, Savannah, built in 1881. From an original drawing by Pamela Lee. Copyright by Pamela Lee

Sour Cream-Honey Dressing

Yield: 1¼ cups

1 cup sour cream
¼ teaspoon salt
1 tablespoon lemon juice
1 tablespoon orange juice
¼ cup honey

Combine ingredients and beat until stiff. Cover and chill until needed.

Yogurt-Curry Dressing

Yield: 1 cup

1 cup plain yogurt
2 teaspoons confectioners'
 sugar
1 teaspoon grated orange
 peel
¼ teaspoon curry powder, or
 to taste

Blend ingredients; cover and chill until serving time.

Yogurt-Sesame Dressing

Yield: 1¼ cups

1 cup plain yogurt
2 tablespoons toasted sesame
 seeds
2 tablespoons honey
1 teaspoon grated orange
 peel
1 teaspoon grated lemon peel
⅛ teaspoon salt

Blend ingredients; cover and chill. Excellent on a fruit salad.
  Note: For variety, vanilla-flavored yogurt may be substituted.

Sallad

Take equal quantities of cabbage and green tomatoes. Season with green onions and green peppers to your taste. Chop all very fine and put in a pan. Cover with a handful of salt, letting them remain a few hours. Then squeeze out, and put in vinegar, for 24 hours. Squeeze out of the vinegar, and put in a large jar with layers of ground and seed mustard, cloves, cinnamon and horse radish to your taste. Fill the jar with fresh vinegar. Cover. In a week, this will be fit for the table.

—Family cookbook of Mrs. Lucinda Williams, Milledgeville, 1857

Crisp Onion Rings

In adding fresh onion rings to a salad, they will be crisp if you put them in ice water for an hour in the refrigerator, then drain and dry between paper towels before adding to the salad bowl.

Breads

That Dieter's Downfall, Cracklin' Bread

A Macon food columnist and author of *Hearth Cookery: Authentic Recipes From America's past,* writes about a Georgia specialty:

> *"There is no flavor comparable, I will contend, to that of the crisp, tawny, well-watched and not over-roasted crackling," the English essayist Charles Lamb wrote over 150 years ago. Sounds as though he really enjoyed well-prepared pork, even in a country devoted to great haunches of beef!*
>
> *That Southern favorite, cracklin's, or bits of fried pork fat used to flavor Dixie dishes in the days before so many became calorie conscious, were once associated with butchering time and fresh pork on the plantation. However, it is now possible to have them anytime by trimming the fat parts of fresh pork chops, ribs or roasts, chopping them into bits with the kitchen cleaver, and storing them in the freezer until needed.*

They may be "rendered" by roasting for half an hour in a preheated 325 degree oven—I like my old black iron skillet for this. The process gives you both cracklin's and some pretty white lard. (Once you've made your cracklin's, use about ½ cup in your favorite corn bread recipe. You can use some of the rendered pork lard for the shortening, and to grease the pan or skillet—however, remember that more lard will still cook out of the cracklin's in baking.)

The pan is traditionally greased and heated in the oven as the stove is preheated, to give a good crusty bread. Don't burn yourself!

I have a friend, a nutritionist, who adds peanut butter to her cracklin' bread: says it takes care of protein deficiency, and makes a full meal. Anyway, to me, cracklin' bread is a special delight: cracklin' bread and soupy dried limas; cracklin' bread and collard greens, cooked with a ham hock. . . . It was what you might call a basic food, invented in pioneer times by people who used what was at hand, and worked so hard with the axe, hoe and hammer, they didn't have time to worry about cholesterol!

—Violet Moore, Montezuma

Angie's Corn Bread

The following recipe is good as it is, or can be combined with cracklin's as described above. It is also the basis for a fantastic cornbread and oyster stuffing for poultry (see page 122).

Yield: 1 8-inch pan

1 cup enriched cornmeal
1 cup flour
1 tablespoon baking powder
1 teaspoon salt
1 egg, beaten
1 cup milk
¼ cup vegetable oil

Preheat oven to 425 degrees F. Combine dry ingredients in a large bowl. Add egg, milk, and oil. Beat about 1 minute, or until smooth. Bake in greased 8-inch square pan for 20 to 25 minutes.

—Angie Chilen, Port Wentworth

Mrs. Ryder's Corn Bread

Whole corn gives this bread a distinctive texture. Baking it in a pre-heated pan adds the appealing crust.

Yield: 1 9-inch square

⅓ cup vegetable oil
1 cup self-rising cornmeal
½ cup self-rising flour
2 eggs, beaten
1 cup buttermilk
½ teaspoon baking powder
½ teaspoon salt
1 cup cream-style corn

Pour oil into a lightly greased 9-inch square pan. Place pan in oven, and begin to preheat to 350 degrees F.

Meanwhile, mix the cornmeal and flour together in a bowl and add beaten eggs. Add buttermilk, baking powder, salt, and corn, mixing enough to moisten well. Remove hot pan from oven, pour hot oil into batter, and stir to mix well. Pour batter into pan and bake about 25 to 30 minutes, or until golden brown.

—Marilyn Whelpley

Ola Rogalski's Jalapeno Corn Bread

This hearty recipe makes enough for a crowd, or extra loaves which freeze well.

Yield: 1 13-by-9-by-2-inch
*   pan, or 3 9-inch loaves*

2½ cups cornmeal
1 cup flour
2 tablespoons sugar
1 tablespoon salt
1⅓ tablespoons baking
*   powder*
3 eggs
1½ cups milk
½ cup vegetable oil
2 cups cream-style corn
6 to 8 jalapeno peppers,
*   seeded, finely chopped*
1 cup chopped onion
2 cups grated Cheddar
*   cheese*

Preheat oven to 425 degrees F. Place a well-greased 13-by-9-by-2-inch baking pan, or 3 9-inch pans, in the oven to preheat, for a crispy crust on the bread.

In a large bowl, stir the dry ingredients together. In a separate small bowl, beat the eggs and add the milk and oil. Mix well, add to flour mixture; then stir in corn, peppers, onions, and cheese, mixing well to moisten batter ingredients. Pour into hot pan or pans, and bake for about 45 minutes (less for smaller pans) or until golden brown on top.

Antebellum Scott-Tate house in Milledgeville, where Mary Howell Scott was living at the time she recorded her family recipes, circa 1918. Drawing by Sterling Everett

Confederate Spoon Bread

Beat 2 tablespoons lard, 1 egg, and 1 teaspoon sugar well together. Add 1 pint milk, 1½ cups cornmeal, 1 teaspoon salt, and 1 teaspoon baking powder. Mix well, pour into [greased] oven dish, and bake slowly [at 325 degrees F. for about an hour, or] until brown.

—Family cookbook of Mary Howell Scott,
Milledgeville, circa 1918

Omendaw Corn Bread

Take about 2 cups boiled hominy while it is hot, and put in a large tablespoon of butter or lard. Beat 4 eggs and stir into the hominy, along with 1 pint milk and ½ pint sifted cornmeal. It should be about as thick as boiled custard. Bake in a deep greased pan [at 400 degrees F. for 20 to 25 minutes].

—Bryan family cookbook, Savannah, circa 1885

Louise's Sour Cream-Banana Bread

Yield: 1 loaf

*¾ cup (1½ sticks) butter or
    margarine, at room
    temperature
1½ cups sugar
1½ cups mashed bananas
2 eggs, well-beaten
1 teaspoon vanilla extract
1 teaspoon baking soda
2 cups sifted flour
¾ teaspoon salt
½ cup sour cream
¾ cup chopped pecans*

Preheat oven to 325 degrees F. Cream butter and sugar together thoroughly. Blend in bananas, eggs, and vanilla and combine well. Sift dry ingredients together and add to mixture, alternating with sour cream and mix thoroughly after each addition. Stir in nuts and mix well.

Grease and flour a 9-by-5-by-3-inch loaf pan and pour in batter. Bake for about 1 hour and 15 minutes, or until a nice golden brown. Excellent with whipped butter or cream cheese spread.

—Louise Hinely

Benne-Cheese Bread

Yield: 1 8-inch loaf

*½ cup milk
2 tablespoons sugar
1 teaspoon salt
1 envelope active dry yeast
¼ cup warm water
2½ cups sifted flour
1 cup grated Cheddar cheese
½ cup toasted benne seed*

Scald milk. Stir in sugar and salt; set aside to cool to lukewarm. Sprinkle yeast over warm water to soften. Stir into lukewarm milk mixture. Add half the flour and beat until smooth. Stir in cheese and benne seed, beating until smooth. Work in enough of the remaining flour to make an easily handled, not sticky, dough. Turn out onto lightly floured board; knead until smooth and elastic.

Place in a greased bowl. Grease top, cover with a towel, and set aside to rise in a warm place, free from drafts, until doubled in bulk, about 1 hour and 15 minutes. Punch down, and shape into a loaf to fit a greased 8-by-4-inch loaf pan. Cover and set aside to rise as before, for about 45 minutes.

Preheat oven to 375 degrees F. Bake for about 30 minutes, or until loaf shrinks from sides of pan and top is browned. Remove from pan and cool thoroughly on a rack before cutting, two to three hours.

Note: This recipe may be doubled or tripled, but use a little less salt if you do so, as salt has a tendency to build up in such recipes.

—Emma R. Law

Ellen Young's Cuban Bread

Yield: 2 loaves

2 packages active dry yeast
2 cups lukewarm water
2 teaspoons salt
2 tablespoons sugar
6½ cups plus 2 tablespoons
  sifted flour, divided
Cornmeal as needed
Cold water as needed
Butter as needed

In a room-temperature bowl, crumble yeast in water. Stir in salt and sugar, preferably with a wooden spoon. Then stir in 6½ cups sifted flour, 1 cup at a time.

Turn dough onto a lightly floured board, using some of the extra 2 tablespoons flour. Knead lightly but enough for the dough to be smooth and elastic. Form into a ball and place in a greased bowl. Turn dough once, so that all is coated.

Set aside to rise in a warm, draft-free place until double in bulk, about 40 minutes. Make finger indentation in dough. If imprint remains, it has risen enough. Place on lightly floured board, using some or all of the remainder of the extra flour.

Punch dough down. Cut in half and shape into two round loaves. Place on baking sheet that has been greased and sprinkled generously with cornmeal. Cover dough with a tea towel, and set aside to rise 5 minutes. Cut an X on the top of each loaf. Brush top with cold water for a crisp crust. Place in a cold oven.

Set oven to 400 degrees F. with two pie or cake pans filled with boiling water placed in the oven also, on rack under bread or on same middle rack. Bake for 45 to 55 minutes. If bread is getting too brown, cover loaves lightly with a piece of foil. When done, bread should be golden brown and thump with a "hollow" sound. Remove to a rack to cool, and brush tops with soft butter. Bread is best served warm, as crust is most crisp then, but it is good cold also.

Instant Bread Board

If your kitchen lacks a bread board, a large piece of extra-wide foil or plastic wrap, taped to your counter or kitchen table, will also serve the purpose.

Some types of plastic wrap will not slip if laid on a moist counter—no taping necessary.

Whitfield Square Lemon Bread

Wheat germ makes this loaf extra nutritious.

Yield: 1 loaf

2¾ cups flour
½ teaspoon baking soda
1 tablespoon baking powder
½ teaspoon salt
⅓ cup butter or shortening,
  or a half-and-half mixture
  of the two
1 cup sugar
½ cup wheat germ
3 or 4 tablespoons grated
  lemon peel, or to taste
2 eggs, slightly beaten
½ cup lemon juice
½ cup water
½ cup finely chopped pecans
  or ½ cup currants
  (optional)

Preheat oven to 350 degrees F. Sift together flour, soda, baking powder, and salt into a bowl. With finger tips or a pastry blender, work in butter or shortening until texture is like coarse meal. Stir in the sugar, wheat germ, peel, and eggs. Stir in lemon juice mixed with water, and optional nuts or currants. Mix well to moisten all ingredients. Turn into a greased 9-by-5-by-3-inch pan. Bake one hour, or until golden brown on top and loaf springs back when touched lightly. Cool 10 minutes in the pan, and then finish cooling on rack after removing from pan.

Note: This also freezes well.

—Emma R. Law

Dalton Peach Bread

Yield: 2 loaves

1½ cups sugar
½ cup vegetable shortening
2 eggs
2 cups flour
1 teaspoon cinnamon
1 teaspoon baking soda
1 teaspoon baking powder
¼ teaspoon salt
2½ cups finely chopped or
  pureéd peeled peaches
1 teaspoon vanilla extract
1 cup finely chopped pecans

Preheat oven to 325 degrees F. Cream sugar and shortening. Add eggs and mix thoroughly. Add sifted dry ingredients and mix well. Stir in peaches, vanilla, and nuts.

Pour batter in two greased, floured 9-by-5-inch loaf pans. Bake for 55 minutes to 1 hour, or until top is golden and springs lightly back when touched with fingers. (If bread is browning too fast, cover loaf pan lightly with foil.) Cool for a few minutes on a rack before removing from pan, and then finish cooling on rack.

Honey-Oatmeal Loaf

Yield: 2 8-inch loaves

1½ cups warm water
¼ cup honey
1 package active dry yeast
2 teaspoons salt
2 egg yolks
⅓ cup vegetable oil
1 cup dry milk powder
1 cup quick-cooking rolled
   oats (not instant)
4 cups sifted flour

In a large bowl, mix together the water and honey. Sprinkle in the yeast, and set aside for 10 minutes. Blend in remaining ingredients except the flour, and with a rubber spatula gradually work in the flour until well blended. Mixture will be very thick.

Cover and set in a warm, draft-free place for 30 minutes. With a spatula, work dough well again. Cover and set aside to rise until doubled, about 1 hour and 15 minutes.

Turn out onto a floured board. Cut in half. Pat each half into a loaf shape: dough will be very soft. Drop each half into a greased loaf pan, 8-by-4-by-3-inches, and turn to oil top. Set aside to rise as previously, until dough is about ½-inch from top of pan.

Place in a cold oven with a shallow pan of water on the rack underneath. Set oven to 350 degrees F. and bake for about 45 minutes, or until golden brown. Turn out carefully on rack, as bread will be soft. Turn right side up to cool.

—Emma R. Law

Emma's Buttermilk-Pecan Bread

Yield: 1 loaf

⅓ cup butter or margarine,
   at room temperature
½ cup sugar
1 egg
2 cups sifted flour
½ teaspoon salt
2 teaspoons baking powder
¼ teaspoon baking soda
¾ cup minced pecans
1¼ cups buttermilk

Preheat oven to 325 degrees F. Cream butter and sugar together until light and fluffy. Beat in egg. Sift together flour, salt, baking powder, and baking soda. Add pecans, and stir well. Fold in dry mixture alternately with buttermilk, saving some dry mixture for the last addition. Pour evenly into a 9-by-5-by-3-inch loaf pan, greased and lined on the bottom with waxed paper. Bake 1 to 1½ hours, or until loaf is brown and shrinking slightly from sides of pan. Turn out on rack, turn right side up, and cool thoroughly before cutting.

—Emma R. Law

Betty Rahn's Persimmon Bread

A delicious bread, or perhaps cake, to eat with butter or cream cheese! An unusual recipe for your family, or a coffee treat.

Yield: 1 9-inch loaf

1 cup sugar
⅓ cup butter or margarine, at room temperature
1¼ cups flour
½ teaspoon baking soda
½ teaspoon ground ginger
1 teaspoon ground allspice
1½ teaspoons ground cinnamon
¼ teaspoon ground cloves
1 egg
1 cup very ripe peeled, chopped persimmons, divided
¼ cup raisins, currants, or chopped nuts (optional)

Preheat oven to 375 degrees F. Cream sugar and butter or margarine well in a large bowl until light and fluffy. Meanwhile, sift together dry ingredients in another bowl. Add egg to butter mixture and beat well. Add half of persimmons and mix well. Add half the flour mixture and beat well. Add remaining persimmons and beat well, ending with remaining flour and beat well again. Fold in raisins, currants, or nuts if desired.

Grease a 9-by-5-inch loaf pan well and dust with flour before pouring in the batter. Bake about 50 minutes, or until top springs back when touched lightly with the fingers. Cool on a cake rack for at least 10 minutes and then turn out of pan. Finish cooling on a rack. When cool, wrap and store in a cool place if not being served immediately.

Note: This recipe may also be baked in greased, floured one-pound coffee cans and frozen in them.

—Betty Rahn

Sally's Strawberry Bread

Yield: 1 loaf or 12 muffins

2 cups regular flour
1 teaspoon baking soda
½ teaspoon salt
1 teaspoon ground cinnamon
⅔ cup sugar, or to taste
1 10-ounce package frozen sweetened strawberries, thawed, or 2 cups fresh, sliced
2 eggs, well beaten
¼ cup vegetable oil
¾ cup chopped pecans
¼ cup milk

Preheat oven to 375°F. Sift together dry ingredients in large bowl. Add remaining ingredients, including juice, stirring just to mix well. Pour into greased 9x5x3-inch loaf pan or 2¾-inch muffin tins. Bake loaf for about an hour or muffins for about 20 minutes, until golden, and top springs back when touched lightly. Serve warm or cold with whipped butter or cream cheese. Freezes well.

Prater's Mill was built in 1859 by Benjamin Franklin Prater at Dalton. Corn is still ground here during the Prater's Mill Country Fair, held semi-annually on Mother's Day weekend in May and Columbus Day weekend in October.

Irish Soda Bread

Yield: 1 loaf, about 20 slices

4 cups sifted flour
¼ cup sugar
1 teaspoon salt
1 teaspoon baking powder
2 tablespoons caraway seeds
4 tablespoons butter or margarine
1 cup raisins or currants
1⅓ cups buttermilk
1 egg
1 teaspoon baking soda
1 egg yolk

In a large mixing bowl, sift the flour, sugar, salt, and baking powder. Stir in seeds. With a pastry blender or two knives, scissor fashion, cut the butter in until like coarse corn meal. Stir in raisins. Combine buttermilk, egg, and soda. Stir into flour mixture just until moistened.

Preheat oven to 375 degrees F. Grease a 2-quart casserole. Turn dough onto lightly floured surface. Knead lightly until smooth. Shape into a ball. Place in casserole. With a sharp knife, make a 4-inch cross, ¼-inch deep, in center. Brush top with egg yolk. Bake about 1 hour, or until golden brown. Cool in pan 10 minutes, and then remove and finish cooling on a rack.

Note: This may be made the day before, and wrapped in foil until time to serve.

—Jerry Downey

Cornmeal Yeast Rolls

These rolls have that Southern cornmeal flavor, but the lighter texture of yeast bread.

Yield: 12

1½ cups flour, divided
¾ cup cornmeal
1 package active dry yeast
1 teaspoon baking powder
¾ cup milk
⅓ cup vegetable shortening
3 tablespoons sugar
1 teaspoon salt
1 egg

Combine ¾ cup flour, cornmeal, yeast, and baking powder in a large mixing bowl. Heat and stir together the milk, shortening, sugar, and salt just until warm enough for shortening to melt. Add to dry ingredients in the mixing bowl. If you have an electric mixer, beat on low speed about 30 seconds. (Mixture may also be beaten by hand.) Then add the egg, and beat for three minutes at high speed. At low speed, beat in the remaining flour for two minutes, or until smooth. Cover and refrigerate for several hours, or overnight.

Remove batter from refrigerator, stir down, and leave for 10 minutes. Grease muffin tins, (2½-inch size), and fill ½ full. Cover and set aside to rise one hour, or until dough is double in size.

Preheat oven to 325 degrees F. Bake for 20 to 25 minutes, or until golden brown.

Marietta Cottage Cheese Rolls

Yield: about 24

2 packages active dry yeast
½ cup warm water
2 cups cottage cheese
¼ cup sugar
2 teaspoons salt
½ teaspoon baking soda
2 beaten eggs
5 cups flour, divided

Dissolve yeast in very warm water. Heat cottage cheese in a small saucepan over low heat until very warm, but not hot; remove from heat. Combine cottage cheese, yeast, sugar, salt, soda, eggs, and 1 cup flour in a large mixing bowl and beat with an electric mixer on medium speed for 2 minutes, if you have one; otherwise, mix well by hand. Gradually add remaining 4 cups flour to form a soft dough. Place in a greased bowl, turning dough to grease all sides.

Cover and set aside to rise in a warm place away from drafts until doubled, 1½ hours. Turn dough onto floured surface and shape into rolls. Cover and set aside to rise in a warm place about 30 minutes on greased baking sheets.

Preheat oven to 350 degrees F. Bake for about 20 minutes, or until a nice golden brown.

Vineboro Crescent Rolls

Yield: 48

Rolls:
1½ cups milk
1 cup (2 sticks) butter
½ cup sugar
1 teaspoon salt
3 eggs
1 package active dry yeast
2 teaspoons sugar
5 to 5½ cups flour
Butter, at room temperature

Scald milk. Add butter, ½ cup sugar, and salt. Blend and cool. Add eggs, one at a time, beating well after each. Add yeast and 2 teaspoons sugar, following package directions. Add the flour to make a firm batter. Beat well. Set aside in warm place until double in bulk.

Punch down and place covered in the refrigerator overnight. Next day, divide into 3 parts. Roll into a round, as for pie crust, and spread with softened butter. Cut each round into 16 wedges, and begin to roll from the wide to the pointed end. Bend to form a crescent. Set aside to rise on a greased cookie sheet or pan for about 2 hours.

Preheat oven to 375 degrees F. Bake for about 15 minutes, or until golden brown. Frost while still hot with glaze.

Place confectioners' sugar in a small bowl. Slowly stir in milk and extract to make a glaze of spreading consistency.

Glaze:
1 cup confectioners' sugar
6 tablespoons milk
⅛ teaspoon almond extract,
*   or to taste*

—Jane Swanson

Tifton Peanut Butter Rolls

Yield: 36

2 packages active dry yeast
2 cups lukewarm water
⅓ cup butter or margarine
1 cup peanut butter
4 cups flour
1½ cups whole wheat flour
1 tablespoon salt
⅓ cup non-fat dry milk
*   powder*

Dissolve yeast in lukewarm water. Stir in the butter and peanut butter. Beat until smooth. Add remaining ingredients, and stir until a stiff dough is formed. Knead on a lightly floured board until smooth and elastic. Set aside to rise in a warm place, free from drafts, until double in bulk. Punch down dough and cut into 36 pieces. Shape balls into smooth rounds by pinching down dough under the ball. Place balls side by side in a layer in 2 well-greased 13-by-9-by-2-inch baking pans. Set aside again until double in bulk.

Preheat oven to 375 degrees F. Bake for 20 to 25 minutes, until rolls are well browned.

—Georgia Peanut Commission

Bartow Pecan Rolls

Yield: about 20

1 package active dry yeast
¼ cup warm water
1¾ cups sugar, divided
½ teaspoon salt
½ cup milk
1 egg, beaten
1 teaspoon cinnamon
2½ cups sifted flour, divided
¾ cup (1½ sticks) butter,
  divided
1 cup chopped pecans

Soften yeast in warm water in a large bowl. Add ¼ cup sugar, salt, milk, and egg. Add cinnamon and 2 cups flour; beat until smooth.

Roll out on floured board to ¼-inch thick. Divide ½ cup butter (1 stick) into 8 parts. Place 4 of them on the middle third of the dough. Fold outer third over middle; place remaining 4 pieces of butter on top, and cover with final third of the dough.

Roll out. Fold in thirds again and roll again. Do this 3 or 4 times, ending with a 15-by-13-inch piece of dough. Brush with remaining ¼ cup butter, melted.

Mix pecans and remaining 1½ cups sugar. Sprinkle ¼ mixture over pastry. Cut sheet in half, and roll each half like a jelly roll. Cut off in 1½-inch pieces. Place cut side down in a shallow pan, and chill covered, for 30 minutes.

Remove from refrigerator, and set aside 5 minutes. Spread remaining sugar-pecan mixture on work surface. Coat each roll by rolling to ¼-inch thickness (4 to 5 inches in diameter), turning during rolling to coat both sides.

Place on greased baking sheet. Set aside in a warm, draft-free place, about 45 minutes. Preheat oven to 375 degrees F.

Bake for about 15 minutes, or until golden brown. Serve hot with butter.

—Mrs. James H. Lynch, Jr.

Color and Flavor

For both a nice golden color and extra flavor, brush biscuit and roll tops before baking with a little extra soft butter.

Mary Beth Busbee's Cream Biscuits

Yield: 12

2 cups sifted flour
1 tablespoon baking powder
1 teaspoon salt
2 eggs, beaten
¾ cup heavy cream

Preheat oven to 400 degrees F. Sift dry ingredients together. Add eggs and cream. Stir to mix. (Dough should be lumpy and soft.) Drop from tablespoon onto greased baking sheets. Bake for about 15 minutes, or until a nice golden brown.

—Mary Beth Busbee, Atlanta

Eufaula Sour Cream Biscuits

Yield: 12

2 cups sifted flour
2 teaspoons baking powder
½ teaspoon baking soda
1 teaspoon salt
1 teaspoon sugar
½ cup vegetable shortening
1 cup sour cream

Preheat oven to 450 degrees F. Sift together dry ingredients; cut in shortening until mixture resembles coarse cornmeal. Add sour cream; mix to a soft dough. Turn out on well-floured surface; knead gently about a minute. Roll dough ½ inch thick. Cut with round cutter dipped in flour, and place on ungreased baking sheet. Bake 10 to 12 minutes, or until a nice golden brown on top.

Mary Lou Phinizy's Beaten Biscuits

Sift 1 quart of flour with a pinch of soda, teaspoon sugar, and teaspoon salt. Mix with 2 tablespoons lard, and then 1 cup sweet milk. Work into a dough, put on a board, and beat it until it flakes, and is smooth, at least 15 minutes. (You can also get beaten biscuit machines now.) Roll it out and cut it in rounds. Punch each all over with a fork. Bake in a moderate oven [at 350 degrees F. for 15 minutes, or] until light brown. Don't cook these too fast.

—Family cookbook of Sophie Meldrim Shonnard, Savannah

Tavern Biscuits

To 1 pound flour, add ½ pound butter, ½ pound sugar, mace, and nutmeg to taste, and a glass of wine or brandy. Wet it with milk to make a dough. Knead well, and roll thin. Cut into shapes, and bake in a quick oven [at 400 degrees F. for 10 to 12 minutes].

Mayonnaise Drop Biscuits

Yield: 16

1 tablespoon baking powder
¾ teaspoon salt
2 cups sifted flour
¼ cup mayonnaise
1 cup milk

Preheat oven to 450 degrees F. Sift dry ingredients together and stir in mayonnaise and milk. Drop batter into well-greased muffin tins, filling them one-third full; batter will be soft. Bake about 10 minutes, or until a nice golden brown.

Note: This batter is even better if it is mixed and then chilled, covered, for several hours before pouring into tins.

—Eleanor Scarbrough

Pine Mountain Whole Wheat Biscuits

These are rather flat and do not rise as much as some biscuits. They may also be made with regular flour.

Yield: 20

2 cups whole wheat flour
2 teaspoons baking powder
⅓ teaspoon salt
3 tablespoons butter or
  vegetable shortening
½ cup milk

Preheat oven to 450 degrees F. Sift together dry ingredients. Cut in shortening until mixture is like coarse cornmeal. Add milk and stir well. Roll dough onto a lightly-floured board until ½-inch thick. Cut with biscuit cutter. Place biscuits on lightly greased cookie sheet. Bake 10 minutes, or until a nice golden brown.

Note: In sifting whole wheat flour, some of it will not go through the sifter. It is all right to add this to the batter.

Stickies

Roll some nice rich pastry into a sheet, and spread over it a mixture of sugar and butter, with a large proportion of powdered cinnamon. Roll the sheet up, over and over, and cut into squares. Lay them in a pan, and sprinkle with sugar, butter, and cinnamon again, thickly. Bake a nice brown [at 400 degrees F. for 12 to 15 minutes].

—Bryan family cookbook, Savannah, circa 1885

Apple Spice Muffins

Yield: 12

¾ cup milk
1 egg, beaten
¼ cup vegetable oil or
   melted shortening
2 cups flour
1 tablespoon baking powder
½ teaspoon salt
½ cup sugar
1 teaspoon ground cinnamon
1 cup peeled, finely chopped
   apples
¼ cup currants or raisins

Preheat oven to 400 degrees F. Add milk to egg in a small mixing bowl; stir in oil or cooled shortening. Sift dry ingredients together in another large bowl; stir in apples and currants or raisins, coating well with flour. Add liquid mixture, and stir just until all ingredients are moistened; do not overmix. Batter should be lumpy. Fill greased 2¾-inch muffin tins ⅔ full. Bake for about 20 to 25 minutes, or until golden brown.

—Georgia Apple Commission

Date-Oatmeal Muffins

Yield: 12

1 cup sifted flour
3 teaspoons baking powder
½ teaspoon salt
½ cup (1 stick) butter or
   margarine, at room
   temperature
⅓ cup brown sugar
½ cup chopped dates
1 egg, beaten
1 cup milk
1 cup quick-cooking oatmeal

Preheat oven to 425 degrees F. Sift first three dry ingredients together. Cut in butter until mixture is all coarse crumbs. Stir in remaining ingredients and blend just until well-moistened. Fill greased 2¾-inch muffin tins ⅔ full. Sprinkle with cinnamon sugar. Bake for 15 to 20 minutes, or until nicely browned.

Cinnamon Sugar: Shake together ½ cup sugar and 2 teaspoons cinnamon until well mixed. Use for cinnamon toast, or to sprinkle on muffins and other treats.

—Claire Lowell Crosby

Albany Pecan Muffins

Yield: 12

2 cups sifted flour
2 teaspoons baking powder
½ teaspoon baking soda
½ teaspoon salt
½ teaspoon cinnamon
½ cup light brown sugar
¼ cup wheat germ
1 egg, beaten
1 cup buttermilk
3 tablespoons melted butter
1 cup coarsely chopped
  pecans

Preheat oven to 350 degrees F. Sift flour, baking powder, baking soda, salt, and cinnamon together in a large bowl. Stir in sugar, wheat germ, egg, buttermilk, and butter. Stir just enough to moisten all ingredients. Fold in pecans.

Grease 2¾-inch muffin tins, and spoon in batter. Bake for 25 to 30 minutes, or until nicely browned.

Warm Muffins

If muffins get done a little ahead of the rest of the meal, tip them slightly in the pans, and cover with foil. Leave on the back of the stove or in other warm place until time to serve.

Epworth Popovers

Yield: 8

1 cup milk
⅞ cup unsifted all-purpose
  flour (Measure one cup
  and remove 2 tablespoons)
1 tablespoon cooking oil
½ teaspoon salt
2 eggs

Grease well 8 5-ounce muffin tins or custard cups. Combine milk, flour, oil and salt. Beat with electric mixer on high for one minute, or with rotary beater for at least two. Add eggs, one at a time, beating well after each. Fill cups ⅔ full. Set in cold oven. Turn heat to 425 degrees F. Bake 35 minutes, or until puffed and golden brown. Remove from oven and let stand a few minutes before removing from pan.

—*The Epworth Cookbook*, Savannah

Dill Seed Crisps

Yield: about 30

¾ cup sifted flour
¾ teaspoon baking powder
⅛ teaspoon baking soda
¼ teaspoon salt
¼ teaspoon paprika
2 tablespoons vegetable oil
¼ cup buttermilk
1 egg, beaten
1 tablespoon water
Dill seeds

Preheat oven to 425 degrees F. Sift flour well with baking powder, soda, salt, and paprika. Make a well in the center of flour mixture. Mix oil with buttermilk and pour into flour mixture. Stir quickly until mixture forms a ball of dough. Turn out onto lightly floured surface and knead about eight times. Roll very thin. Cut into 2-inch rounds. Pierce well with fork. Brush lightly with a mixture of the beaten egg and water. Sprinkle with dill seeds. Transfer to greased cookie sheet. Bake for about 9 minutes.

Note: Of course, untoasted benne (sesame) seed may be used in place of the dill.

—Emma R. Law

Darien Cream Scones

Yield: 16

4 cups sifted cake flour, or
*   3½ cups sifted flour*
4½ teaspoons baking powder
2 teaspoons sugar
1 teaspoon salt
½ cup (1 stick) butter or
*   margarine*
4 eggs, well-beaten
⅔ cup light cream
2 teaspoons water

Sift dry ingredients together into a large mixing bowl. Cut butter into dry material until the size of very tiny peas. Measure 4 tablespoons of beaten egg into a small cup; set aside. Beat cream into remaining beaten eggs. Make a "well" in the flour mixture and pour in egg mixture. Stir together quickly, handling as little as possible. Place on lightly-floured board. Pat with floured hands into a square ½-inch thick. With a floured knife, cut into four squares. Cut each square into four sheets.

Preheat oven to 450 degrees F. Transfer, with spatula, the squares to greased baking sheets. Mix 2 teaspoons water with reserved beaten egg, and brush over tops. Bake for 10 to 12 minutes, or until golden brown.

—Emma R. Law

Forsyth Drop Doughnuts

Delicious and fun to make on a Saturday morning.

Yield: about 30

2 cups flour
¼ cup sugar
3 teaspoons baking powder
1 teaspoon salt
1 teaspoon nutmeg or mace
¼ cup vegetable oil
¾ cup milk
1 egg, beaten
Fat for frying
Confectioners' sugar as
*   needed*

Sift the flour, sugar, baking powder, salt, and nutmeg or mace together in a large bowl. Add oil, milk, and egg; stir until thoroughly mixed. Drop by teaspoonfuls (too large a puff will not cook through) into deep hot fat (375 degrees F.). Fry until golden brown, about 3 minutes. Drain on absorbent paper, and then roll while warm in a plate of confectioners' sugar.

Note: For variety, you could roll some in a mixture of cinnamon-sugar, or glaze by dipping into a thin confectioners' sugar and water icing.

—Mrs. O. W. Newman

Miss Ellie's Dough Nuts

Mix one tablespoon lard or butter with 1½ cups sugar, 2 or 3 eggs, and a small cup of sour milk, with 1 teaspoon [baking] soda. Add a little salt, a grated nutmeg, and flour enough to roll it all out nicely. Cut into rings, and fry in hot lard [until golden], constantly turning with a fork as it cooks.

—Bryan family cookbook, Savannah, circa 1885

Celia's Battercakes

Beat 1 egg well with ½ cup milk and 2 or 3 tablespoons melted butter. Add ½ cup cornmeal, ½ cup flour, 1 teaspoon sugar, 2 teaspoons baking powder, and ½ teaspoon salt, sifted together. Add a little more milk if needed for the batter, and spoon on hot griddle greased with lard. Turn when underside is cooked, and bubbles appear in batter.

—Family cookbook of Sophie Meldrim Shonnard, Savannah

Buckwheat-Buttermilk Pancakes

Yield: about 16

2 cups buckwheat flour
¾ teaspoon salt
1 teaspoon baking soda
2 cups buttermilk or sour milk
1 egg, beaten
1 tablespoon melted vegetable shortening or oil

Mix flour, salt, and soda. Add milk, egg, and shortening. Pour on hot, greased griddle and cook until brown, turning once. Serve hot.

Note: 1 cup buckwheat and 1 regular flour may be used for milder buckwheat flavor.

Maple Flavor

For an extra touch of maple, add 1 tablespoon maple syrup for each cup of flour in mixing pancakes, and decrease sugar slightly if desired.

Grandma's Cornmeal Griddle Cakes

Yield: about 18

1 cup cornmeal
1 cup flour
1 teaspoon salt
1⅓ tablespoons baking powder
1 egg, beaten
2½ cups milk
¼ cup melted vegetable shortening

Mix dry ingredients in a large bowl. Combine egg and milk in a small bowl, and stir into dry ingredients. Stir in shortening. Add more milk if necessary. Bake on a hot greased griddle, turning when underside is brown and batter bubbly.

For Browner Griddle Cakes

A teaspoon of brown sugar added to griddle cakes, will make them brown nicer.

—Family cookbook of Mary Howell Scott,
Milledgeville, circa 1918

The Ante-Bellum Plantation at Atlanta's Stone Mountain Park was created from nearly a score of eighteenth and nineteenth century buildings moved to the location and furnished with area antiques, to give an idea of life on a plantation of the period before the War Between The States.

Apple Waffles

Some peeled, chopped apple, mixed with a little sugar and cinnamon, adds a spicy touch to plain waffle batter.

Georgia Peanut Butter Waffles

Yield: 4 to 6 servings

1¾ cups sifted flour
1 tablespoon baking powder
3 tablespoons sugar
¼ teaspoon salt
6 tablespoons peanut butter
4 tablespoons butter or
margarine, at room
temperature
2 eggs
1¾ cups milk

Sift flour, baking powder, sugar, and salt into a bowl. Cream peanut butter with butter or margarine until smooth. Beat eggs and milk until well blended. Add to peanut mixture. Beat well. Add sifted dry ingredients and mix just until smooth. Bake in a hot, greased waffle iron. Serve with butter and jelly or syrup.

—Georgia Peanut Commission

Nutmeg Sauce

Yield: 1½ cups

1 cup dark brown sugar,
firmly packed
2 tablespoons flour
¼ teaspoon nutmeg
¼ teaspoon cinnamon
1 cup boiling water
1 tablespon butter or
margarine

Combine sugar, flour, and spices in a small saucepan. Gradually add water, stirring constantly. Cook and stir over medium heat until thickened. Blend in butter. Serve warm over waffles, griddle cakes, or French toast.

Mother's French Toast

Beat 4 eggs light, and stir into them a pint of milk. Dip into this mixture some slices of nice light bread, and fry them brown. Sprinkle over a little [confectioners'] sugar, and cinnamon on each piece. Serve hot.

—Bryan family cookbook, Savannah, circa 1885

Main Dishes

> *"I long for that moon country,*
> *That 'possum and 'coon country,*
> *That 'good for the soul' country,*
> *I long for that ol' country,*
> *That 'good for the soul' country,*
> *Good for cookin' things that melt in your mouth . . ."*
>
> —Savannahian Johnny Mercer, from "Moon Country"
> with music by Hoagy Carmichael, copyright 1934
> by Southern Music Company, New York

Yorkshire Pudding for Roast Beef

Mix 6 large tablespoons of flour and a little salt with 1½ pints of milk and three eggs. Beat well to free from lumps. Put in a greased pan and bake [at 350 degrees F.] for an hour, then cut into squares and put under the beef.

—Bryan family cookbook, Savannah, circa 1885

Meat

Examine the meat before you accept it. If you do not know the looks of good meat, you should go to a butcher's shop, and ask the butcher to show you how to know it. Much gristle is a sign of old age. . . . Beef should be of a bright red color, and juicy and elastic. The fat should be firm, and of a pale straw color. Mutton should feel dryish, and the fat look white. All papers must be taken off at once. The feet of fowls should be soft and flexible, not dry, and the skin of the back should not be discolored.

—"How Girls Can Help Their Country,"
Handbook For Girl Scouts by W. J. Hoxie, 1913

Carter's Marinated London Broil

Yield: 4 to 6 servings

1 teaspoon salt
½ teaspoon black pepper
¼ teaspoon basil
¼ teaspoon rosemary
1 garlic clove, crushed
½ medium onion, chopped
1 tablespoon wine vinegar
2 tablespoons vegetable oil
1 flank steak, about 1¾ pounds

Combine all ingredients except steak in a shallow pan. Place steak in mixture and marinate, brushing sauce over the top, for at least two hours. Broil about 3 inches from heat for five minutes, then turn and coat with remaining mixture. Broil another 4 minutes, or until done as desired. (This timing is for a rare steak.) Slice steak across the grain as thinly as possible. Spoon remaining pan juices over meat to serve.

—Carter Olive

Bordelaise Steak

Cut sirloin steak of one pound each, and rub on both sides with salt and pepper. Let stand for ½ hour, then rub on both sides with ½ tablespoon sweet [vegetable] oil. Place them on a broiler over a hot charcoal fire, and broil for 6 minutes on each side. Place on a hot platter and keep warm. Mix for each steak a tablespoon of nice butter, a teaspoon of finely chopped parsley, ½ teaspoon lemon juice, ½ teaspoon very finely chopped onion. Mix smooth, rub over steak, cover closely, let stand for 5 minutes in a hot place, and serve.

—Mrs. Arnold, *Some Choice Receipts of Savannah Homemakers*, Savannah, 1904

Visitors to the living history Village of Westville can sample sausages and biscuits cooked by an open fire as well as gingerbread baked in a wood-burning stove.

Lemon Marinade

A marinade made from the juice of a lemon mixed with several tablespoons of olive and vegetable oil and a little onion or garlic salt can serve as a tenderizer when applied to both sides of the steak several hours before cooking. Be sure to use an earthenware or glass, not metal container, because of the acid effect of the lemon juice. This also adds flavor to the meat.

Tomato juice is a good tenderizer, too, when cooking stew beef, chuck roasts, and other meats, and also adds flavor and color.

Hash for a Crowd

Take a 15 to 18 pound round of beefsteak. Take the skin off, and boil for a long time; save the water. Grind meat with about 2 or 3 pounds of fat bacon. Add 2 or 3 large Irish potatoes, and some onions and hard boiled eggs while grinding meat, along with garlic and red and black pepper, [hot sauce] and Worcestershire sauce to taste. A little curry helps; not enough to detect. Cook hash mixture on the stove until soft. Hash does not keep as long with eggs in it. This is good at a barbecue.

—Family cookbook of Sophie Meldrim Shonnard, Savannah

Deviled Short Ribs

Yield: 4 to 6 servings

*4 pounds beef short ribs,
  lean*
4 teaspoons brown sugar
1½ teaspons salt
1 teaspoon dry mustard
½ teaspoon ground ginger
⅛ teaspoon pepper
¾ cup ketchup
¼ cup soy sauce
2 tablespoons lemon juice
1 cup water
1 bay leaf
1 onion, sliced
Flour (optional)

In a large skillet with a lid, brown short ribs on all sides. Pour off drippings. Cover tightly, and cook slowly for 1½ hours, adding a little water if desired. Combine all remaining ingredients except flour, and add to ribs. Cover and simmer one hour longer, or until meat is tender, adding more liquid if necessary. Before serving, discard bay leaf and thicken gravy with a little flour if desired. This is also good cooked in a crock pot, and is even better reheated the next day.

—Gail Hart

Mrs. Cohen's Fine Spiced Beef

Take a very large piece of rib beef. Take out all the bones, and put meat in salt or salt meat pickle for two or three weeks. Then take it out and soak it in fresh water overnight. Next morning wipe it dry, and lay flat on a large dish. Prepare seasoning of pepper, allspice, ginger, mace, and nutmeg. Add to this some onions and parsley, chopped very fine, and two chopped [hard-cooked] eggs, along with thyme, and sage. Mix all these together well; it will require a breakfast plate full.

Spread mixture over the whole length of the meat, and on the sides from which the bones were taken. Roll over and over, very tight, and tie with strong string. Roll this up in a towel, tied at each end. Boil well, and then press with a heavy weight for 2 to 3 hours to get out all the juice. Take the towel off, remove strings, and cut in slices. Eat at your pleasure.

—Bryan family cookbook, Savannah, circa 1885

Sauce for Stew

Rub a level tablespoon of flour with one of butter, until smooth. Then stir it into a cup of the beef juice or broth, and cook a few minutes. Season with salt, pepper, and a teaspoon of prepared mustard and a tablespoonful of ketchup. Let it get very hot, and pour around the beef.

—Family cookbook of Sophie Meldrim Shonnard, Savannah

Round Steak in Wine Sauce

Yield: 6 servings

3 pounds round steak, about
   1½ inches thick
2 tablespoons butter
1½ cups chopped onion
2 tablespoons prepared
   mustard
1 teaspoon Worcestershire
   sauce
1 cup sliced fresh
   mushrooms, or canned,
   drained
½ teaspoon salt
¼ cup dry red wine
½ cup water
1 or 2 tablespoons flour

Brown steak on all sides in butter in a large skillet, one with a lid. Add remaining ingredients except flour, and combine well. Cover and simmer 2 hours or until meat is tender. If desired, add more liquid in the percentage of 1 part wine to 2 parts water. Remove meat and keep warm. Add flour to pan juice, blend well, and simmer 3 minutes. Add more liquid if needed. Serve with meat.

A Good Cream Sauce

Add ½ pint thick cream to your meat liquid, and some paprika and red pepper to taste. Cook and stir until thick, but do not boil; check seasoning. Add a little more salt or pepper if desired.

Sweetbreads à la Reine

Cut 4 blanched sweetbreads in slices, and fry them in one tablespoon good butter, until lightly browned. Add ½ wineglass of white wine, 3 tablespoons canned mushroom liquor, and salt, pepper and nutmeg to taste. Boil for 10 minutes, and add 2 yolks hard-boiled eggs, 6 sliced canned mushrooms, 2 sliced truffles, cut fine, and 1 gill (½ cup) strong white stock. Boil 5 minutes more, take from fire, and stir in 1 gill (½ cup) sweet cream, and a squeeze of lemon juice to taste. Serve in a hot chafing dish with toast; or fill shells, cover with browned breadcrumbs, sprinkle a few drops of melted butter over the top, and brown in the oven for 5 minutes.

—Mrs. Baldwin, *Some Choice Receipts from Savannah Homemakers*, Savannah, 1904

Ann's Mexican Lasagne

Yield: 6 servings

2 tablespoons vegetable
  shortening
½ cup minced onion
2 pounds lean ground beef
2 1¼-ounce packages Taco
  seasoning mix
1 5½-ounce package taco-
  flavored corn chips,
  slightly crushed
1 pound shredded Cheddar
  cheese

Heat shortening in 12-inch skillet over moderate heat. Sauté onion and brown meat until well done. Drain fat. Stir in seasoning mix according to package directions, and blend well.

Preheat oven to 350 degrees F. Lightly grease a 13-by-9-by-2-inch baking pan, and alternate layers of chips, meat and cheese, ending with the cheese. Bake for 30 minutes, or until hot and bubbly.

—Ann Wenner Osteen

Julia Kiminsky's Veal Loaf

Grind 3 pounds of round of veal, 1 pound of fresh pork, and 1 pound salt pork, all together as for sausage meat. Mash 6 soda crackers fine, and sift into the meat. Beat 2 eggs light, and add to meat to bind together. Season highly with pepper and salt, working it well into the meat and making into loaves as if for bread, pressing it to be very compact. Put the meat into a pan with a tablespoonful of butter and cracker dust on top of each loaf. Put a pint of water in the pan, and baste the meat frequently. It takes two hours of slow cooking [at 325 degrees F.] to bake done. Eat cold, with ketchup.

—Family cookbook of Sophie Meldrim Shonnard, Savannah

Noble Jones' Venison

Before cooking, place the meat in a solution made of 2 cups vinegar to 2 cups salt (ice cream type), and water to cover. Soak until time to cook. Brown the meat in the oven, and baste during cooking with a dressing made of bacon grease, Worcestershire sauce, salt, pepper, cloves, and other spices if desired. [Bake at 325 degrees F. for 20 to 25 minutes *per pound.*] Place this all over the meat, and in slits cut in the meat large enough to sink four fingers into.

—Family cookbook of Sophie Meldrim Shonnard, Savannah

Emma's Meatballs in Dill Sauce

Yield: 4 to 6 servings

⅔ cup cracker crumbs (may
   be part wheat germ)
½ cup milk
1 egg, beaten
1 teaspoon salt
¼ teaspoon pepper
2 tablespoons minced onion
⅛ teaspoon ground nutmeg
1½ pounds meat loaf
   mixture (equal parts beef,
   pork, and veal)
⅓ cup vegetable oil

Allow cracker crumbs to soften in milk while combining remaining ingredients except oil in a large mixing bowl. Blend in crumb mixture and mix well. Roll into balls about an inch in diameter. Sauté in oil over moderate heat until brown, turning as necessary. Remove from skillet. Drain on paper towels. Discard oil and wipe out skillet with paper towels. Prepare sauce.

Dill Sauce:
3 tablespoons butter or
   margarine
4 tablespoons flour
1 10-ounce can beef broth
½ cup light cream
Salt and pepper to taste
1 teaspoon chopped fresh
   dill, or ¼ teaspoon dried

Melt butter over moderate heat in skillet in which meatballs were browned. Blend in flour and cook a few minutes. Do not brown. Stir in broth and cream. Cook, stirring constantly, until thick and satiny. Add seasoning to taste. Stir in dill. Add meatballs and simmer over low heat, turning several times, for about 10 minutes. Serve with noodles or rice.

Note: Meatballs may be made ahead of time and reheated with sauce to serve. If meatballs are frozen, thaw in the refrigerator before warming in sauce.

—Emma R. Law

Hamburger Steak

Have one pound round steak and one pound veal ground together three times. Add 1 large onion that has been chopped fine and fried just a little; 4 canned whole tomatoes; ½ teaspoon mace; ½ teaspoon ginger; and salt and pepper to taste. Beat all together with a fork at least 10 minutes, until well mixed. Make into small meat cakes, and broil or pan fry.

For good juicy hamburgers, mix each pound meat with 2 eggs, 1 ground onion, and 1 tablespoonful cooked rice.

—Family cookbook of Sophie Meldrim Shonnard, Savannah

Emma's Moussaka

Yield: 4 to 6 servings

2 eggplants, about 2 pounds
1½ pounds ground beef
½ cup (1 stick) butter,
*   divided*
1 cup chopped onion
1 cup peeled and chopped
*   tomato*
1 teaspoon salt
¼ teaspoon pepper
⅛ teaspoon thyme
⅛ teaspoon oregano
½ cup fresh bread crumbs
½ cup grated Cheddar
*   cheese*
3 eggs
⅔ cup milk
2 tablespoons chopped
*   parsley*

Peel eggplants and parboil in salted water about 8 minutes. Remove from water and cool. Meanwhile, break up and brown meat in 2 tablespoons butter over moderate heat, stirring several times. Drain fat. Add onion, tomato, salt, pepper, thyme, and oregano to the meat, with a little more butter if desired. Simmer over low heat, stirring several times, for 15 to 20 minutes. Meanwhile, cut eggplant into ½-inch slices and brown in remaining butter.

Preheat oven to 375 degrees F. Grease a shallow 2-quart baking dish and sprinkle lightly with bread crumbs. Make a bottom layer of ⅓ of meat mixture; then ⅓ of eggplant; then ⅓ of the crumbs and cheese. Repeat, making last layer of remaining eggplant, with crumbs and cheese. Beat eggs well, and combine with milk. Pour evenly over the top. Bake for about 45 minutes to one hour, until firm. Sprinkle with parsley and serve hot.

—Emma R. Law

This dwelling is one of 25 buildings at Westville, a recreated 1850 rural village near Lumpkin. Courtesy Westville

Hamburger Pie

A dish teenagers like, and a change from pizza.

Yield: 6 to 8 servings

*1½ pounds ground beef
  chuck
1 teaspoon Worcestershire
  sauce
¼ cup ketchup
2 tablespoons prepared
  mustard
1 egg, beaten
½ cup fresh bread crumbs
1½ teaspoons salt
½ cup minced onion
½ cup minced green pepper
1 9-inch pie crust, unbaked
4 slices Mozzarella cheese*

Preheat oven to 350 degrees F. Combine first nine ingredients, and place in pie crust. Spread evenly, and bake for about 1 hour. Arrange cheese slices on top of pie, making a design if desired. Return to oven for 15 minutes or until cheese melts. Set aside 10 minutes before cutting. Serve with pickle slices or pickle relish.

—Emma R. Law

Summer Salami Sausage

Yield: about 1½ pounds

*2 pounds ground beef chuck
2 tablespoons Morton's
  Tender-Quick curing salts
  (see note)
½ teaspoon pepper
¼ teaspoon garlic salt
1 cup cold water*

Mix all ingredients together well. Shape into rolls two inches in diameter. Wrap in foil and refrigerate overnight.

Preheat oven to 350 degrees F. Bake in foil in a shallow pan for 1½ hours. Remove from foil immediately. Place on a rack over the pan to drain and cool. Wrap well and refrigerate. These may also be frozen. Slice thinly for cocktails or sandwiches in small rolls. This recipe may be doubled.

Note: Salt may be ordered from the Morton Company, or your grocer can order it for you.

—Mrs. Max Condon, La Grange

Meat Loaf with Bacon

When baking a meat loaf, if you lay a couple of slices of bacon in the bottom of the baking pan before putting in the meat loaf, it will not stick to the pan. It adds a little flavor, too.

This simple cottage, built about 1932, was the residence of President Franklin Delano Roosevelt during his many visits to Warm Springs. He died here April 12, 1945. The home is now the Little White House Historic Site, maintained by Georgia's Department of Natural Resources.

Storage Tip

When planning meals, remember that the smaller the cut of meat, the sooner it should be used. For instance, plan to use the ground beef in the refrigerator before the chuck roast.

Mandarin Pork Roast

Have the butcher prepare this roast by cutting it along the back, so it can easily be carved into chops when done.

Yield: 8 servings

1 pork loin roast, about 3½ pounds
1 teaspoon ground ginger
1 garlic clove, crushed or finely minced
1 teaspoon salt
2 teaspoons soy sauce
2 tablespoons sherry
2 tablespoons honey

Preheat oven to 325 degrees F. Place meat on rack in a shallow pan, fat side up. Combine remaining ingredients and brush well all over. Roast meat for about 3 hours, or until a meat thermometer registers 185 degrees F. During cooking time, baste every 45 minutes with marinade mixture.

Note: Chinese snow peas are especially good with this.

How To Barbecue a Pig

The size of the pig makes little difference; anywhere from 40 to 150 pounds, depending on number to be served. Around 75 pounds is the most convenient. Allow 1 pound meat per person, exclusive of head and feet, which are removed. First, wipe the pig off with vinegar, after thoroughly cleaning with a sharp knife.

Make your pit about 3 feet wide by 4 feet long. Have plenty of green oak or hickory wood. Have two fires, one for the pig and one to make coals. Have grate or wire fencing on sticks over fire, or flat on pit. Put pig over fire; it takes about 18 hours, as you want to cook it very slowly.

Have a pan ready with melted butter (if you want), garlic, onion, vinegar, red and black pepper, Worcestershire sauce, and a little sugar to take edge off vinegar. Mop pig constantly with the sauce. Just before it is done, mop it all over with the same sauce, but add a good amount English mustard. (Do not add mustard at the first, as it will cause the skin to scorch.)

With the pig, serve rice or white potatoes or hash, amount depending on the number of people.

—Recipe of Dr. E. C. L. Adams, from the family cookbook of Sophie Meldrim Shonnard, Savannah

Danish Pork Chops

Yield: 6 servings

6 large center-cut pork chops
4 tablespoons butter
¾ cup chopped onion
¾ cup peeled, chopped tart
*   apple*
½ cup dry white wine

Trim chops of excess fat. Brown in butter in skillet. Remove to baking dish. Preheat oven to 350 degrees F. Brown onion and apple in butter. Spread over chops. Add wine. Bake covered for 30 minutes, then uncovered for 15 minutes, or until brown.

—Emma R. Law

Country Sausage

Yield: 12 to 15 patties
*   (4 to 6 servings)*

2 pounds lean ground pork
1 teaspoon salt
½ teaspoon sage
½ teaspoon cumin
¼ teaspoon ground ginger
1 teaspoon crushed bay
*   laurel leaves*
1 tablespoon dried crushed
*   parsley*
½ teaspoon freshly ground
*   black pepper*

Combine all ingredients. Mix well. Shape into patties. Fry in a hot skillet about 8 minutes per side, turning once. Drain fat and serve.

Fine Sausages

For 10 pounds of pork ground fine, take 1 ounce black pepper, ½ ounce sage, ½ ounce thyme, ¼ ounce cayenne pepper, and not quite a quarter pound salt, but to taste. Have all those ingredients pounded very fine, and mixed well together before seasoning the meat. Either make into balls or stuff in the sausage shape.

—Mrs. George W. Anderson, *Favorite Recipes From*
Savannah Homes, 1904

Ham in Parsley Aspic Savannah

"Oh, the South, where every aspic pleases . . ."

Yield: 4 to 6 servings

3 envelopes unflavored
  gelatin
¾ cup cold water
5 tablespoons chicken-flavor
  instant bouillon, or 5
  cubes
3¼ cups of boiling water
¼ teaspoon dried tarragon,
  well-rubbed
½ teaspoon celery seed
2 tablespoons cider vinegar
3 cups finely chopped lean
  cooked ham, chilled
2 cups minced parsley,
  chilled

Sprinkle gelatin over cold water and set aside to soften. Stir bouillon into boiling water. Add softened gelatin and stir until dissolved. Sprinkle in tarragon and celery seed. Cool. Stir in vinegar. Chill, stirring occasionally, until consistency of unbeaten egg white. Stir in chopped ham and parsley, mixing well. Pour into lightly greased loaf pan, 9-by-5-by-3-inches, or 6 cup mold. Chill until firm. Unmold on serving plate, and garnish.

—Emma R. Law

Ham with Red-Eye Gravy

After ham has been fried in the skillet, remove to serving platter and keep warm. In the skillet, for each pound of ham, stir in ½ cup strong coffee, 1 teaspoon light brown sugar, and 1 teaspoon Worcestershire sauce (optional). Cook, uncovered, stirring well, at least 3 minutes. Pour over ham and serve. Cornbread is good with this.

Hattie's Beer-Baked Ham

Wash ham well, and put in a large boiler, skin side up. Over it, pour 1 can black molasses and 4 quarts weak tea, rinsing out the molasses can well with the tea to get it all. Let ham soak in a cool place overnight in this sweet bath. Next morning, put ham in a steamer, fat side up, and pour over it 2 quarts water. Bake in a covered steamer for 3 to 4 hours. Take out, and skin. Plaster ham with a paste made of ketchup and mustard. Return to the oven, and let cook about another 30 minutes, basting well with beer. Then, sprinkle with brown sugar. Bake a little browner, and serve hot.

—Family cookbook of Sophie Meldrim Shonnard, Savannah

Emma's Ham and Corn Pudding

Here's a good luncheon dish using leftover ham.

Yield: 6 servings

1 tablespoon cornstarch
1 tablespoon sugar
1 cup milk
2 eggs, well-beaten
½ cup (1 stick) melted butter
1 16-ounce can corn, undrained
2 cups finely minced cooked ham
¼ cup minced green pepper
2 tablespoons minced onion
¼ teaspoon salt
⅛ teaspoon black pepper
Dash hot sauce

Preheat oven to 350 degrees F. Mix cornstarch well with sugar; mix with remaining ingredients. Turn into greased 6-cup shallow casserole. Bake about 60 minutes, or until firm.

—Emma R. Law

Rose of Sharon Ham Slice

Yield: 4 to 6 servings

1 cooked slice of ham (1 to 1½ inches thick)
2 tablespoons prepared mustard
Juice of one lemon (2½ tablespoons)
⅓ cup honey

Score ham fat edge to prevent curling by cutting it through in several places. Place in baking dish and combine remaining ingredients. Pour over ham. Bake at 325 degrees F. until ham is tender, 45 minutes to one hour.

Chicken Variation: With the addition of garlic salt to taste, this glaze is also good on chicken, and is enough for 1 3-pound chicken, quartered. Brush with glaze several times while broiling.

—Emma R. Law

Ham in a Crust

This ham will be hot, juicy, and tender.

Yield: 4 servings.

For a flavorful ham dish, lay a ¾-inch thick center-cut slice of cooked ham in a heavy ovenproof skillet. Open a can of pineapple slices and drain. Place pineapple rings on the ham. Gradually mix some flour with the juice to make a thick sauce. Pour this on top of the ham until it covers it well on all sides.

Place in a preheated 325 degrees F. oven, and cook for 45 to 60 minutes. Peel off crust and discard, or give to the birds.

—Carter Olive

Honey-Ham Glaze

Yield: 1 cup

½ cup honey or maple syrup
½ cup apple juice
2 tablespoons prepared
    mustard
½ teaspoon ground cloves

Combine ingredients and pour over ham during last 30 minutes of baking. Glaze every 10 minutes, and at end of baking time before removing from oven.

Note: Beer may be substituted in place of juice for an equally good flavor.

Emma's Frisky Franks

Pierce all-beef hot dogs several times with a fork and drop into boiling beer. Cover and remove from heat. Set aside eight minutes before serving. You can save the beer, skim the fat, and keep it in the refrigerator to use again for this purpose if you wish. With this, some like the classic Boston brown bread with butter, and fruits for dessert.

—Emma R. Law

Southern Ham Hocks and Turnip Greens

Wash and place ham hocks in two quarts water. Bring to a boil. Reduce heat, and cook until tender, about 35 or 40 minutes.

Meanwhile, pick and wash turnip leaves. Stack the leaves, and roll together lengthwise. Cut the roll in three or four parts. Peel the turnip roots, and slice in halves, or leave whole.

Add both leaves and turnip roots to the hocks, along with a teaspoon salt and one of sugar. Bring all to a boil, and simmer until roots are tender. This is good with cornbread.

—Family cookbook of Diane Harvey Johnson, Macon

Cumberland Ham Sauce

Yield: 2 cups

*1 cup currant or other red
    jelly
1 tablespoon prepared
    mustard
1 teaspoon grated onion
⅛ teaspoon ginger
Grated peel of one orange
Grated peel of one lemon
½ cup orange juice
2 tablespoons lemon juice
½ cup port wine
1½ tablespoons cornstarch*

In a saucepan combine jelly, mustard, onion, ginger, peels, and juices. Place over low heat, stirring constantly until jelly melts. Mix wine with cornstarch and stir into the jelly mixture. Stir constantly while cooking over a low heat, until sauce bubbles and thickens. Serve either warm or cold with sliced ham or other meats.

How Much Meat Should I Buy?

In serving boneless meats, such as cutlets, liver, stew beef, lean ground meat, and rolled roasts—allow ¼ pound per serving.

For meat with an average amount of bone—bone-in roasts, steaks, and ham—allow ⅓ to ½ pound per serving.

Meat with a large amount of bone, such as short ribs and spareribs—better allow ¾ to 1 pound per serving.

Jarrell Plantation State Historic Site in Jones County near Juliette consists of 20 historic buildings dating as far back as 1847. Annual exhibitions at the site include cane grinding, syrup making, and a corn harvest festival. Drawing by Mary Rutherford, courtesy Jarrell Plantation

Macon Ham Loaf

Yield: 6 servings

¾ pound ground ham
¾ pound ground pork
¼ teaspoon pepper
½ cup milk
*½ cup graham or plain
  cracker crumbs*
1 egg, beaten
1 cup crushed pineapple

Preheat oven to 350 degrees F.
Mix all ingredients except pineapple. Shape into loaf and place on rack in roaster with ½ inch water in the bottom. Bake uncovered one hour. Spread top with pineapple and bake 40 minutes more.

—Elizabeth Solomon Smith, *Sharing Southern Secrets: Recipes of the Deep South*, Macon, 1948.

Creamy Mustard Sauce

Yield: 1 cup

1 cup sour cream
*1 teaspoon wine vinegar or
  lemon juice*
*2 teaspoons prepared
  mustard*
1 teaspoon honey
½ teaspoon salt

Mix ingredients together well and serve.

Rum-Raisin Sauce

Yield: 1¾ cups

2 tablespoons brown sugar
1 tablespoon cornstarch
½ cup water
½ cup orange juice
1 tablespoon rum
⅓ cup apple or currant jelly
1 cup currants or raisins
⅛ teaspoon ground allspice
¼ teaspoon salt

Combine sugar and cornstarch in a small saucepan. Gradually add water, stirring until well blended. Add remaining ingredients and cook over medium heat until clear and thickened. Serve over baked ham.

Cheese Hint

If end pieces of cheese become dry and hard, don't throw them away. Instead, grate them and store in refrigerator in glass jars, or in freezer. Use to top casseroles, vegetables, soups, and sauces.

Betty's Cheese and Chili Pie

A salad and fruit are all you need with this, for a satisfying summer meal. It's a little hot, but also unusual and delicious.

Yield: 6 servings

3 4-ounce cans green chili peppers, seeded, drained and cut so they lie flat
1 pound sharp Cheddar cheese, grated
6 eggs
1 5-ounce can condensed milk, or 5 ounces heavy cream

Preheat oven to 350 degrees F. Line a greased flat casserole or 10-inch pie pan with the peppers. Mix remaining ingredients and pour over peppers. Bake until a knife inserted comes out clean, about 30 to 40 minutes. Cool slightly and serve as a main course for lunch, or cut in small pieces as appetizers. Serve with fruit.

—Betty W. Rauers

Quiche Hint

For a better flavor in your quiche, fry the bacon in a little butter before adding to the other ingredients.

—Carter Olive

Macaroni and Cheese

Boil a quantity of macaroni in plenty of water until nearly soft, then pour off the water and boil in milk until done. Butter your pan, and put in a layer of macaroni, then cheese, mustard, black pepper, and butter, alternating layers until the pan is full or nearly so. Then put breadcrumbs over the top. Beat up two or three eggs with milk enough to cover the whole, pour over, and bake [at 350 degrees F. for 30 minutes or until gold and bubbly].

—Bryan family cookbook, Savannah, circa 1885

Cheese Croquettes

Rub together ⅓ cup of sifted flour and 3 tablespoons of melted butter, and cook into a sauce with ⅔ cup sweet milk, a pinch of salt, and red pepper to taste. Beat into this the yolks of two eggs. Stir into this 1½ cups grated fresh Parmesan cheese, and ½ cup any other kind of cheese you like. Let it get cold, and then form into shape for croquettes. Roll each in egg whites and then cracker crumbs well, and fry quickly in boiling grease.

—Family cookbook of Sophie Meldrim Shonnard, Savannah

The Gazebo at Overlook Mansion, now the Woodruff House, Macon. Drawing by Sterling Everett

Eggs Everglade

Yield: 8 servings

2 envelopes unflavored
   gelatin
2 cups chicken broth, cold
6 shelled hard-cooked eggs
2 cups mayonnaise
2 tablespoons curry powder

Sprinkle gelatin over cold chicken broth in a 1-quart saucepan. Place over low heat, stirring constantly, until gelatin dissolves, about 3 minutes. Remove from heat. Combine broth, eggs, mayonnaise and curry in blender until well blended. Pour into oiled 12-cup mold, and chill at least 12 hours. This is better if made the day before to allow flavors to blend.

To serve, unmold on a lettuce-lined plate, with salad tomatoes, black olives stuffed with blue cheese, or olives stuffed with cold salmon in the center of the ring. Serve with chutney.

—Betty W. Rauers

Easter Monday Casserole

Yield: 4 servings

6 hard-cooked eggs, peeled
   and sliced
4 tablespoons butter or
   margarine
4 tablespoons flour
1 teaspoon salt
⅛ teaspoon pepper
1 teaspoon grated onion
2 cups milk
1 cup grated Cheddar cheese
1 cup dry bread crumbs
Butter for topping

Butter 2-quart casserole and spread eggs evenly in it. Melt 4 tablespoons butter in a saucepan and make a sauce by stirring flour into it, then adding the other seasonings and the milk gradually. Cook and stir over medium heat, folding in cheese as sauce thickens.

Pour sauce over eggs. Top with bread crumbs, and dot with a little extra butter. Bake in a 350 F. oven about 25 minutes, or until hot. May also be prepared ahead of time and refrigerated until time to bake. This is a good brunch dish with corn sticks or split, buttered English muffins.

If you are in a hurry, a can of Cheddar cheese soup, diluted with a little milk, may be used in place of the cooked sauce.

—Helena DeBolt

Augusta Celery Sauce

Yield: about 2 cups

1 cup chopped celery
1 tablespoon finely chopped
  onion
4 tablespoons butter or
  margarine
¼ cup flour
2 cups milk
2 envelopes dehydrated
  chicken broth or 2
  chicken bouillon cubes

Sauté celery and onion in butter for about 5 minutes, until tender but not brown, over moderate heat. Blend in flour and stir about a minute. Slowly add milk and bouillon. Stir sauce constantly until as thickened as desired, checking seasonings and adding more salt or pepper as desired.

Note: This is especially good with an egg dish.

Creole Barbecue Sauce

Yield: 2 cups

1 cup finely chopped onion
3 tablespoons vegetable oil
2 cups tomato sauce
¼ cup cider or wine vinegar
¼ cup lemon juice
3 tablespoons Worcestershire
  sauce
2 tablespons firmly packed
  brown sugar
2 tablespoons prepared
  mustard
¼ to ½ teaspoon hot pepper
  sauce, to taste
1 crushed garlic clove
1 bay leaf
¾ teaspoon chili powder

Sauté onion in oil until tender, but not brown. Add remaining ingredients and bring to a boil. Reduce heat and simmer for 20 to 25 minutes, uncovered, or until mixture begins to thicken. Good with beef, pork, or chicken. Keeps well if covered and refrigerated.

Nutmeg Hint

Add an extra touch of flavor to your barbecue, baked beans, and other such dishes with a few dashes of ground nutmeg.

Poultry

An Island Thanksgiving

A Savannahian remembers Thanksgiving dinner as a child in the early years of the century, as a guest of Captain Joseph Manigault at his Low Country home on Pennyworth Island:

Dinner was served at two; probably the gentlemen and a few rather daring ladies had toddies beforehand. . . . It began with a turtle soup for which Grace, the family cook, was famed. Shrimp pie followed, rice slightly pink with tomato, and filled with big pieces of cauliflower. With this was served turkey stuffed with oysters, and thin slices of well-cured ham. Vegetables were there but to children these were an added burden, and not the delicacy they have now become. Dessert was always the same, vanilla ice cream, a huge mound of it, and the little crescent and diamond cakes, with jelly between, and thin frosting on top.

—From a *Savannah News-Press* feature, November 1943

111

Benne-Baked Chicken

Yield: 4 servings

1 broiler-fryer (2½ to 3 pounds) cut into serving pieces
½ cup flour
1 teaspoon garlic or celery salt
1 teaspoon onion salt
¼ teaspoon pepper
½ teaspoon paprika
3 tablespoons melted butter or margarine
2 tablespoons vegetable oil
1 tablespoon lemon juice
1 cup benne (sesame) seeds

Preheat oven to 350 degrees F. Place chicken in a plastic bag with the flour, salts, pepper, and paprika and shake well. Combine butter, oil, and lemon juice in a shallow dish. Dip each piece of seasoned chicken in this, and then roll in benne seeds. Place chicken pieces in a single row in a baking pan and bake for about an hour, or until tender, turning once.

Broiled Game Hens St. Julian Street

Yield: 6 servings

3 Cornish game hens, 2 pounds each, split
⅓ cup orange juice
1 teaspoon lemon juice
⅓ cup dry white wine
½ teaspoon celery salt
1 teaspoon ginger
1 teaspoon salt
½ teaspoon paprika
1 garlic clove, crushed
⅓ cup vegetable oil

Place chickens in a flat container and cover with marinade made with remaining ingredients. Cover lightly and refrigerate for 3 hours or longer, turning several times. Drain and broil over moderate charcoal heat or in your oven broiler 25 to 30 minutes, or until tender, turning once and basting each side with marinade.

—Emma R. Law

Rice Pie

Nicely roast one or two chickens, saving all the gravy. Have ready a quart of rice, boiled. Mix it with butter, pepper and salt, and the gravy from the fowls, also several eggs. Mix all together. Put it round the sides and bottom of a pan and fill the center with chicken meat and some [hard-cooked] eggs, cut in slices. Cover with rice, and bake.

—Bryan family cookbook, Savannah, circa 1885

Curried Fried Chicken

Yield: 4 servings

1 cup flour
1 teaspoon salt
¼ teaspoon pepper
½ teaspoon paprika
1 teaspoon curry powder
2 eggs, well-beaten
2 tablespoons water
8 chicken legs or other
  serving pieces
Oil for frying

Mix flour and seasonings. Beat eggs and water. Roll chicken in flour, then in the egg mixture, and then again in the flour. Set aside for about 20 minutes. Fry in about an inch of hot oil until golden, turning as necessary, for about 10 minutes. Cover, lower heat, and cook about 15 minutes more. Remove cover and cook another 10 minutes, turning as necessary. Drain on paper towels. This is good either hot or cold.

—Emma R. Law

Curried Chicken

Cut up the chicken, and fry a nice light brown. Stew it gently for 20 minutes in a cream gravy, to which you have added a tablespoon curry powder. Serve with boiled rice around edge of dish.

—Mrs. George W. Anderson, *Favorite Recipes From Savannah Homes*, 1904

Rice for Chicken

Chop one onion very fine and cook it in butter until limp. Pour 2½ cups chicken stock over 1½ cups rice in the same pot, and bring to a boil. Then let simmer for about 20 minutes, or until rice is done. Fluff with fork to serve.

—Family cookbook of Sophie Meldrim Shonnard, Savannah

Fried Chicken

Clean chicken carefully, and lay in salted water for awhile. Have your lard boiling hot. Dip each piece of chicken, well-floured, in egg batter, and fry quickly. With what remains of the batter, make a rich gravy.

—Mrs. George W. Anderson *Favorite Recipes From Savannah Homes*, Savannah, 1904

Honey-Glazed Chicken

Yield: 4 to 6 servings

2 small broiler-fryers (about
  2½ pounds), halved
½ cup (1 stick) butter, at
  room temperature
⅛ teaspoon dried sage, well-
  rubbed
⅓ cup chopped mild
  Valdosta onions or green
  onions
1 teaspoon salt, or to taste
¼ teaspoon freshly-ground
  black pepper
½ cup dry sherry
¼ cup honey

Preheat oven to 350 degrees F. Skewer wings of chicken to sides with wooden pegs or small skewers if desired. Brush chicken well all over with a mixture of the butter and dry seasonings. Roast for about 1¼ hours, turning at least once. Meanwhile mix sherry with honey and bring to simmering in a small saucepan. Brush chicken well on both sides with honey mixture and bake another 15 minutes. Cooking time will depend on chicken.

—Emma R. Law

Lemon Barbecue Chicken

A favorite recipe from Macon author and newspaper food columnist, Violet Moore.

Yield: 4 servings

2 tablespoons butter
1 tablespoon sugar
1 tablespoon prepared
  mustard
3 tablespoons lemon juice
2 teaspoons salt
¼ teaspoon seasoned salt
  (optional)
¼ teaspoon black pepper
8 serving pieces chicken
1½ teaspoons paprika,
  divided

Preheat oven to 350 degrees F. Melt the butter in a baking pan large enough to accommodate all the chicken in one layer without crowding. Stir in next six ingredients and mix well. Lay the chicken in the pan skin side up. Set aside for several minutes. Then turn skin side down, so that all pieces are well covered with the sauce. Sprinkle with half the paprika. Bake ½ hour uncovered, and then turn and sprinkle with remaining paprika. Bake another half hour.

Note: This could also work on the grill, basting with the sauce. It could be used on ribs, and is a nice change from the usual color and flavor of barbecued chicken.

—Violet Moore, Montezuma

Chicken Hint

In stewing chicken for salads and other dishes, one 5-pound stewing hen yields about 4 cups cut-up meat, and about 3 or 4 cups stock.

Emma's Italian Braised Chicken

Yield: 4 servings

1 broiler-fryer (about 3
  pounds), cut up
2 tablespoons olive oil
⅓ cup minced onion
1 garlic clove, crushed or
  minced
1 teaspoon salt, or to taste
⅛ teaspoon freshly-ground
  black pepper
1 cup peeled, seeded minced
  tomato, fresh or canned
½ cup dry red wine
2 teaspoons instant chicken
  bouillon
1 teaspoon Italian herb
  seasoning, or ¼ teaspoon
  each *thyme, basil,
  marjoram, and sage
  (optional)*

Brown chicken in oil in large skillet, one with a lid, over moderate heat. Combine remaining ingredients and spoon over chicken. Cover and simmer over low heat until chicken is tender, about 45 minutes.

Note: Oven method—brown chicken, and place in baking dish. Combine remaining ingredients and spoon over chicken. Cover and bake for about an hour at 350 degrees F.

—Emma R. Law

Mrs. George Hull's Chicken Dumplings

Joint a large chicken, dividing breast and back into pieces fit to serve. Put in sauce pan with water enough to cover well, 1 teaspoon salt, ¼ teaspoon black pepper, 1 tablespoon chopped parsley, 1 teaspoon finely chopped onion, and stew for ½ hour.

Make your dumplings with 1 quart flour, 1 tablespoon lard, 1 tablespoon butter, 1 teaspoon salt, 2 teaspoons baking powder, and 1 large well-washed boiled Irish potato, mashed. Mix all with just enough water to make a dough to roll out. Cut into small biscuits, and add to boiling chicken. Cook about 20 to 25 minutes more, setting the pot back a little on the fire so it will not boil too hard.

Keep pot covered. If you lift the lid even once after the dumplings are in, and let out the steam, they will be tough.

—*Some Choice Receipts of Savannah Homemakers,*
Savannah, 1904

Drawing by Georgia artist Barry Champion

Chicken Pie with Mushrooms

Take 5 spring chickens, cut in fours, or one pair fowls. If chickens, stew in milk. Boil until tender. Take out bones, and throw the bones back into the water the chickens were boiled in, with one onion, salt and pepper. Boil down and strain, and save. Cut up the white meat of the chicken. Take all the dark meat, and run it through a food chooper; then add it to the rest. Melt ½ pound of butter with 4 tablespoons white flour, and the chicken jelly to it, along with 1 can of mushrooms (drained), 6 [hard-cooked] eggs chopped fine, and the chicken meat, pepper, and salt. Let all cook together. Meanwhile, line a large pie dish with a good crust at the bottom and side, and bake lightly [at 325 degrees F. for 30 minutes or] until a very light brown. Now pour in the chicken and mushrooms, and then put a top crust on it. Put back in the oven, and bake brown. Serve at once.

—Family cookbook of Sophie Meldrim Shonnard, Savannah

St. Simons Chicken with Mushrooms

Yield: 4 servings

1 chicken (about 2½
  pounds), cut for serving
1 tablespoon lemon juice
Salt and pepper to taste
2 tablespoons vegetable oil
½ cup chopped onion
1 garlic clove, crushed
¼ pound sliced mushrooms
1 tablespoon flour
⅛ teaspoon cayenne pepper,
  or to taste
½ cup dry white wine
1 tablespoon chopped parsley

Rub chicken pieces with lemon juice and sprinkle with salt and pepper. Heat oil in a large skillet, one with a lid. Saute chicken to a light brown color. Add onion, garlic, and mushrooms. Cook about 5 minutes, or until onion and mushrooms are limp.

Sprinkle flour and cayenne pepper over chicken and vegetables and stir until flour is well absorbed. While stirring, add wine and bring to a boil. Cook until smooth. Add a little more wine, water, or broth if necessary.

Cover pan partially, or use a steam-vented lid if you have one, and simmer 25 to 30 minutes more, until chicken is done. Sprinkle with parsley before serving.

Mrs. Meldrim's Chicken Fricassee

Cut up chicken as for frying. Put in a saucepan and cook slowly, adding water and a little onion cut fine. When tender, take several [hard-cooked] eggs, and mash the yolks in a bowl. Add to this 1 tablespoon butter, ¼ cup [heavy] cream, and some grated nutmeg. Chop the whites fine, and add to this. Pour all over chicken, stirring well. Cook 10 to 15 minutes more. Add a glass of sherry, and a little lemon juice if desired. Heat and serve.

—Family cookbook of Sophie Meldrim Shonnard, Savannah

Chicken and Oyster Croquets

Boil two young chickens, and cut up fine. Drain one quart oysters, and put on the fire for a few minutes; then cut up fine. Make a custard of a pint of milk with some butter and flour, salt, and two eggs. Cut up some celery and parsley, and mix this well together. Cool and form into rolls. Dip in the whites of eggs and then cracker crumbs. Fry in boiling lard until brown.

—Family cookbook of Sophie Meldrim Shonnard, Savannah

Athens Chicken Rosemary

Rosemary is for remembering . . . this chicken.

Yield: 4 servings.

1 3-pound fryer chicken, cut up, buttermilk as needed, bread crumbs as needed, salt and pepper to taste, rosemary to taste.

Preheat oven to 350 degrees F. Take one fryer chicken, cut in serving pieces, and dip each piece in a shallow dish of buttermilk. Then roll in fine dried bread crumbs and arrange in a shallow buttered baking pan. Sprinkle each piece with salt, pepper, and crumbled rosemary. If any buttermilk is left over, you can sprinkle it over the chicken in the pan before baking. Bake for about one hour, or until chicken is tender.

—Jacqueline Harter, Athens

Economical Chicken

You can save real money by learning to cut up a chicken yourself when a recipe calls for chicken breasts and other choice serving parts. Cook unused portions and use them in soup, chicken salad, or a creamed dish at another meal. Or save extra pieces in the freezer until you have enough for a certain dish.

When making a chicken dish, skin chicken whenever possible. It is not only easier to eat, especially with a sauce, but you are eliminating the fat deposits just under the skin, saving calories and avoiding cholesterol. For the same reason, chicken broth should always be cooled and skimmed before using in recipes.

A Nice Sauce for Fowl

Put a nice piece of butter in a skillet, and stir in 1 heaping teaspoon flour. Stir in 2 cups of chicken stock, and cook about 10 or 12 minutes, stirring well. Then squeeze juice of ½ lemon into it, and take out ½ cup of the liquid. To this, add 2 well-beaten egg yolks. Put back in the sauce, and stir well together, but do not allow to boil.

For a nice serving, cook some sliced mushrooms separately in butter. Put your rice around a platter, then the chicken on top, mushrooms around platter, and sauce on top or around chicken.

—Family cookbook of Sophie Meldrim Shonnard, Savannah

Sherry-Marinated Chicken

Yield: 4 servings

*1 garlic clove, crushed or
   finely minced*
3 tablespoons lemon juice
2 tablespoons vegetable oil
¾ cup dry sherry
1 teaspoon salt
*1 broiler-fryer (2½ or 3
   pounds), cut up*
Paprika to taste

Combine first five ingredients. Pour over chicken pieces in a shallow baking pan. Marinate in the refrigerator at least three hours, turning often. Sprinkle with paprika.

Preheat oven to 375 degrees F. Sprinkle chicken with paprika and bake until tender, about 45 to 55 minutes. Remove from pan, and keep warm.

A Nice Dressing for Fowls

Make a batter with two eggs, milk, and sifted cornmeal, and season it with pepper, salt, and onions chopped fine. Beat well. Dip chicken pieces in it, and fry brown, turning occasionally. You might use flour instead of cornmeal if desired.

—Bryan family cookbook, Savannah, circa 1885

Drawing courtesy Savannah Visitors Center

Chicken Livers with Wine

Yield: 3 servings

1 cup sliced onions
1 garlic clove, crushed or
   finely minced
1 pound chicken livers
4 tablespoons butter or
   margarine
½ teaspoon salt
¼ teaspoon pepper
¼ cup dry red wine
1 tablespoon Worcestershire
   sauce

In a large skillet, one with a lid, sauté onions, garlic, and livers in melted butter. Sprinkle livers with salt and pepper while sautéing until lightly brown. Stir in wine and Worcestershire sauce. Cover and simmer about 10 minutes, or until tender. Serve as desired with buttered noodles or cooked rice.

Pimento-Parsley Sauce

Yield: 1 cup

1 tablespoon butter
1 tablespoon flour
¾ cup milk or light cream
2 teaspoons lemon juice
2 tablespoons finely chopped
   pimento
2 tablespoons finely chopped
   parsley
½ teaspoon salt (or onion,
   celery, or garlic salt)
⅛ teaspoon black pepper

Melt butter in small saucepan over medium heat. Blend in flour smoothly. Stir in milk or cream. Cook, stirring constantly, until mixture begins to thicken. Add seasonings and simmer a few minutes until flavors are well blended. Check for seasoning and serve hot.

Roast Chicken

Prepare same as turkey. For a pair of chickens weighing six or seven pounds, they should be roasted about an hour and a half. A great deal depends on the age of the chicken: an old hen takes longer.

A nice dressing for chickens is a loaf of stale bread broken in very fine crumbs, scant ½ cup of butter, salt and pepper, teaspoon of chopped parsley, ½ teaspoon of sage. Mix well together in pan before putting in chicken. Rub chicken well with butter, and dredge rather quickly with flour. Baste every 15 or 20 minutes with the gravy in the pan from the fowl.

—Mrs. George W. Anderson, *Favorite Recipes From*
Savannah Homes, 1904

Eatonton Chicken Spaghetti

Yield: 6 to 8 servings

1 4- to 5-pound stewing hen
Water as needed
1 sprig fresh parsley
2 celery stalks with leaves,
  cut up
1 small onion, quartered
2½ teaspoons salt, divided
¾ teaspoon pepper, divided
4 tablespoons chicken fat
4 tablespoons flour
2 cups milk
3 tablespoons butter or
  margarine
1 cup sliced mushrooms, or
  1 8-ounce can, drained
1 cup chopped celery
¼ cup chopped green pepper
½ cup sliced stuffed olives,
  drained
2 pimentos, cut into strips
8 ounces thin spaghetti
½ cup blanched almonds for
  garnish
Parmesan cheese for garnish

Cook hen in boiling water to cover, to which parsley, celery, onion, 2 teaspoons salt, and ½ teaspoon black pepper have been added. Simmer 2 or 3 hours, or until tender, adding more water if necessary.

Remove chicken from stock and strain stock. Skin and bone chicken, cutting meat into bite-sized pieces. Allow stock to chill, and remove fat from the top. (This may be done one day, and dish completed the next. After straining stock, some like to have the chicken cool in it, for extra flavor.)

Make a medium white sauce, using chicken fat in place of butter. Melt 4 tablespoons fat over low heat in a heavy saucepan, preferably stirring with a wooden spoon. Blend in flour and ½ teaspoon salt and ¼ teaspoon pepper. Cook over low heat, stirring, until mixture is smooth and bubbly. Gradually stir in milk, stirring constantly, until mixture thickens. (If you use canned mushrooms, the liquid from them may be used in place of part of the milk here.) Set sauce aside.

Melt butter in a large skillet or pan, and sauté mushrooms, celery, and green pepper until limp but not brown. Stir these and cut-up chicken pieces into the white sauce. Warm all gently in the top of a large double boiler or over moderate heat. Add olives and pimentos and heat, allowing flavors to blend, while cooking spaghetti according to package directions. (If you do not want the chicken stock for another purpose, it may be used as part of the liquid in cooking spaghetti, for extra flavor.)

Drain spaghetti and combine with sauce in a large serving dish. Garnish with almonds and cheese.

—Wink Walker, Eatonton

Mushroom Addition

One-half cup or more fresh or drained canned sliced mushrooms, sautéed with the onions and celery, add a special touch to baked dressings, and almost no calories.

Port Wentworth Oyster Dressing

Yield: 3 quarts

1 8-inch pan corn bread, crumbled (see page 68)
6 cups whole wheat bread cubes
2 teaspoons poultry seasoning
1½ teaspoons salt
¼ teaspoon pepper
2 cups celery slices
1 cup chopped onion
½ cup (1 stick) butter or margarine
1 9½-ounce can frozen oysters, thawed in the refrigerator, or fresh oysters, undrained
2 eggs, beaten

Preheat oven to 325 degrees F. Combine crumbs or corn bread, whole wheat cubes, and seasonings in a large bowl. Sauté celery and onion in butter until tender. Add to bread mixture, tossing lightly.

Drain oysters, reserving liquid. Add enough water to oyster liquid to make 1 cup, or for a more moist dressing, use 2 cups liquid. (Broth or bouillon might also be used for part of liquid.) Add this to bread mixture with oysters and eggs, tossing all lightly until thoroughly moistened. Place in greased 3-quart casserole and cover. Bake about 1 hour, uncovering last 15 minutes to brown.

Note: Stuffing may be lightly stuffed into body and neck cavity of one 16 to 18 pound turkey.

—Angie Chilen, Port Wentworth

To Roast a Turkey

See that the turkey is well cleansed and washed. Salt and pepper inside. Take a loaf and a half of baker's bread, rub fine with the hands, and have in a pan a lump of butter a little larger than an egg. Cut into this half of an onion. Let it cook a few minutes, but not brown. Then stir in the bread, add 1 tablespoon each of salt and pepper, and let it get thoroughly heated. If thyme and sage are liked, add to the dressing. Oysters can also be added.

Fill the turkey with this dressing. If any is left, put it in one end of the pan. Put the turkey into a dripping (roasting) pan, and dredge with a little flour. Put about 1 coffee cup of water in the pan, and baste very often. Have a moderate fire, and roast 15 minutes to the pound.

Pâté Romaine

Cut the remains of any white cooked meat into julienne strips; also boil some spaghetti pieces, 2 inches long. Strain spaghetti. Have some cream hot, and grated cheese. Toss the meat and spaghetti together. Add cream, put in a gratin dish, and sprinkle a little more grated cheese on the top. Brown in the oven and serve.

—Family cookbook of Sophie Meldrim Shonnard, Savannah

Pecan-Corn Bread Stuffing

Yield: 2½ quarts

1 cup chopped pecans
1 cup celery slices
½ cup chopped onion (may
   be part sliced green
   onions)
¾ cup melted butter or
   margarine
6 cups crumbled corn bread
   (see note)
6 cups dry bread cubes
1½ teaspoons poultry
   seasoning
1½ teaspoons salt
¼ teaspoon pepper
2 eggs, beaten
1¼ cups stock, bouillon, or
   water

Sauté nuts, celery, and onion in butter. Add to combined corn bread, cubes, and seasonings. Mix with eggs and liquid. Stuff cavity of a 12-pound bird, or roast separately at 325 degrees F. for about an hour, covered for first 45 minutes and uncovered last 15 minutes to brown.

Note: One 8- or 9-inch pan of cornbread yields about 6 cups crumbs for cornbread stuffing. A good recipe for corn bread is on p. 68.

Calhoun Turkey Hash

Yield: 4 servings

2 cups chopped cooked
   turkey
2 cups chopped cooked
   potatoes
¼ cup finely chopped onion
2 tablespoons chopped green
   pepper
1 teaspoon salt, or to taste
⅛ teaspoon ground black
   pepper
½ cup turkey broth or
   chicken consommé, or
   gravy
Dash thyme or sage
Parsley, chopped, to taste

Preheat oven to 350 degrees F. Mix all ingredients except parsley and place in greased 1½-quart casserole. Sprinkle with parsley. Bake covered for 30 minutes; then remove foil and cook another 10 to 15 minutes, or until brown.

Pan Gravy

Blend 1 tablespoon soft butter with 1 tablespoon flour, and stir into pan in which chicken was cooked, combining well with juices in pan. Stir over moderate heat until bubbly and thick. Serve in a sauceboat.

Dressing for Turkeys

Delicious dressing for turkeys may be made from peanuts or chestnuts, or toasted bread crumbs, or oysters, or potatoes, or onion and celery. Pound the peanuts, season to taste with salt and black pepper, and bind with yolk of egg. Do likewise with the chestnuts. Toast your bread very crisp. Season with salt, pepper, and butter, and bind with raw egg.

Drain and wash oysters and season to taste with salt and pepper and celery and butter. Boil Irish potatoes and mash them, season while hot with onion chopped up, and with pepper and salt and butter; also, celery cut up. Mix all thoroughly.

—Favorite Recipes from Savannah Homes, 1904

Turkey Reuben

Toast 2 slices whole wheat bread on one side, for each sandwich. Butter lightly. Arrange slices of white turkey meat over the bread. Spread well-drained sauerkraut over the meat, and top with sliced Swiss cheese. Broil until cheese is melted and sandwich is heated. Serve with a garnish of dill pickle and radish roses.

—Emma R. Law

Sweet-Sour Orange Sauce for Duckling

To the gravy in the pan in which the duck has been roasted, add 1 tablespoon cornstarch, 2 tablespoons wine vinegar, and 2 tablespoons sugar, and cook over medium heat 5 minutes, stirring until sauce thickens. Add ⅛ teaspoon thyme, 2 tablespoons finely chopped fresh or dried parsley, 1 teaspoon salt, ¼ teaspoon white or black pepper, and the grated peel and juice of five oranges, preferably navel. Finally, stir in 2 tablespoons curacao. Heat, but do not allow to boil. Pour over warm duckling and serve.

Poultry Hints

When flouring chicken parts for frying, try adding a teaspoon of curry to the flour. Or a half-teaspoon basil, tarragon or thyme leaves, crushed, will add extra flavor.

Larger chickens and turkeys have more meat in proportion to the bone. Whole chickens also cost less than cut-up ones.

Seafood

How To Plank A Fish

Butter and brown your plank in the oven before using the first time. Do not let it blacken; with every use, the board will improve.

Before placing your fish on the board, butter the board, and heat it through in the oven. Never use bacon, pork, or any other kind of animal fat; butter is the only thing. Place fish on plank, skin side down, and fasten the corners with thumb tacks. Brush with butter, and season with salt.

Never wash the board; scrape with the back of a knife, and wash it off after use with a cloth wrung out of cold water.

Bake your fish 30 to 45 minutes, according to the size of fish. Any firm white-meated fish is good planked.

—Frances Meldrim, (Mrs. Peter)
from the family cookbook of her daughter Sophie Meldrim Shonnard, Savannah

Fish

The gills of fish, if fresh, should be bright red. . . . Fish is a food which you can get more good from, considering the price, than if you bought meat, and the most nourishing fish is one of the cheapest—that is, the herring. Pieces of fish, buttered, can be deliciously steamed or baked if laid between two plates over a saucepan of water.

—"How Girls Can Help Their Country,"
Handbook for Girl Scouts by W. J. Hoxie, 1913

125

Scene at Isle of Hope near Savannah. The area is actually a peninsula, with a name dating from Colonial days. Drawing by Alberta R. Beckwith

Salt the Skillet

When frying fish, if you salt the bottom of the skillet the fish will not stick.

To Remove Fish Odor

To remove fish odor from hands, wash them with lemon juice or vinegar before using soap.

Emma's Baked Whole Fish with Wine

Yield: 8 servings

1 whole fish, such as striped
  bass, cod, or red snapper,
  cleaned
2 teaspoons salt
1 cup chopped green onion
2 tablespoons vegetable oil
¼ cup fresh chopped parsley
1 teaspoon grated lemon peel
½ teaspoon marjoram, well-
  rubbed
⅛ teaspoon freshly-ground
  black pepper
2 tablespoons fresh lemon
  juice
½ cup cracker crumbs
4 tablespoons butter
¾ cup dry white table wine
1 lemon, thinly sliced
1 medium onion, thinly
  sliced
2 small tomatoes, cut in
  about 8 wedges each
Parsley sprigs
Lemon wedges for garnish

Preheat oven to 350 degrees F. Wash fish inside and out in cold running water. Dry inside and out with paper towels. Sprinkle with salt. Set aside.

Sauté onions for about 2 minutes in 8-inch skillet in oil. Stir in chopped parsley, grated lemon peel, marjoram, pepper, and lemon juice. Place half of onion mixture in a baking dish large enough to hold fish without leaving much space on either side. Place fish on this, and spread with remaining onion mixture. Sprinkle with crumbs and dot with butter. Pour wine around, but not over, fish.

Bake for 15 minutes. Arrange lemon and onion slices over fish and place tomato wedges at the sides. Bake 20 minutes more, or until fish flakes easily when gently tested with a fork. Serve with pan juice spooned over fish. Garnish with parsley and lemon wedges as desired.

—Emma R. Law

Dixie Cornmeal-Fried Fish

Yield: 4 servings

1 egg, beaten
1 tablespoon Worcestershire
  sauce
1 cup yellow cornmeal
¾ teaspoon salt
1 pound flounder or other
  fish fillets, fresh or frozen,
  thawed
Vegetable oil for frying

In a shallow dish, combine egg and Worcestershire sauce. In a flat dish, combine cornmeal and salt. Dip fish in egg mixture and then coat evenly with cornmeal. Fry fish in hot oil until browned, about 5 minutes on each side.

Baked Fillets with Lemon and Sour Cream

Yield: 2 to 3 servings

1 pound fish fillets, fresh or
  frozen, thawed
1 tablespoon butter
¼ cup sour cream
¼ cup mayonnaise
1 tablespoon fresh lemon or
  lime juice
Parsley and lemon wedges
  for garnish

Preheat oven to 350 degrees F. Place fish in a buttered baking dish in a single layer, dot with a little more butter, and bake about 10 minutes. Blend sour cream, mayonnaise, and juice and spread over fish. Bake 10 to 15 minutes longer, or until fish flakes easily with a fork. Serve garnished with parsley and lemon wedges as desired.

—Emma R. Law

Rachel's Fish in Beer Batter

Yield: 4 servings

1½ cups flour
2¼ teaspoons baking powder
¾ teaspoon baking soda
1½ teaspoons salt, or to taste
⅛ teaspoon pepper
1 pound fish fillets, fresh or
  frozen, thawed
⅓ cup lemon juice
⅔ cup beer
Vegetable oil for frying
Lemon wedges (optional)

Combine first five ingredients in a large flat dish. Pat fish dry on paper towels and coat with about ⅓ of the flour mixture. Now pour remaining mixture into a bowl with the lemon juice and beer (mixture will foam up). Stir until mixture is consistency of pancake batter. Dip fish in batter and fry in hot oil about 3 minutes on each side, or until golden brown. Drain on paper towels and serve immediately, with lemon wedges if desired.

Note: This is also a good batter for deep-fried shrimp, with a dash of ground nutmeg added if desired.

Fish Steaks

The steaks should be one pound each. Wipe well, and rub on each side with salt and pepper. Lay on a dish, and pour over them a very little sweet [vegetable] oil, and let stand for 10 minutes. Lay on a double broiler, and broil over a brisk fire 8 minutes on each side. Rub soft a tablespoonful of butter for two steaks, with a tablespoonful of nicely chopped parsley, spread this over your hot steaks, and serve on a hot dish.

—Mrs. Wallace Cumming, *Some Choice Receipts of Savannah Homemakers*, Savannah, 1904

Fran's Fillets with Cheese Sauce

Yield: 4 servings

1½ pounds fresh or frozen
  fillets, thawed
Salt and pepper to taste
½ cup mayonnaise
Dash cayenne pepper
2 tablespoons capers, drained
1 tablespoon chopped chives
1 tablespoon finely chopped
  fresh parsley, or dried
  parsley to taste
½ cup grated sharp Cheddar
  cheese
1 egg white
Pimento strips for garnish

Wipe fillets with a damp clean cloth or paper towel and place on oiled broiler rack. Broil under medium heat for 10 or 12 minutes. Sprinkle with salt and pepper and turn if desired. Combine mayonnaise, cayenne, capers, chives, parsley, and cheese. Beat egg white until stiff and fold into dressing. Spread on fish and broil for 5 minutes, or until sauce is puffed. Garnish with pimento.

Wilkes County Tartar Sauce

To ½ cup mayonnaise, add 1 finely chopped dill pickle and 1 small onion, finely chopped. Season as desired with red pepper, paprika, salt, and lemon juice. Serve with fried fish or fish croquettes. Makes nearly 1 cup sauce.

—*Colonial Kitchens of Washington-Wilkes*, Washington

Baked Shad

Split the shad wide enough to enable you to carefully clean, wash and salt. Prepare a dressing of Irish potatoes, onion, salt and pepper, a good size piece of butter, and a very small piece of breakfast bacon. Stuff the shad with this, and sew it up. Put it in a pan with a little water and a piece of butter, and baste constantly. Have a steady fire.

—Mrs. George W. Anderson, *Some Choice Receipts of
Savannah Homemakers*, Savannah, 1904

Herb-Broiled Fish Steaks

Yield: 4 servings

1 tablespoon butter or margarine
1 tablespoon finely chopped parsley or dried parsley flakes
1½ teaspoons salt or celery salt
½ teaspoon crumbled oregano leaves
¼ teaspoon white pepper
1 tablespoon lemon juice
1½ pounds fish steaks
Fresh parsley for garnish

Melt butter in a small saucepan and add next five ingredients. Arrange fish on oiled rack in a broiler pan and brush mixture over fish, using about half of mixture. Broil for 5 minutes. Turn and brush with remaining herb mixture; then broil for another 5 minutes, or until fish flakes easily when tested with a fork and is nicely browned. Garnish with parsley to serve.

Note: Lemon pepper or freshly-ground black pepper may be used in place of white pepper if desired.

Baked Crabs with Cheese

The meat of one dozen crabs, 1 pint milk, 1 heaping tablespoon flour, 1 tablespoon butter, ¼ pound grated cheese, salt and pepper.

Let the milk come to a boil. Cream the flour and butter together, add to the milk, and boil 5 minutes, stirring so that it will be smooth. Add to this half of the grated cheese, and the meat of the crabs.

When ready to use, put either into the backs of the crabs, or in a baking dish. Sprinkle the top with a little butter, breadcrumbs, and the remainder of the cheese. Put in the oven and brown. This recipe will fill 9 crab backs.

—Mrs. W. H. Daniel, *Some Choice Receipts of Savannah Homemakers*, Savannah, 1904

Tracy's Crab Newberg

Cream 2 tablespoons butter and 1 of flour together well. Put these in a pot and add 1 pint milk and ½ pint cream gradually, with a little salt and 1 tablespoon finely chopped onion for flavor. Cook until sauce is as thick as desired. Now stir in 2 cups mushrooms, sliced and lightly browned, and 2 cups crab or lobster meat, pulled into small pieces. Cook long enough to heat well, with 3 tablespoons of sherry added last, but do not overcook. Serve on toast.

—Family cookbook of Sophie Meldrim Shonnard, Savannah

Crab-Cheese Puff

Yield: 4 servings

6 slices white bread, trimmed
   and cut in small cubes
1 pound crab meat, or
   2 6½-ounce cans, drained
1 8-ounce package Old
   English process cheese,
   chopped, or 1 cup grated
   Cheddar cheese
4 tablespoons melted butter
3 eggs
2 cups milk
½ teaspoon salt, or to taste
½ teaspoon dry mustard, or
   to taste

Preheat oven to 350 degrees F. In a greased 2-quart casserole, arrange bread cubes, crab and cheese in layers. Top with melted butter. Beat eggs with milk and seasonings and pour over casserole. Bake for about an hour, or until golden and puffy. May be made ahead of time and refrigerated, covered, overnight or until needed.

Puff Variation

This same recipe, without the crab, may be used as a brunch dish with broiled tomatoes and link sausage.

—Emma R. Law

Miss Saidie Hunter's Brown Fricasee of Fish

Take two large fish, about 2½ pounds each. Boil in a pot, half covered with water, to which 1 bay leaf, 7 cloves, 1 onion cut up fine, 1 teaspoon celery seed, and salt and pepper, have been added. When done, remove from water when cool, and skin and bone. Drain and save cooking water.

Now rub 3 heaping teaspoons of brown flour with 1 pint of hot water and 1 teaspoon butter to make a sauce, adding water gradually and stirring until thick. Now add fish stock and cook until a nice sauce, adding Worcester [sic] sauce, nutmeg, red pepper, lemon juice to taste, and 2 sliced hard-boiled eggs. Put the fish in the sauce and let it all come to a boil. Then add 1 glass sherry, stir all well, and serve.

—Family cookbook of Sophie Meldrim Shonnard, Savannah

Alligator Creek Crab

Yield: 4 to 6 servings

2 tablespoons flour
3 tablespoons butter
1 cup light cream, at room temperature
⅛ teaspoon allspice
⅛ teaspoon cayenne pepper
⅛ teaspoon mace
1 teaspoon dry mustard
¾ teaspoon seafood seasoning (optional)
1 lemon, finely chopped, seeded, peel included
1 pound crab meat (should be ½ claw meat)
2 teaspoons Worcestershire sauce
Paprika to taste
Butter as needed

Brown flour in butter. Slowly add the cream, stirring continuously, and cook over low to moderate heat until thickened, but do not allow to boil. Add spices, lemon, flaked crab meat, and Worcestershire sauce. Mix well. Spoon into lightly-greased baking dishes or shells. Sprinkle with paprika and dot with butter. Brown under the broiler, or bake in a preheated 350 degrees F. oven for about 20 minutes.

Crab Oh's!

Boil one large eggplant, and scald six tomatoes. Skin them, and drain in a sifter, until the water is out of them. When cold, chop both together with pepper and salt. Add meat of four crabs, and 3 eggs; beat well together. Fry it in a skillet with a tablespoonful of butter, then brown it in a dish in the oven with breadcrumbs on the top and a little butter, and send it to the table.

—Family cookbook of Sophie Meldrim Shonnard, Savannah

Daisy Phillips' Stuffed Crabs

For 6 crabs, cream 1 tablespoonful of flour with 1 tablespoonful of butter, and add 1 cup milk slowly to make a sauce, cooking until it thickens, along with a little chopped onion and celery and some nutmeg. When it is thick, add the crab meat, stir well, and put in shells. Sprinkle each with breadcrumbs and a dab of butter. Bake and serve with some chopped parsley.

—Family cookbook of Sophie Meldrim Shonnard, Savannah

Shrimp boat. Drawing by Fran Kebschull

Macon Crab Mold

Yield: 6 cups

*2 tablespoons unflavored
gelatin*
1 cup cold water
1 large onion, divided
2 cups tomato juice
2 whole cloves
1 bay leaf
2 tablespoons sugar
3 tablespoons lemon juice
4 drops hot sauce
*1½ cups cooked, shredded
lump crab meat*
*¼ cup finely chopped green
pepper*
½ cup finely chopped celery
*½ cup sliced stuffed green
olives*
Greens as needed
Parsley for garnish

Soften gelatin in cold water according to package instructions. Grate one tablespoon of onion and set aside. Chop the rest in quarters into a small saucepan. Add tomato juice, whole cloves, and bay leaf. Bring to a boil and simmer for about five minutes. Strain into a large mixing bowl, discarding cloves, bay leaf, and large onion pieces. Add softened gelatin and water mixture to tomato juice. Mix until well dissolved. Add the sugar, lemon juice, hot sauce, and reserved grated onion. Cool until jelly-like. Then add crab meat, green pepper, celery, and olives; mix well. Pour into large decorative mold; cover. Chill until firm. Unmold on plate of greens; decorate with parsley.

Port Royal Crab Quiche

*Yield: 6 servings
(12 as appetizers)*

3 eggs
*1 9-inch pie or quiche shell,
unbaked*
*1 cup fresh or 1 6½-ounce
can crab meat, drained and
shredded*
*1¼ cups light cream or half-
and-half*
1 cup shredded Swiss cheese
½ teaspoon salt
⅛ teaspoon black pepper
*½ teaspoon dried dill weed
or 1 teaspoon finely
chopped parsley*
*½ cup sliced mushrooms,
drained*

First, separate one egg and take about two teaspoons egg white. Brush this around the edge of the pie shell to keep the crust tender and yet crisp. Set rest of egg aside.

Preheat oven to 400 degrees F. Sprinkle crab meat evenly over bottom of pie shell and set aside. Blend cream with cheese until smooth. Beat remaining egg with the other two eggs; combine with cream mixture and seasonings. Add mushrooms. Pour over crab meat. Bake for about 30 minutes or until firm, puffy, and golden. Cool on a rack for about 10 minutes before cutting.

Note: Shrimp, lobster, or chopped cooked ham may be used in place of crab.

Moultrie Crab Cakes

Yield: 4 servings

1 pound crab meat
½ cup fine bread crumbs
½ teaspoon salt
¼ teaspoon pepper
¼ teaspoon celery salt
1 egg, well-beaten
2½ tablespoons mayonnaise
1 tablespoon dry mustard
½ teaspoon dried parsley
   flakes, or 1 tablespoon
   finely chopped parsley
Vegetable oil

Combine all ingredients except the oil. Mix well and shape like hamburgers. Fry in hot oil until done, turning once.

Note: Instead of bread crumbs, try using herb-seasoned stuffing mix in mixing crab cakes. A little chopped onion, green pepper, and celery in the mixture is also good.

—Diane Harvey Johnson

Emma's Browned Oysters

Yield: 4 to 5 servings

1 quart oysters
Flour as needed
3 tablespoons butter, divided
Salt and pepper to taste
Worcestershire sauce to taste
Lemon wedges for garnish
Parsley sprigs for garnish

Drain oysters well and examine for any pieces of shell. Dredge with enough flour to cover. Heat 2 tablespoons butter over moderate heat in a large skillet and brown oysters, turning as desired. Strain, reserving juice and butter mixture in skillet. Set aside. Make a roux of remaining butter and one tablespoon flour in skillet by browning flour and then stirring in brown pan juices. Add seasonings to taste, and replace oysters in the pan. Warm over low heat and serve hot, garnished with lemon and parsley as desired.

—Emma R. Law

Bridget's Creamed Oysters

Put one pound butter in a pan and let it melt. Rub in one pint flour until smooth, and then add 2 quarts milk gradually, along with some finely chopped celery, and a little mace.

Wash 1 gallon oysters in cold water, and drain well. When the milk mixture is well heated, add the oysters, and cook a few minutes, but do not boil.

—Family cookbook of Sophie Meldrim Shonnard, Savannah

Angels on Horseback

Yield: 24 rolls

2 dozen large oysters
12 slices bacon
½ teaspoon salt
⅛ teaspoon pepper
⅛ teaspoon paprika
Lemon wedges for garnish
Fresh parsley for garnish

Shuck and drain oysters on a towel. Set aside. Cut bacon slices in half. Lay oysters on bacon and sprinkle with salt, pepper, and paprika. Roll each in a piece of bacon and fasten with a pick. Arrange on a greased baking sheet.

Preheat broiler and broil on each side until bacon is cooked and crisp; do not overbake. Remove toothpicks to serve, and garnish with lemon and parsley as desired.

Note: Oven variation: Preheat oven to 450 degrees F. and bake for about 10 minutes, turning once if desired, until bacon is crisp.

Andrea's Oyster Soufflé

Yield: 4 to 6 servings

1 pint oysters
2 tablespoons butter
2 tablespoons flour
1 teaspoon salt
⅛ teaspoon pepper
1 cup light cream
1 teaspoon Worcestershire
* sauce*
3 eggs, divided
Buttered crumbs for topping

Drain oysters well, chop fine, and set aside. Make a thick white sauce by melting the butter in a small pan, stirring in the flour, seasonings, gradually adding the cream, and cooking over moderate heat until thickened. Add Worcestershire, oysters, and beaten egg yolks. Allow to cool to lukewarm.

Preheat oven to 325 degrees F. Spread sides and bottom of a 6-cup soufflé dish or deep casserole with butter. Beat egg whites stiff, and carefully fold into the cream mixture. Pour into soufflé dish. Top with buttered crumbs. Bake about 35 to 40 minutes. Serve at once.

Escalloped Oysters

Drain oysters. Use only an earthware dish for the oven. Put a layer of oysters in it, then a layer of crushed breadcrumbs, salt, pepper, nutmeg, and small lumps butter. Repeat until dish is full, and bake a dark brown.

—Bryan family cookbook, Savannah, circa 1885

Ralph's Escalloped Oysters

Yield: 6 to 8 servings

1 quart oysters
Milk as needed
2 cups cracker crumbs,
*   medium fine*
½ cup (1 stick) butter or as
*   desired*
Freshly ground pepper to
*   taste*
¼ teaspoon ground mace, or
*   to taste*
Salt to taste

Preheat oven to 350 degrees F. Drain oyster liquid into a quart measuring cup. Add enough milk to make one pint. Place over low heat in a saucepan. Meanwhile, mix crumbs with seasonings while butter is also melting over moderate heat or in a preheating oven. Add butter to crumbs and mix well.

Place half of crumbs in a shallow 2-quart baking dish, then half of oysters; repeat, ending with oysters. Pour heated liquor evenly over oysters. Bake for about 30 minutes.

Note: Not much salt is needed for this because of the salt in most crackers. Buttery-flavored crackers are preferred, not plain saltines.

—Emma R. Law

Mrs. T. M. Cunningham's Oyster Cocktail

Mix well together one (small) bottle of ketchup, ½ bottle horseradish, juice of four lemons, 1 cup finely chopped celery, 4 tablespoons of Worcestershire sauce, 1 teaspoon salt, 1 tablespoonful of sugar, and one tablespoonful vinegar. This will keep in the icebox, and is the same receipt for crabs or shrimp.

—Family cookbook of Sophie Meldrim Shonnard, Savannah

Caro Alston's Oyster Terrapin

Cream ½ cup of flour with ½ pound of butter in double boiler.

Add 1 pint of cream, and stir until smooth. Add 3 hard-cooked egg yolks, ½ cup celery cut fine, ½ grated medium onion, 1 medium green pepper chopped fine, paprika and hot sauce to taste, and 1 tablespoonful of Worcestershire sauce. Cook 1 quart of oysters until gills open. Drain and chop with scissors. Cook ¾ pound of fresh mushrooms in butter. Add oysters and mushrooms to the sauce. Heat well, but do not boil. Lastly, add ½ cup of sherry. This will serve 8 persons.

—Family cookbook of Sophie Meldrim Shonnard, Savannah

Sapelo Seafood Newburg

Yield: 4 servings

½ cup (1 stick) butter or
  margarine
1½ cups crab meat
1 cup medium shrimp, peeled
  and deveined
1 cup sliced mushrooms,
  fresh, or canned, drained
1 tablespoon dry sherry
1 tablespoon brandy
1½ cups light cream
⅛ teaspoon nutmeg
⅛ teaspoon cayenne pepper
Salt and freshly-ground
  pepper to taste
4 egg yolks, slightly beaten

Melt butter in a heavy 2-quart saucepan over low heat. Add crab, shrimp, and mushrooms and cook slowly until shrimp turns pink but is still crisp. Add sherry and brandy. Cook one minute and add cream and seasonings, stirring constantly. Stir some hot cream into the cup with the yolks, stirring well, and then stir egg yolks into hot sauce. Continue to stir over low heat until thickened. Serve with thick slices of toasted French bread.

—Barry D. Waters

Kellee's Frogmore Stew

Yield: 12 servings

½ pound bacon, chopped
1 cup chopped onion
6 quarts water
1 tablespoon salt
2 tablespoons commercial
  seafood seasoning, or 1
  large bag commercial
  seasoning for boiled
  seafood
Few dashes hot sauce
3 pounds smoked sausage,
  cut into 2-inch pieces
3 dozen crabs, cleaned for
  cooking
2 dozen ears corn, with
  husks and silks removed
3 pounds shrimp, headed, in
  the shells

Fry bacon in a very large pot. Remove bacon, and fry onion until limp but not brown. Replace bacon and add water and seasonings. Add sausage and simmer 20 minutes to allow flavors to blend. Add crab, bring to a boil, and simmer 10 minutes. Add corn, bring back to a boil, and simmer 10 minutes. Add shrimp and simmer 6 to 8 minutes, or until done. (Shrimp will turn pink.)

Drain and serve on a very large platter along with butter, salt, pepper, and seafood sauce as desired.

Drawing by Margaret Berry

Spicy Baked Shrimp

Yield: 4 servings

1 teaspoon salt
1½ pounds shrimp, shelled
  and deveined
2 tablespoons vegetable oil
1 garlic clove, minced or
  crushed
¼ cup chopped green onions
¼ cup chopped green pepper
½ cup dry white wine
⅛ teaspoon hot sauce, or to
  taste
¼ teaspoon ground mustard
½ cup soft bread crumbs

Sprinkle salt over shrimp on all sides. Heat oil in 12-inch skillet over moderate heat. Add garlic, shrimp, onion, and green pepper. Sauté 2 or 3 minutes. Reduce heat and stir in wine and seasonings. Cover and simmer 5 minutes.

Preheat oven to 400 degrees F. Arrange shrimp in a single layer in a greased 1-quart baking dish. Pour sauce evenly over and top with crumbs. Bake about 15 minutes, or just until tender.

—Emma R. Law

Thunderbolt Barbecued Shrimp

Yield: 4 servings

2 tablespoons finely minced
    green pepper
¼ cup finely minced onion
2 tablespoons finely minced
    celery
1 small garlic clove, minced
    or crushed
⅔ cup vegetable oil
2 tablespoons lemon juice
⅔ cup dry white wine
1 pound shrimp, cleaned and
    deveined

Combine all ingredients but shrimp in a shallow bowl. Stir in shrimp, covering completely with marinade. Cover, refrigerate, and marinate at least two hours.

Place shrimp on an oiled broiler pan and broil 4 inches from heat for about 2 minutes. Turn and broil about 2 minutes longer, or until shrimp are cooked but still tender, brushing with a little of the marinade. Serve plain with the heated marinade, or with a cocktail sauce or dip.

Note: In place of marinade above, shrimp may also be marinated in commercial Italian dressing, lemon juice, and wine before cooking.

Curried Shrimp Sauce

Yield: about ¾ cup

⅓ cup mayonnaise
1 tablespoon lemon juice
¾ teaspoon curry powder
¼ cup finely chopped green
    onions

Combine ingredients and serve chilled in a small bowl.

Note: This makes enough for two pounds of cooked shrimp.

A Nice Dressing for Crab or Shrimp

To ½ cup mayonnaise, add ¼ cup chili sauce, ¼ cup tomato sauce, 3 or 4 tablespoons of finely chopped celery, 2 medium size well-cooked beets, chopped fine, 1 teaspoon chopped bell pepper, a little red pepper, and salt to taste. Use a little garlic rubbed in the bowl, for crab.

—Family cookbook of Sophie Meldrim Shonnard, Savannah

A delightful example of Georgia's Victorian architecture is the Toole-Lewis House, built about 1890 in Macon. Drawing by Sterling Everett

Mrs. Huger's Shrimp Pillaux

Take one pint of rice, and boil until grainy. While hot, add a heaping table-spoonful of butter, one pint of milk, mace, salt, and pepper to taste. Have two plates of shelled shrimp ready. Put alternate layers of rice and shrimp in a dish, letting the first and last be of rice. Beat up the yoke [*sic*] of an egg, pour over all, and bake.

—Family Cookbook of Sophie Meldrim Shonnard, Savannah

Emma's Savannah Shrimp

The word shrimp comes from the Middle English "shrimpe," or "puny." Small, but oh, so good!

Yield: 6 servings

3 tablespoons minced green onion or mild onion
4 tablespoons butter or margarine
2 pounds shrimp, shelled and deveined
1 cup peeled, seeded, chopped tomatoes
2 teaspoons chili powder
2 teaspoons salt or to taste
⅛ teaspoon cayenne pepper or to taste

Simmer onion in butter in a large skillet or saucepan over medium heat until transparent but not brown. Stir in shrimp and simmer for about 5 minutes. Add remaining ingredients and simmer just until shrimp are tender, but do not overcook (exact time depends on size of shrimp).

Serve over hot rice, toast, patty shells, or as desired.

—Emma R. Law

Taliaferro Remoulade Sauce

Yield: nearly 2 cups

1 cup mayonnaise
1 hard-cooked egg, peeled and finely chopped
½ cup finely chopped celery
1 large garlic clove, crushed or minced
1 tablespoon dry mustard
1 tablespoon red wine vinegar
⅛ cup horseradish "hot" mustard
1 teaspoon Worcestershire sauce
1 teaspoon sugar, or to taste
½ teaspoon salt, or a seasoned salt such as celery salt
¼ teaspoon pepper

Combine ingredients and mix thoroughly. Store in a tightly covered jar. Keep refrigerated. Serve with shrimp, asparagus, or as a fresh vegetable dip.

Note: White pepper may be used if desired.

Diane's Shrimp Stew

Hearty and spicy, good for brunch.

Yield: 8 to 10 servings

½ pound chopped celery
¼ cup chopped green pepper
1 cup chopped onion
2 tablespoons butter or
   margarine
3 pounds shrimp, shelled,
   and deveined
2 teaspoons cornstarch or
   flour
1 teaspoon salt
1 teaspoon pepper
1 teaspoon seafood or
   poultry seasoning, or to
   taste
3 tablespoons Worcestershire
   sauce
1 cup chopped red radishes
   (optional)
2 cups water
Grits

Sauté celery, green pepper, and onion in butter or margarine in a large saucepan over medium heat until tender but not brown. Add shrimp, cornstarch, seasonings, and radishes. Stir quickly to coat shrimp with seasonings. Add water and bring to a boil. Reduce heat and simmer 15 to 20 minutes. Prepare grits according to package directions. Simmer stew to desired thickness, check seasonings, and serve over grits. Cornbread sticks are good with this.

—Diane Harvey Johnson

Yogurt-Dill Sauce

Yield: about 1¼ cups

½ cup plain yogurt (or sour
   cream)
1 tablespoon lemon juice
1 teaspoon prepared mustard
1 tablespoon finely chopped
   fresh dill, or dried dillweed
½ teaspoon salt or celery salt
1 tablespoon grated onion
½ cup finely chopped
   cucumber, well-drained

Combine or mix in blender until well blended; serve chilled.

Chioppino Sauce

Yield: 6 servings

1½ cups chopped onions
1 garlic clove, crushed or
   finely minced
1 tablespoon finely chopped
   parsley
3 tablespoons finely chopped
   celery
2 tablespoons finely chopped
   green pepper
Olive oil as needed
2 cups chopped tomatoes,
   fresh or canned, drained
1 cup tomato sauce
2 teaspoons salt, or to taste
1 teaspoon paprika
¼ teaspoon pepper
½ cup dry red wine
2 cups water or tomato juice

Cook onions, garlic, parsley, celery, and green pepper in a little olive oil until limp but not brown. Add remaining ingredients but water and stir well. Cook over moderate heat for about 15 minutes, but do not allow to boil. Add water, stir well, and cook uncovered over low heat about an hour, stirring occasionally. Check seasonings. Serve with any fresh or shell fish.

Drawing by Fran Kebschull

Vegetables

Vegetable Cookery

Vegetables which are grown below the ground should begin cooking in cold water. Those grown above the ground should begin the cooking process in boiling water.

When cooking vegetables in boiling water, always begin with cold tap water, and bring to a boil. Using warm water from the tap as a short-cut gives the vegetables a rather stale taste.

To "sweat" a vegetable, place in a Dutch oven, or a heavy skillet with a tight-fitting lid. Frozen vegetables may also be cooked in this way. Place a tablespoon of butter on the vegetable, and cover with a sheet of waxed paper. Cover and place on very low heat. Cook about 10 to 15 minutes for a crisp but not overdone vegetable.

A pinch of cinnamon added to mashed potatoes will bring out the flavor.

—Carter Olive

Vegetables, Southern Style

In cooking such vegetables as greens, beans, and cabbage, Southern cooks like to add some chopped bacon or ham while the vegetables are being boiled. The cooking water is often later used in soup.

145

Basil-Buttered Asparagus

Yield: 6 servings

2 tablespoons butter or
  margarine
¼ teaspoon crushed dried
  basil leaves
Salt and pepper to taste
2 pounds (or 2 10-ounce
  packages) cooked
  asparagus

Melt butter or margarine in small saucepan. Add basil, season to taste, and stir well. Pour over asparagus, and serve hot.

Hot Vinaigrette Sauce for Asparagus

Yield: about ¾ cup

½ cup vegetable oil
1½ tablespoons white wine
  vinegar
1 tablespoon finely chopped
  sweet or dill pickle, or 1
  tablespoon pickle relish
½ teaspoon dry mustard
½ teaspoon salt
⅛ teaspoon pepper
2 teaspoons finely chopped
  fresh chives
2 teaspoons finely chopped
  fresh parsley
2 teaspoons capers

Heat oil, vinegar, pickle, mustard, salt, and pepper in a small saucepan. Stir in chives and parsley. Pour over hot cooked asparagus or other vegetables and top with capers.

Note: This is enough sauce for about 1½ pounds fresh asparagus, or 4 servings.

Southern Green Beans with Ham Hock

Yield: 10 to 12 servings

1 ½-pound ham hock
5 cups water
3 pounds fresh green beans
2 teaspoons salt
¼ teaspoon pepper

Bring ham hock and water to boil in a Dutch oven. Reduce heat and simmer 1 hour. Meanwhile, wash beans and remove strings. Cut in 2-inch pieces. Add beans and seasoning and cook 30 minutes more, or until beans are tender.

—Georgia Extension Service

Bourbon Baked Beans

Yield: 6 servings

1 cup chopped, peeled apple
¼ cup raisins or currants
½ cup chopped onion
1 cup chopped cooked ham
1 tablespoon prepared
 mustard
¼ cup chili sauce
1 tablespoon brown sugar, or
 to taste
½ cup bourbon
4 cups canned baked beans
 (1 quart)

Preheat oven to 300 degrees F. Combine ingredients, and pour into a two-quart baking dish. Bake for one hour.

Note: If desired, the first 4 ingredients may be chopped together in a blender to combine before stirring into beans.

Creole Green Beans

Yield: 4 to 6 servings

1 pound fresh green beans
 prepared for cooking
Water as needed
Salt as needed
½ cup chopped green pepper
½ cup chopped celery
2 tablespoons chopped onion
2 tablespoons butter,
 margarine or vegetable oil
1 tablespoon chopped
 pimento
⅓ cup ketchup or chili sauce
½ teaspoon salt (optional)

Cook beans in water and a little salt until tender. Drain. Sauté green pepper, celery, and onion in butter or oil until tender, but not brown. Add seasonings and beans; stir until just heated through.

Note: 1 pound fresh green beans equals 3 cups cooked beans.

—Elizabeth Brown

Topping for Beans

A cup of grated Cheddar cheese is a nice topping for baked beans, added the last 15 minutes of baking time.

Ground ginger, or a few ground gingersnaps, is another good way to improve the flavor of this budget-wise dish.

Beets in Cream

Yield: 6 servings

2 pounds (about 4 cups),
  cooked beets, small whole,
  sliced, or shoestring
3 tablespoons sugar or honey
1 6-ounce can orange juice
  concentrate, thawed and
  undiluted
¼ cup sour cream, or to
  taste
Ground ginger for garnish

Drain beets; add sugar and juice concentrate. Bring to a boil in a 2-quart pan and then remove from the heat. Marinate beets in the liquid for about 2 hours. (It is even better if they can be left overnight.) Bring just to a boil again before serving them. Drain liquid. Add sour cream to beets and mix well. Garnish with a little ground ginger, and serve.

—Annie Nutting, Macon

Herbed Broccoli

Yield: 6 servings

3 pounds broccoli
2 cups water
2 teaspoons chicken-base
  stock, or 2 bouillon cubes
½ cup chopped onion
1 teaspoon marjoram
1 bay leaf
½ teaspoon fines herbes (see
  note)
3 tablespoons melted butter

Wash broccoli well and remove large leaves. Cut off ends of stalks. Cut large stalks in half lengthwise. Bring water to a boil in a large skillet with a lid. Add all ingredients except butter. Cook covered 10 to 15 minutes, or just until tender. Drain and add butter.

Note: 2 cups chicken stock may be used instead of two cups water and bouillon or chicken base stock.

Note: Fines herbes are mixtures of equal parts of minced chives, chervil, tarragon, parsley, or other herbs of your choice.

Milledgeville Cabbage

Boil one head freshly chopped cabbage in salted water until barely done. Drain well. Make a cream sauce with butter, corn starch, salt, pepper, and milk. Mix cabbage and sauce in a baking dish, and sprinkle with grated Parmesan cheese. Bake in 350 degree F. oven until warm all the way through, and brown on top.

—Hogan's House of Fine Foods, Milledgeville

Cabbage with Caraway

Yield: 4 to 6 servings

1 head (about a pound)
   young green cabbage,
   cored and thinly sliced
¼ cup water
1 teaspoon salt
1 teaspoon sugar
2 tablespoons butter or
   margarine
½ cup peeled, cored, and
   sliced apple
⅛ teaspoon pepper
1 or 2 teaspoons caraway
   seeds

Place cabbage in a 2-quart saucepan with boiling water, salt, sugar, butter, and apple. Cover and bring to a boil again, and then simmer for about 15 or 20 minutes, just until tender. Drain any remaining liquid, or allow to steam uncovered for a minute or so. Add pepper and caraway and serve.

Creamy Cabbage

Cook one medium head cabbage in boiling salted water until tender; drain. Add 3 ounces cream cheese, salt, pepper, and celery seed to taste. Mix well and serve hot.

Rote Kraut

Yield: 8 servings

1 small onion, chopped
4 tablespoons bacon grease
1 2½ pound head red
   cabbage, shredded
¼ cup vinegar
¼ cup water
4 tablespoons sugar
Salt and pepper to taste
1 large cored pared apple,
   quartered

Brown onion in bacon grease in a large pot. Add remaining ingredients, apple on top. Cover and bring to a boil, then simmer until tender, about 20 minutes.

If desired, fry a few strips of bacon in the pot first. Remove bacon, drain and crumble. Add to cooked cabbage before serving.

This dish may also be made in the pressure cooker, at 15 pounds for about 4 minutes. Cool and release pressure immediately.

—Bill R. Hoffner

Wilkes County Carrot Ring

Yield: 4 to 6 servings

*2 cups mashed cooked
    carrots*
2 tablespoons butter
3 eggs, divided
*½ cup dry bread or cracker
    crumbs*
1 cup milk
¼ cup finely chopped onion
⅛ teaspoon pepper
1 teaspoon salt
*½ teaspoon Worcestershire
    sauce*
Dash paprika (optional)

Preheat oven to 350 degrees F. Combine carrots and butter with egg yolks and all other ingredients but egg whites. Beat whites stiff but not dry, and gently fold into other ingredients. Pour into a greased 1½-quart ring mold, set in a pan of hot water 1 inch deep. Bake 40 to 45 minutes. Serve with cooked peas and mushrooms in the center! It may also be served with an egg sauce.

Spiced Carrots

Yield: 3 to 4 servings

1 pound carrots
½ teaspoon salt
¾ cup water
*2 tablespoons butter or
    margarine*
*1 teaspoon fresh grated
    lemon peel*
1 tablespoon lemon juice
½ teaspoon ground cloves
1 tablespoon sugar
Parsley

Remove tops and cut carrots into ¼ inch slices. Cook carrots with salt and water in a covered saucepan until just tender, 10 to 15 minutes. Drain and keep warm while combining remaining ingredients, except for parsley, in the saucepan. Stir to make a smooth sauce and return carrots to pan, stirring well until coated and heated through. Serve garnished with parsley.

Stewed Celery

Cut your celery into small pieces and boil until tender. Pour over this melted butter, salt, and pepper.

—*Hints From Southern Epicures*, Savannah, 1890

Southern Corn Pudding

Yield: 6 servings

*3 cups (12 ears) uncooked
  cut corn*
3 eggs, slightly beaten
1 teaspoon salt
⅛ teaspoon pepper
*2 tablespoons grated onion,
  or to taste*
3 tablespoons butter
3 tablespoons sugar
1⅛ cups scalded milk

Preheat oven to 350 degrees F. Combine in order listed and pour into a greased 1½-quart baking dish. Bake 60 minutes, or until firm.

Margaret Gordon's Corn Pudding

Cut the corn off 12 ears of fresh sweet corn, and place in a bowl with three eggs, well-beaten; 2 tablespoons butter; pinch of salt; pinch of sugar; and 2½ cups milk. Bake in a [greased] dish in a moderate (350 degree F.) oven until brown. Enough for six servings.

—Family cookbook of Sophie Meldrim Shonnard, Savannah

Corn Oysters

Grate young sweet corn into a dish. To a pint of this, add one egg, well-beaten, a small teacup of flour, half a gill (2 ounces) of cream, and a teaspoonful of salt. Mix well, and fry like oysters, dropping in the hot fat by spoonfuls about the size of an oyster.

—Family cookbook of Mrs. Lucinda Williams, Milledgeville, 1857

For White Vegetables

In preparing white vegetables, the color may be preserved by adding a little lemon juice to the cooking water.

Scalloped Cucumbers

Yield: 6 servings

3 slices bread
3 large cucumbers, peeled and sliced ⅓ to ½ inch thick
Salt and pepper to taste
½ cup (1 stick) butter, or to taste
¾ cup milk
½ cup grated sharp cheese (optional)

Preheat oven to 350 degrees F. Into a greased 1½ quart baking dish, crumble one slice of bread. Add about half the cucumber slices over it and sprinkle with salt and pepper. Add a little butter here and there on the slices. Repeat with second slice of bread and remaining cucumbers. Crumble the last slice of bread over the top and dot again with butter. Pour milk carefully around sides of the dish. Bake about 30 minutes or until brown. If desired, sprinkle with grated cheese the last 15 minutes of baking time.

—Peggy Gunn

Glazed Cucumbers

Yield: 4 servings

2 large cucumbers
1 tablespoon butter
¼ teaspoon salt
¼ teaspoon sugar
1 teaspoon lemon juice
Minced parsley, optional

Peel and cut cucumbers in half lengthwise. Remove seeds with a small spoon or potato baller. Slice across in half-inch slices. Place in a skillet and barely cover with water. Add butter, salt, sugar, and lemon juice. Cover and bring to a boil. Lower heat and simmer about 2 or 3 minutes. Drain and serve. Sprinkle with parsley if desired.

—Emma R. Law

Prater's Mill Foundation

St. Mary's Baked Eggplant

Yield: 6 servings

1 medium eggplant
  (1 pound)
Flour as needed
Salt and pepper to taste
¼ cup vegetable oil
3 medium onions, thinly
  sliced (1½ cups)
3 medium tomatoes (about 1
  pound), in ¼-inch slices
1 pound grated Cheddar
  cheese

Peel eggplant and slice horizontally in slices about ¼-inch thick. Flour, salt, and pepper these, and fry until crisp in hot oil. Drain.

Preheat oven to 350 degrees F. In a greased 2-quart casserole, alternate layers of eggplant with onion, tomato and cheese, ending with cheese on top. Bake 45 minutes.

Note: This may be prepared as much as day ahead of time, and refrigerated covered until time to bake.

Mrs. Lawton's Baked Eggplant

Boil the contents of 1 large eggplant in sufficient water to cover it. About 20 minutes should suffice to cook it thoroughly tender. Mash well through a colander, and return to the pot for a few minutes to dry out a little. Then add to this 1 cup of grated breadcrumbs. (Let them not be too stale, as they should be flaky and light.) Also 2 eggs, well-beaten, 1 heaping teaspoon butter, a dash of onion juice, pepper, and salt to taste. A little grated ham improves the flavor, but is not necessary. Put this mixture in a baking dish, and if too dry, add a little milk to soften. Sprinkle breadcrumbs on top, to which a little butter and milk are added to keep in the moisture while baking. Bake in a moderate oven until the top is brown. This can also be served in the shells of the eggplant, in which case the shells should be steamed to be slightly cooked. It will take 1½ eggplants to nicely fill 1 shell.

—*Some Choice Receipts of Savannah Homemakers,* Savannah, 1904

Augusta Baked Hominy

Cook 1½ cups of hominy, and mash fine. Add to this 3 eggs, beaten; 1 cup grated cheese; 2 tablespoonsful butter; 2 cups milk; and salt and pepper to taste. Mix all together and put in greased baking dish. Bake slowly to a nice brown. This can also be made without the cheese.

—Family cookbook of Sophie Meldrim Shonnard, Savannah

Mushrooms in Sherry Sauce

Make a thick cream sauce of 3 cups milk thickened with 6 tablespoons flour, and 6 tablespoons butter. Add two beaten eggs, salt and pepper, onion juice, nutmeg, and sherry to taste. Add sliced mushrooms browned in butter, and simmer for at least one half hour before serving. Brown your toast, and serve with sauce.

—Bryan family cookbook, Savannah, circa 1885

Ogeechee Okra

Yield: 4 servings

1 garlic clove, finely chopped
  (optional)
½ cup chopped onion
½ cup chopped green pepper
2 tablespoons butter
2 cups okra, cut into ½-inch
  pieces
2 cups chopped tomatoes
1 teaspoon sugar or to taste
⅛ teaspoon oregano
  (optional)
Salt and pepper to taste

Sauté garlic, onion, and green pepper in butter in a 10-inch skillet for about 3 or 4 minutes, until tender but not brown. Add okra and cook for 5 minutes more, stirring frequently. Add remaining ingredients and cover. Simmer for about 10 minutes, or until vegetables are tender. Check seasonings and serve hot.

Peas and Onions Cooked with Lettuce

The outer leaves of a head of Iceberg lettuce add flavor to new peas, called English peas in the South.

Yield: 4 servings

3 or 4 outside leaves of
  lettuce
2 cups fresh peas, shelled
½ cup chopped green onions
  (optional)
1 teaspoon sugar
3 tablespoons water
¼ teaspoon salt, or to taste
⅛ teaspoon pepper
2 tablespoons butter or
  margarine
¼ cup light cream (optional)

Rinse lettuce and use to line a 1-quart saucepan. Add peas, onions, sugar, and water. Cover tightly and cook over medium heat just until peas are tender, 10 to 15 minutes. Discard lettuce leaves. Add remaining ingredients and heat for a few seconds.

Vidalia Onions

May and June in Georgia are Vidalia onion season, the time of those uniquely sweet, mild ones which by law are only grown in an area whose soil gives them their unforgettable flavor. They excel in salads, on sandwiches, and may even be eaten raw, like an apple.

However, Vidalias do not keep as well at room temperature as other varieties. Many cooks buy them by the 25-pound bag, and tie each separately in an old pair of stockings, then hang them in a cool place, snipping one off as needed. They may also be stored in foil in the refrigerator.

Baked Vidalias

Only the Vidalia onion can be baked like a potato. Scoop out a small hole in the top of each peeled onion. Fill with a bouillon cube, topped with a pat of butter, and salt and pepper. Wrap each separately and tightly in aluminum foil.

These may then be grilled on hot coals for about 30 minutes, turning frequently. Or, bake in a moderate (350 degrees F.) oven until tender, 45 minutes to an hour, depending on size.

Spicy Variation

Some cooks peel and slice Vidalias and place them in a baking dish with a small amount of melted butter. Then Catalina French Dressing is poured over them, and they are baked in a 350 degree F. oven until tender.

Onion Sandwiches

Vidalias are excellent sliced, on any type of bread, and spread with softened butter, cream cheese, sour cream, or mayonnaise.

To Remove Onion Odor

To remove the scent of onions on the hands, rub hands with lemon juice or celery salt after chopping onions.

Deep Dish Onion Pie

This recipe features Vidalia onions, known for their sweet, mild flavor.

Yield: 6 servings

2½ cups chopped Vidalia
  onions
4 tablespoons butter
6 eggs, divided
½ cup light cream
1 teaspoon salt
⅛ teaspoon pepper
1 cup dry white wine
1 9-inch deep-dish pastry
  shell, unbaked

Preheat oven to 350 degrees F. Simmer onions in butter about 20 minutes in an open skillet, or until onions are golden but not brown. Cool onions slightly and place in a large mixing bowl. Add to them the slightly beaten egg yolks, cream, salt, pepper, and wine. Gently mix well. Beat whites until stiff but not dry and gently fold mixture into them. Pour into pastry shell and bake for about 30 minutes.

Vidalia Onion Casserole

Yield: 8 to 10 servings

8 large Vidalia onions, cut in
  chunks
¼ cup butter or margarine
½ cup uncooked rice
1 cup salted boiling water
1 cup grated Swiss cheese
⅔ cup half and half cream

Sauté onions in butter until transparent but not brown. Meanwhile, add rice to salted boiling water and cook 5 minutes on low heat, covered. Place rice, onions and cheese in a 2-quart baking dish. Combine well and stir in half and half. Bake 1 hour at 325 degrees F.

Note: If onions have an unusually strong flavor, soak in milk for two hours prior to baking; drain well.

—Cyndee Goeffroy

Minted Peas

When cooking fresh peas, a little chopped mint added, all cooked with as little water as possible, gives a flavor that is unusual and refreshing.

—*Savannah Morning News*, 1923

Oven-Creamed Potatoes

Yield: 6 servings

4 tablespoons butter
¼ cup flour
½ teaspoon salt
½ teaspoon prepared mustard
⅛ teaspoon pepper
2 cups milk
1½ tablespoons horseradish
6 medium potatoes, peeled and chopped
½ cup grated Cheddar cheese

Preheat over to 375 degrees F. Melt butter in a one-quart saucepan over low heat. Stir in flour, salt, mustard, and pepper; then gradually add the milk, stirring to mix well. Cook, stirring, over medium heat until thickened. Add horseradish and stir well. Combine with potatoes in a large mixing bowl; pour into a greased 1½ quart baking dish. Sprinkle with cheese. Bake in oven for about 45 minutes.

—Betty W. Rauers

Emma's Potatoes Rosti

Yield: 4 servings

2 large potatoes (about 1 pound)
Salted water as needed
⅓ cup vegetable oil
Salt and pepper to taste
Butter to taste

Parboil potatoes in boiling salted water to cover until barely done, about 30 minutes. Drain and cool; then peel and shred. (Potatoes may be pre-cooked the day before use.) Heat oil in a 10-inch skillet. Spread potatoes in a layer and gently pat down with spatula. Cook over moderate heat, uncovered, until tender, and bottom is golden; then fold in half. Sprinkle with salt and pepper, and a little butter if desired.

Variations: grate or chop some onion with the potato. Some also like a little grated cheese, Cheddar or Gruyere.

Harbor Colcannon

A dish from the South's Scotch-Irish tradition.

Yield: 4 to 6 servings

1 medium head cabbage
1 medium turnip
5 medium potatoes
Salted water as needed
Butter to taste
Salt and pepper to taste

Cook cabbage, coarsely chopped, turnip, peeled and sliced, and potatoes, peeled and sliced, in salted water until tender. Drain and mash, seasoning with butter, salt, and pepper.

These traditional quilt patterns, from a Georgia Folk Art Festival poster designed by Dottie Mercer, represent the Goose Tracks, Mexican Star and Cross and Crown motifs. For pioneer women, quilting was an art form as well as a household necessity.

Potatoes and Squash

Boil the squash until done, and mash fine; also, about an equal quantity of Irish potatoes. Season both with butter, salt, and pepper and mix them well together. Put in a [greased] pan, and bake them brown.

—Bryan family cookbook, Savannah, circa 1885

For Crisp French Fries

Allow raw cut potatoes to stand in cold water for at least half an hour before frying for crisper french fries.

Also, potatoes soaked in salt water for 20 minutes before baking will bake more rapidly.

Potatoes with Sugar

Peel some nice size sweet potatoes. If very large, divide them, and lay them in a baking pan. Cut up some butter and lay on them, and sprinkle with sugar freely. Add a very little water, and bake a nice brown.

—Bryan family cookbook, Savannah, circa 1885

Sherry-Glazed Sweet Potatoes

Yield: 6 servings

½ cup brown sugar, divided
6 medium sweet potatoes
  (about 2 pounds), cooked
  and peeled
Salt to taste
4 tablespoons butter or
  margarine
½ cup dry sherry

Preheat oven to 350 degrees F. Spread half the sugar in the bottom of a greased 9-by-13-inch baking pan. Cut potatoes in half lengthwise. Arrange cut-side down over sugar. Sprinkle with salt and dot with butter. Sprinkle remaining brown sugar over potatoes, and pour sherry over. Bake uncovered for at least 30 minutes, or until browned and glazed, turning at least once and spooning syrup over during baking.

—Robert M. Hollingsworth, Macon

Sesame Sweet Potatoes

When baking candied sweet potatoes, a sprinkling of sesame seed or sunflower seeds add an interesting topping.

Hogan's Sweet Potatoes

Cook sweet potatoes. Peel and mash, adding a little orange juice, a dash of cinnamon, and nutmeg, plenty of butter, and a beaten egg, if desired. Put in a baking dish, and heat thoroughly [at 350 degrees F. for 30 minutes].

—Hogan's House Of Fine Foods, Milledgeville

Savannah Potato Pone

Take a quart of grated sweet potato, ¾ pound sugar, 10 ounces soft butter, ½ pint milk, powdered ginger to taste, grated peel of an orange, and a teacup of molasses. Beat all well together, and bake in a slow oven [at 325 degrees F. for 1 hour, or until golden].

—Bryan family cookbook, Savannah, circa 1885

Absolutely Perfect Rice

Yield: 4 to 6 servings

6 cups water
1 teaspoon vegetable oil
1 teaspoon salt
1 cup rice
Hot water as needed

Bring water to a boil in a large kettle. To this, add oil and salt, plus rice. Cook 15 minutes, covered. Stir with a fork. Pour into a colander, and rinse with hot water. Put the colander in a boiler, with ½ to 1 inch of hot water. Steam for a few minutes. Every grain of rice will be separate, and perfect.

—Carter Olive

Savannah Red Rice

This version of one of Savannah's favorite recipes, also called "dirty rice," can finish cooking in the oven.

Yield: 6 to 8 servings

¼ pound bacon, cut in small pieces
½ cup chopped onions
2 cups raw rice
2 cups canned tomatoes
½ teaspoon salt
¼ teaspoon pepper
⅛ teaspoon hot sauce
1 teaspoon Worcestershire sauce

Preheat oven to 350 degrees F. Fry bacon crisp. Remove from pan and cook onions until tender in bacon fat. Add washed rice, tomatoes, seasonings, and cooked bacon. combine and cook over low heat about 10 minutes. Pour into a 1-quart casserole. Cover tightly. Bake for 60 minutes, stirring with a fork a couple of times during that period.

Note: ⅓ cup chopped green pepper may be cooked with the onion, if desired.

—Debra Rogalski

For Separate Rice Grains

In cooking rice, a tablespoon of vinegar added to the cooking water will help keep grains separate.

Sea Islands Herbed Rice

Yield: 6 servings

4 tablespoons butter
1 cup converted rice
2 cups chicken broth or 2
    cups boiling water and 2
    bouillon cubes, dissolved
3 tablespoons minced onion
1 teaspoon salt
½ teaspoon rosemary
½ teaspoon marjoram
½ teaspoon thyme

Combine in a heavy saucepan with a tight-fitting lid. Heat to boiling, stir and cover. Simmer for 20 minutes. Remove lid, stir with a fork, and allow to steam uncovered 2 or 3 minutes to fluff rice.

Braised Rice

Chop a little onion very fine. Fry in a little butter until slightly brown. Then add 1 cup of rice and two of stock, seasoning to taste. Let boil up, and then put on a cover, and stand in a warm oven [350 degrees F.] for 20 minutes, when it will be ready to serve.

If bacon is liked, cut up strips of it and fry with the onion before adding the rice.

—Family cookbook of Sophie Meldrim Shonnard, Savannah

Rutabaga with Wine

Yield: 4 servings

1 medium rutabaga
    (about 1 pound)
Salt as needed
Water as needed
1 teaspoon sugar
Pepper
2 tablespoons butter
¼ cup dry white wine

Pare and slice or chop rutabaga. Boil, covered, in salted water to which sugar has been added for about 30 to 40 minutes, or until tender. Drain off any liquid and mash with potato masher. Add more salt, pepper to taste, butter, and wine; mix well, and serve.

Onion option: Some prefer 2 medium onions, roughly chopped, cooked with the rutabaga.

—Ian Robertson

Sesame Squash

Yield: 2 to 4 servings

1 pound acorn squash
2 tablespoons butter
4 tablespoons honey
¼ cup sesame seeds

Preheat oven to 350 degrees F. Cut the squash in half and remove the seeds. Cut off the stem piece. Bake halves in a pan containing hot water for 50 minutes. Then turn right side up and brush with butter. Coat with honey and sprinkle with sesame seeds. Bake 25 minutes more, and serve hot.

Apple-Squash Variation: cook squash as above, for 30 minutes. Meanwhile, peel and chop 2 medium cooking apples (about 2 cups sliced apple.) Toss apple with 4 tablespoons honey. When you turn the squash, brush with butter and then fill with apple mixture. Dot with a little more butter and a dash of cinnamon or nutmeg if desired. Bake for about 60 minutes more. If apples are getting too brown, cover with foil. Serve with fresh pork, or ham.

Squash Fritters

Boil the squash until soft, and mash them fine. Then make a batter with some egg, milk, flour, pepper, and salt. Mix in the squash, and fry until the fritters brown.

—Bryan family cookbook, Savannah, circa 1885

Mashed Squash

For a nutritious vegetable and change from potatoes, mash cooked summer squash with butter and milk, and season with a little ginger and/or nutmeg.

Vegetable Storage

Fresh tomatoes will keep longer in refrigerator if stored with stems down.

When storing fresh vegetables in the refrigerator, they will keep longer and be more nutritious if not washed until just before use. Also, paper towels in the crisper tray will help absorb excess moisture, which causes spoilage.

Dalton Summer Casserole

Yield: 6 servings

*3 to 4 medium yellow squash
(1 pound), sliced about ¼
inch thick*
*3 medium tomatoes (1
pound), sliced about ¼
inch thick*
*Thinly sliced onion (about
½ cup)*
*⅓ cup grated Cheddar or
Parmesan cheese*
1 teaspoon basil
½ teaspoon thyme
*1 teaspoon celery or onion
salt*

Preheat oven to 350 degrees F. In a 2-quart casserole, layer half the vegetables. Combine the cheese and seasonings. Sprinkle half the cheese mixture over the vegetables. Repeat, with cheese on top. Bake about 30 minutes, or until golden brown.

Summer Broiled Tomatoes

Yield: 8 servings

*4 large tomatoes (about 1½
pounds) cut in
half horizontally*

Place in 13-by-9-inch baking dish, and broil three or four minutes. Remove, and top with either Yogurt or Cheese Topping. Return to broiler, and broil another 4 or 5 minutes, until bubbly.

Cheese Topping:
*¼ cup butter, at room
temperature*
*2 tablespoons chives or
chopped green onions*
¼ teaspoon basil
*½ cup grated Cheddar or
Parmesan cheese*

Blend butter, chives or onions, and basil. Spread on tomatoes and top with cheese.

Yogurt Topping:
2 teaspoons sugar
*1 tablespoon prepared
mustard*
*½ cup plain yogurt or sour
cream*

Blend ingredients and spread on tomatoes.

Cherry Tomatoes in Cream

Yield: 6 servings

3 tablespoons butter
2 tablespoons light brown sugar
½ teaspoon salt
1 quart cherry tomatoes
1 pint heavy cream

Blend butter, sugar, and salt in a 12-inch skillet. Add tomatoes. Stir gently over moderate heat. When they begin to split, pour in cream. Serve hot.

Curry Sauce for Vegetables

Yield: about ¾ cup

¼ cup sour cream
½ cup mayonnaise
1 tablespoon white wine vinegar
¼ to ½ teaspoon curry powder, to taste
⅛ teaspoon dried tarragon leaves

Mix ingredients in a small saucepan. Heat, but do not boil. Serve over hot cooked vegetables.

—Emma R. Law

Tracy's Hollandaise Sauce

Yield: ½ cup

½ cup (1 stick) butter
1 tablespoon lemon juice
Yolks of two eggs
¼ teaspoon salt
Dash cayenne pepper

Divide butter into three pieces. Place one in the top of a double boiler with lemon juice and egg yolks. Stir constantly over medium heat with a wire whisk. Add second piece and continue to stir as the mixture thickens. Add the third piece and remove from heat. (If kept on the heat, it will separate.) Add salt and pepper. Beat to desired consistency.

—Sophie Meldrim Shonnard

Fuel-saving Hint

Top-of-the-stove cooking uses less energy than heating an oven. An electric skillet appliance uses the least of all. If you use the oven method, plan ahead to heat French bread, cook a vegetable, or bake a custard for dessert at the same time.

The 1820 Federal period Church-Waddel-Brumby House, home of two presidents of the University of Georgia, is believed to be the oldest surviving residence in the city. Restored by the city and the Athens-Clarke Heritage Foundation, it is now the Athens Welcome Center.

Dilled Vegetable Sauce

Yield: 1 cup

2 tablespoons butter
2 tablespoons flour
1 cup water and/or liquid
  from cooking vegetables
1½ teaspoons dill seed
½ teaspoon instant minced
  onion or onion powder
½ teaspoon wine vinegar
¼ teaspoon salt, or to taste
⅛ teaspoon pepper (some
  prefer white pepper)

In a 1-quart saucepan, melt butter and blend in flour. Slowly stir in liquid, stirring continuously. Heat and stir until sauce thickens. Stir in remaining ingredients and check seasonings. Serve over hot cooked vegetables, such as green beans.

The Self-Sufficient Life

We live entirely within ourselves, except for a few necessaries which we cannot do without, and are obliged to purchase elsewhere. Twice a day we eat hominy of our own raising, at present without molasses. For dinner we eat beef of our own stock, and peas for bread, of which we have a plenty. Our garden is very fruitful of greens, turnips, etc., and we expect a good crop of potatoes.

—James Habersham, first administrator at Bethesda Orphanage, now Bethesda Home for Boys, Savannah, 1741

Parsley Sauce for Vegetables

Yield: 1 cup

⅓ cup mayonnaise
⅓ cup sour cream
¼ teaspoon dried dill weed
2 cups parsley leaves
1 tablespoon chopped chives

Place all ingredients in blender container. Cover and blend until parsley is chopped. Pour into a small saucepan and heat, but do not boil. Pour over hot cooked vegetables, such as green beans, braised celery, or mixed vegetables.

Yogurt Sauce with Pecans

Yield: 1 cup

½ cup shelled pecans,
* coarsely chopped*
1 tablespoon butter
Salt to taste
¼ cup green onions
1 teaspoon ground dill seed
1 cup plain yogurt
Pepper (white pepper if
* desired)*

Sauté pecans in butter in a 10-inch skillet just until brown. Sprinkle with salt. Remove from skillet and set aside. Add onions and dill to skillet and cook 1 minute. Add yogurt, stirring over medium heat for about 3 minutes. Add favorite cooked drained vegetables, check seasoning, and heat through. Serve sprinkled with pecans.

Note: This is especially good with green beans or broccoli, cooked just until tender.

Desserts

Quitman Apple Pudding

Yield: 6 to 8 servings

⅓ cup butter or margarine,
   at room temperature
1 cup sugar
1 egg
1 cup flour
1 teaspoon baking soda
¼ teaspoon salt
½ teaspoon cinnamon
¼ teaspoon nutmeg
1 teaspoon vanilla extract
2 cups peeled, grated or
   finely chopped apples
1 teaspoon lemon juice
½ cup chopped pecans

Preheat oven to 350 degrees F. Combine butter or margarine in a mixing bowl with the sugar and then the egg, beating until fluffy. Sift together dry ingredients and add to butter mixture, beating well. Stir in vanilla, apples tossed with lemon juice, and pecans, and mix well. Pour into greased 8-inch square pan, and bake about 35 minutes, or until golden brown. Serve warm or cool, with whipped cream or Brandy Sauce.

Brandy Sauce

Yield: about 1 cup

½ cup butter or margarine,
   at room temperature
1 cup confectioners' sugar
1 teaspoon boiling water
2 tablespoons brandy
⅛ teaspoon salt

Combine ingredients in order listed and mix well.

Gordonston Apple-Cranberry Cobbler

Yield: 8 to 10 servings

3 cups peeled, chopped
   cooking apples
1 tablespoon lemon juice
1 teaspoon cinnamon
½ teaspoon nutmeg
2 cups cranberries
1½ cups brown sugar,
   divided
¼ cup water or apple juice
½ cup (1 stick) butter or
   margarine, at room
   temperature
1½ cups uncooked oatmeal
⅓ cup flour
½ cup chopped pecans
Whipped cream or ice cream
   for topping

Preheat oven to 350 degrees F. Combine apples with lemon juice, cinnamon, and nutmeg in a large bowl. Then add cranberries, 1 cup brown sugar, and water or juice. Mix well and pour into greased 2½-quart casserole. In the same mixing bowl, combine remaining ½ cup sugar, butter, oatmeal, flour, and pecans. Mix well and pour over fruit mixture. Bake for about 50 minutes, or until firm and golden. Serve warm, with whipped cream or ice cream as desired.

Note: Recipe may be doubled and baked in a 13-by-9-by-2-inch sheet cake pan.

Apple Float

Boil a dozen large apples in a little water, and pass them through a sieve. When cold, sweeten to taste, and add the beaten whites of two eggs. Beat well until stiff, and grate a nutmeg over it. Serve with cream.

—Bryan family cookbook, Savannah, circa 1885

Apple Hint

When working with sliced apples, keep them from discoloring as they are peeled by sprinkling generously with lemon juice. Or, place them in a bowl of cold water and add a dash of salt for each apple until ready to use. Drain well before using in your recipe.

Emma's Lemon-Baked Bananas

Yield: 6 servings

4 tablespoons butter or
  margarine
⅓ cup finely crushed graham
  cracker crumbs
¼ teaspoon salt
1 teaspoon sugar
¼ teaspoon cinnamon
1 teaspoon grated lemon peel
6 firm bananas
2 tablespoons lemon juice
1 egg, slightly beaten
Whipped or sour cream for
  topping

Preheat oven to 450 degrees F. Melt butter or margarine in the oven in the shallow baking dish you plan to use for the bananas. Set aside.

Mix together the crumbs, salt, sugar, cinnamon, and lemon peel in a shallow dish. Peel bananas and dip each in lemon juice, then in beaten egg, and then in crumbs. Arrange in greased baking dish and turn, to coat well with butter. Bake for about 7 minutes, or until golden, coating well with butter once or twice. Serve hot with whipped or sour cream.

—Emma R. Law

Mrs. Habersham's Carrot Pudding

Yield: 8 to 10 servings

1½ cups finely grated carrots
1½ cups fine dry
  bread crumbs (may be part
  wheat germ)
1 teaspoon cinnamon
½ teaspoon nutmeg
¼ teaspoon salt
6 eggs (small ones are fine)
¾ cup sugar
2 tablespoons melted butter
  or margarine
½ cup currants or raisins

Preheat oven to 350 degrees F. Combine carrots, bread crumbs, and seasonings in a large mixing bowl. Beat eggs with sugar until thick. Blend into carrot mixture with melted butter; stir in currants or raisins. Grease a shallow 2½-quart baking dish, and pour in mixture. Bake for about 45 or 50 minutes, or until set. Serve warm, with a boiled custard sauce or whipped cream.

Atlanta Coffee Custard

Make a cooked custard from one pint of strong coffee and one pint of milk, boiled together, with six well-beaten eggs and one and a half cups of sugar then added, and all cooked together. Serve warm with cake.

—Mrs. F. Perry, *House-Keeping in the Sunny South*,
Atlanta, 1885

Holiday Cheesecakes

Yield: 18 tea-sized cakes

2 8-ounce packages cream
    cheese, at room
    temperature
¾ cup sugar
2 eggs
1 tablespoon lemon juice
1 teaspoon vanilla extract
18 vanilla wafers
Preserves as needed

Preheat oven to 375 degrees F. Beat first five ingredients until light and fluffy. Line small muffin tins with paper baking cups. Place a vanilla wafer on the bottom of each. Fill cups ⅔ full of cheese mixture. Bake for 15 to 20 minutes, or until set.

Top each as desired with about 1 tablespoon of your favorite preserves, such as cherry, strawberry, or blueberry; or mix colors. Chill before serving.

—Maxine Pinson

Emma's Lime Cheese Cake

This recipe trims calories a bit by using cottage cheese instead of cream cheese.

Yield: 8 to 10 servings

1 9-ounce loaf golden pound
    cake
2 envelopes unflavored
    gelatin
¼ cup water
2 eggs, separated
¼ cup milk
¼ teaspoon salt
½ cup sugar
2 cups cottage cheese,
    strained
1 6-ounce can limeade (or
    lemonade), thawed in
    refrigerator
½ cup heavy cream, whipped
Fresh sliced strawberries for
    topping (optional)

Cut cake lengthwise into 4 equal slices. Lay slices flat and cut each, from top to bottom, into 8 strips. Stand strips on flat ends around the inside of an 8-inch spring form mold. By keeping the slices together, the edge will have a scalloped effect on top. Set aside.

Soften gelatin in water in a small saucepan, and melt over very low heat. Remove and keep warm. Then, combine lightly beaten egg yolks, milk, salt, and sugar in the top of a double boiler over hot water. Cook, stirring constantly, until slightly thickened. Remove from hot water and blend in melted gelatin. Stir in cheese and limeade concentrate, stirring well. Fold in whipped cream. Whip egg whites until stiff but not dry, and fold into mixture.

Pour into mold, being careful to keep cake in place. Chill at least 2 hours before serving. Garnish with more whipped cream and strawberries if desired.

—Emma R. Law

Shady Grove Plantation home, Monticello. Drawing by Sterling Everett

Mrs. Charlton's Chocolate Pudding

Stir 4 tablespoons of grated chocolate into a quart of very hot milk. When beaten in smooth, add the yolks of 5 eggs, and 2 tablespoons of cornstarch dissolved in a little cold milk. Stir until it thickens, flavor with vanilla, and put it in a pudding dish. Bake in a moderate oven until very well set. Beat the remaining five egg whites very stiff, beating in 4 tablespoons of sugar, and spread over top for meringue. Bake a nice brown. Serve cold with cream or whipped cream.

—Mrs. Thomas J. Charlton, *Some Choice Receipts of Savannah Homemakers*, Savannah, 1904

Salzburger Custard Hint

Warm your milk before adding it to the egg when you make a custard, and no water will settle in the bottom of the dish.

—*Ye Old Time Salzburger Cook Book*, Savannah

Figs in Wine

Yield: 4 to 5 servings

1 12-ounce package dried
    figs
2 cups dry red wine
½ teaspoon crumbled dried
    basil, or to taste
3 tablespoons honey

Combine ingredients in a saucepan and simmer covered for about ½ hour, or unti figs are tender. Turn from time to time in the liquid if figs are not completely covered. Remove figs to a serving dish and strain liquid. Reduce by about a third, or to a syrup, by cooking over high heat until of desired consistency. Pour over figs. Good either warm or chilled, served with a dry cookie such as a macaroon.

—Emma R. Law

Pape House Lemon Soufflé

Yield: 4 servings

½ cup sugar plus 1
    tablespoon, divided
2 tablespoons flour
½ teaspoon salt
2 eggs, divided
1 cup milk
2½ tablespoons lemon juice
    (1 medium lemon)
2 teaspoons grated lemon
    peel (1 medium lemon)
½ pint heavy cream,
    whipped
Sugar to taste
Vanilla extract to taste

Preheat oven to 350 degrees F. Combine ½ cup sugar, flour, and salt in a large bowl. Beat egg yolks with milk in a smaller bowl and add to large bowl. Add lemon juice and peel. Beat egg whites stiff and fold in gently. Pour into a greased 1-quart soufflé dish, and sprinkle the top with the additional tablespoon of sugar. Place in a pan of hot water, and bake for about 45 minutes. Cool to room temperature, and then chill in refrigerator. Serve with whipped cream, sweetened to taste and flavored with a little vanilla extract if desired.

—Dr. Lance W. Hemberger

Mrs. H. M. Comer's Vanilla Mousse

Whip 1 quart cream with 1 cup sugar, and mix with 2 egg whites, whipped, 1 teaspoon of vanilla, a little sherry, and some candied fruits if desired. Put in cans, and pack in ice and salt until needed.

—Family cookbook of Sophie Meldrim Shonnard, Savannah

This historic arch at the University of Georgia, erected in 1857, is modeled after the Great Seal of the State of Georgia. The three columns represent wisdom, justice, and moderation. Founded in 1785, the University was the first state-chartered one in the nation.

Mousse Hint

For extra flavor in your next chocolate mousse, try adding 1 tablespoon of brandy or rum, or 1 tablespoon instant coffee along with 1 teaspoon vanilla. Serve with whipped cream and a mint pattie.

—Carter Olive

Rhubarb Cobbler

Yield: 6 to 8 servings

1 cup sugar
2 tablespoons cornstarch
4 cups sliced rhubarb
1 tablespoon water
¼ teaspoon cinnamon
1 cup flour
1 tablespoon sugar
1½ teaspoons baking powder
¼ teaspoon salt
¼ cup butter or margarine
¼ cup milk
1 egg, beaten

Mix together first four ingredients. Bring to a boil and boil 1 minute. Pour into 8-inch greased round pan. Sprinkle with cinnamon.

Preheat oven to 400 degrees F. Sift dry ingredients together. Cut in butter until like coarse crumbs. Mix in milk and egg all at once, just to moisten. Drop by tablespoons over the hot fruit. Bake 20 minutes, or until golden brown.

Emma's Cream Sauterne

Yield: 4 to 6 servings

2 cups sauterne
1 cup sugar
Juice and grated rind of
  1 lemon
Juice and grated rind of
  1 orange
1 teaspoon cornstarch
¼ cup dry white wine,
  chilled
7 egg yolks
2 egg whites

In a saucepan, combine sauterne, sugar, juices, and grated rinds. Bring to a boil, stirring, and add cornstarch dissolved in a little cold wine. Cook the mixture, stirring, for 1 minute. Cool slightly. Beat egg yolks lightly and pour cooked mixture over them. Strain and cool. Beat egg whites stiff, and fold in mixture. Pour into serving bowl, cover, and chill before serving.

—Emma R. Law

Orange Coconut Dessert

Grate a large coconut and mix it with [confectioners'] sugar to sweeten. Peel some nice oranges and slice them crosswise, rather thick. Cover the bottom of a large glass bowl or dish with slices of orange, and strew them thick with [confectioners'] sugar; and then add a layer of the grated coconut and another of orange and sugar, until the bowl is full, heaping the coconut high on top.

—Bryan family cookbook, Savannah, circa 1885

Mrs. Henry Cunningham's Orange Jelly

Grate the peel of one orange and mix with 2 pints water and 2 envelopes gelatin, along with 1 cup sugar. More lemon or orange flavor may be added if desired. Put on ice. When firm, break up and mix well with the whites of two whipped eggs. Put back on ice until firm.

—Family cookbook of Sophie Meldrim Shonnard, Savannah

Topping Note

Vanilla yogurt may be used in place of sour cream as a topping in many dessert recipes. Both are better with a sprinkling of ground ginger on top.

Georgia Peach Puff

Here peaches are used to update that thrifty favorite, bread pudding.

Yield: 4 to 6 servings

1½ cups milk
2 cups bread cubes
2 tablespoons melted butter
  or margarine
2 eggs, beaten
¼ cup honey
½ cup sugar
1 teaspoon vanilla extract
⅛ teaspoon salt
1 teaspoon grated lemon peel
2 cups peeled, chopped
  peaches

Preheat oven to 350 degrees F. Scald milk and pour over bread cubes. Set aside 10 minutes. Add melted butter, eggs, honey, sugar, vanilla, salt, and peel; mix well, and then stir in peaches. Pour into greased 8-inch square baking pan or dish. Bake about 45 minutes, or until golden brown. Serve with ice cream or whipped cream as desired.

Note: Sliced apples, fresh or frozen blueberries, or other fruit may be used in this recipe in place of peaches.

—Georgia Peach Commission, Atlanta

Peach Hints

Firm, ripe peaches which are not soft to the touch, may be kept in the refrigerator for several days before using. To ripen further, leave at room temperature. Do not buy green or shriveled peaches, as they will not ripen.

One pound of peaches equals three medium peaches, two cups sliced peaches, or one cup pulp or purée.

To peel peaches, cover with boiling water. Set aside at least a minute; skins will come off easily.

Ripe peaches have a sweet aroma. They are not only delicious, but low in calories, about 38 per medium peach.

Peach Purée

1 pound peaches, peeled and
  sliced
1 tablespoon lemon juice
½ cup sugar
⅙ teaspoon salt

Combine ingredients in blender or through a strainer. Use as a topping for ice cream or as desired.

Peach Buckle

Some say this recipe should be called "Peach Un-buckle," since that's what a lot of it could do to your waistline . . .

Yield: 8 to 10 servings

2 pounds peaches (about 6 medium), or to taste
1 tablespoon lemon juice
¾ cup sugar, divided
4 tablespoons butter or margarine, at room temperature
1 teaspoon vanilla extract
1 egg, lightly beaten
1 cup flour
¼ teaspoon salt
1 teaspoon baking powder
⅓ cup milk

Crumb Topping:
⅓ cup sugar
⅓ cup flour
¼ cup butter or margarine

Preheat oven to 375 degrees F. Slice peeled peaches thinly, and toss with lemon juice and ¼ cup sugar. Set aside. Cream butter or margarine with remaining sugar, and add vanilla and egg. Blend well. Sift together 1 cup flour, salt, and baking powder. Add dry ingredients alternately with milk to the creamed mixture, beating well after each addition. Pour batter into greased 10-inch baking dish. Spoon peaches over batter.

Combine crumb topping ingredients to form coarse crumbs, and sprinkle over fruit. Bake about 40 to 50 minutes, or until top is golden brown. Serve warm, with sweetened whipped cream or ice cream as desired.

Note: Apples or blueberries are also good in this recipe, with cinnamon and nutmeg added to taste; say 1 teaspoon cinnamon and ¼ teaspoon nutmeg, for the apple batter, and a dash of each in the topping.

This same Crumb Topping recipe is also excellent instead of a top crust for fruit pies, and with less calories. For extra nutrition, ¼ cup wheat germ may also be added to the mixture, either plain or the honey variety.

Spirited Pineapple

Cut a fresh pineapple and slice or cube peeled fruit. Place in dessert dishes, and sprinkle with kirsch before serving.

—Sally Pearce, Tybee Beach

Plums In Wine

Yield: 6 servings

*1¾ pounds dark freestone
plums*
1 cup sugar
1 cup red wine
*3 slices lemon, about ¼ inch
thick*

Rinse plums; quarter or halve, according to size. Discard pits. In a medium saucepan, heat sugar in wine until dissolved. Add plums and lemon. Simmer, covered, until plums are tender but still hold their shape, about 10 minutes. Serve warm or chilled.

Pumpkin and Cream Cheese Roll

A change from pumpkin pie at holiday time!

3 eggs
1 cup sugar
*⅔ cup cooked, strained
pumpkin*
1 teaspoon lemon juice
¾ cup flour
1 teaspoon baking powder
½ teaspoon salt
¼ teaspoon cinnamon
⅛ teaspoon ground cloves
¼ teaspoon allspice
½ teaspoon nutmeg
*1 cup finely chopped pecans
or walnuts*
*Confectioners' sugar as
needed*

Cream Cheese Filling:
1 cup confectioners' sugar
*6 ounces cream cheese, at
room temperature*
*4 tablespoons butter at room
temperature*
1 teaspoon vanilla extract

Preheat oven to 375 degrees F. Beat eggs on high speed with electric beater about 5 minutes, or until very light. Gradually beat in sugar. Then fold in pumpkin and lemon juice. Set aside. Sift flour, baking powder, salt, and spices together into a large bowl, and fold in pumpkin mixture. Spread gently into a 15-by-10-by-1-inch greased and floured jelly roll pan, and top evenly with nuts. Bake for 15 minutes.

Meanwhile, spread a tea towel out and sprinkle with confectioners' sugar. Turn cake onto towel and roll, starting at narrow end. Leave 30 minutes in towel to cool. Then gently unroll and fill with Cream Cheese Filling. Reroll and chill until time to serve.

Combine ingredients and mix well.
Note: Roll may also be frozen.

Cream of Strawberry Tarts

Yes, you can be Queen of Tarts . . .

Yield: 8 servings

2½ cups fresh berries, divided
1 cup heavy cream
¼ cup confectioners' sugar
¼ teaspoon aromatic bitters
¼ teaspoon grated lemon rind
8 baked tart shells (about 3¼-inches)

Wash, stem, and chop 2 cups of the berries as desired. For a very delicate filling, purée chopped berries through a strainer. Reserve ½ cup nice berries for garnish, sliced or whole.

Whip cream until it begins to thicken. Stir in sugar, bitters, and rind. Beat until mixture holds very stiff peaks. Add strawberry purée or chopped berries, and beat well. Divide into tart shells and garnish with remaining ½ cup berries. Chill for at least 1 hour before serving.

Note: This would also make a lovely topping for sliced angel food cake.

In selecting berries, remember that a basket of very large berries will not give you as many chopped berries as a basket of smaller ones, which has less air space in the basket between the berries.

—Emma R. Law

How to Serve Strawberries

It is a bad plan to let the berries lie in water while you are capping them. They are softened, and much of the flavor is lost. Either rinse, and drain off the water, or dip them a few at a time in water. Some like to sprinkle sugar over at the table; others prefer to let them lie in sugar an hour or so before serving. It is now fashionable in New York hotels to bring them to table with caps on, to be dipped in sugar as they are eaten.

—*House-Keeping in the Sunny South*, Atlanta, 1885

Whipped Cream Help

If you have whipping cream which does not reach desired volume, try adding the white of an egg.

Rose Garden Fruit Cup with Cointreau

This treat was named for Savannah's famous Bicentennial Rose Garden at Memorial Medical Center.

Slice peeled, seeded grapefruit and oranges into a large glass bowl. Add sliced fresh strawberries and marinate for a few hours, covered with plastic wrap, in the refrigerator with a little cointreau. Stir in some banana slices dipped in lemon juice to preserve color. Sprinkle with freshly grated coconut, and serve with thin lemon cookies. Seedless green grapes are also pretty with this.

—Betty W. Rauers

Savannah Trifle

Place some sponge cake in the bottom of a dish, cut in small pieces, and then add a layer of raspberry jam. Then some more cake, soaked with sherry, and have ready some boiled custard. Pour this over the cake while it is still warm. Leave enough space for whipped cream on top before serving. The sweetened cream must not be put on until the custard is quite cold. If sherry is not procurable, soak the cake with a little hot milk or syrup.

—Family cookbook of Sophie Meldrim Shonnard, Savannah

Grandma's Pudding

Cut some slices of bread moderately thick, and butter them. [Grease] a deep dish, and place a layer of bread in it with the buttered side up. Spread over the bread a layer of raisins and currants, and sprinkle with brown sugar. Cover the bread again in same fashion until dish is filled. Beat five eggs with two glasses of milk and three tablespoons of sugar. Instead of the raisins and currants, you may use citron, cranberries, or apples, minced fine.

—Bryan family cookbook, Savannah, circa 1885

Scissor-cutting with kitchen shears is the best way to mince, snip, chop, or dice dried fruit and such. Dip blades in warm water occasionally as they become sticky.

Buttermilk Ice Cream

Yield: 8 servings

1 quart buttermilk
1 pint heavy cream
1½ cups sugar
1 teaspoon vanilla extract

Blend ingredients and put into freezer unit of refrigerator in a flat metal pan. Stir well after it begins to freeze, and return to the freezer until firm. Then store in covered container until ready to serve.

Note: In place of vanilla extract, you might like to try the grated peel and juice of one lemon, or ¼ cup dry white dinner wine.

—Peggy Gunn

Ft. Pulaski Fig Ice Cream

Until the tree was trimmed a few years ago, the parade ground at Fort Pulaski outside Savannah was famous for having what was said to be the largest fig tree in the world.

Yield: about 2 quarts

1 quart ripe figs, mashed or
*   strained*
½ cup lemon juice
2 cups sugar
3 cups half and half cream,
*   or 2 cups milk and 1 cup*
*   heavy cream*

Combine ingredients well and freeze in churn according to directions with the freezer.

Cranberry Sauce

At the holiday season, whole-berry cranberry sauce makes an elegant dessert over vanilla ice cream. Serve with very thin sugar cookies.

—Emma R. Law

Chutney and Ice Cream

Another good topping for vanilla ice cream is a generous serving of Major Grey's Chutney.

—Jack Crolly

Georgia Peach Ice Cream

Georgia is famous not only for its fresh peaches, but for its excellent peach desserts, from cobblers to pies and ice cream.

Yield: 2½ quarts

5 eggs
2½ cups sugar, divided
¼ teaspoon salt
1 quart milk
4 cups peeled, chopped ripe peaches, divided
½ pint heavy cream
1 tablespoon vanilla extract, or to taste

Whip eggs, 2 cups sugar, and salt together, in the blender if you have one. Scald milk in a double boiler over hot water; add a little hot milk to the egg mixture; then stir remaining eggs into scalded milk. Cook over hot water in a double boiler until the mixture coats a spoon, stirring frequently. Chill thoroughly.

In the blender, purée 2 cups of the peaches with cream, vanilla, and remaining ½ cup sugar. Add this to the chilled custard mixture and mix thoroughly. Freeze according to directions for your ice cream maker. Halfway through the freezing process, add the remaining 2 cups of chopped peaches.

Note: Some like to vary the flavoring in peach ice cream by using ½ teaspoon vanilla extract and ½ teaspoon almond extract, in place of 1 teaspoon vanilla.

Berry Cream: Fresh berries may be substituted for the peaches in this recipe, with additional sugar if desired.

Banana Cream: Ripe puréed or mashed bananas may be added in place of other fruit.

—Dr. Lance W. Hemberger

Georgia Ice Cream

Allow the usual quantity, say six to eight eggs, to a quart of milk; also, one heaping tablespoon of flour, and one of butter from which the salt has been thoroughly washed. Mix the flour and butter together, and add to the eggs and sugar as you bring the milk to a boil. Stir it in the usual manner, cooking all together until it thickens. Custard for freezing requires to be a little sweeter than for other purposes.

—Bryan family cookbook, Savannah, circa 1885

Beaufort Rum-Raisin Ice Cream

Good anytime, but a special treat at holiday dinners. Soak ½ cup raisins in same amount of rum for at least an hour. Let 1 pint vanilla ice cream stay at room temperature long enough to get a little soft. Stir all together and refreeze.

Eggnog Rum-Raisin Ice Cream

Combine 1 quart chilled eggnog with ⅓ cup light rum and ice cream prepared as above. Sprinkle with 1 tablespoon grated orange rind and 1 teaspoon grated nutmeg.

—Orral Ann Moss, Beaufort, S.C.

Noel Tortoni

Toast ½ cup slivered almonds at 350 degrees F. for about 5 minutes, or until golden. Meanwhile, let ½ gallon vanilla ice cream stand at room temperature long enough to get soft. Combine ice cream, nuts, 1 tablespoon rum flavoring, and chopped Maraschino cherries and candied pineapple as desired. Refreeze.

If this is frozen in individual paper liners in muffin tins, covered with plastic wrap, it makes easy individual desserts during the busy holiday season. Pitted sweet canned or frozen cherries may be used in place of the Maraschino ones, if desired.

—Arline Rinkle

Coconut Balls

For an attractive dessert, scoop out balls of vanilla ice cream, and roll in freshly grated coconut. Freeze firm again in a shallow dish, each ball separate until serving time. Serve garnished with Creme de Menthe, or chocolate sauce and finely chopped nuts.

Lime or Lemon Ice Cream Hint

For a delicious and easy lemon or lime ice cream, allow ½ gallon vanilla ice cream (your supermarket's own brand is fine), to thaw slightly. Mix well with 1 6-ounce can lemonade or limeade, thawed in the refrigerator and undiluted, and refreeze.

—Carter Olive

Summer Sherbet

Yield: 4 to 6 servings

1 cup mashed ripe banana
1½ cups orange juice
½ cup lemon juice
2 cups sugar
2 cups skim milk or water

Combine ingredients, in blender if wished. Pour into shallow trays in the freezer and stir every 20 minutes until mushy, about 2 hours. Continue freezing until firm. Sherbet may be served at this point or stored in covered freezer container. Other fruit flavors may be added to this basic recipe as desired, such as tangerine or apricot juice.

Ginger Sauce

For a good and unusual topping in summer for orange or pineapple sherbet, stir two tablespoons finely chopped candied ginger into 8 ounces of sour cream. Chill covered for at least eight hours to allow flavors to combine before serving.

—Lou Dobbs

Orange Dessert

One of the favorite desserts of Juliette Gordon Low, founder of the Girl Scouts, and one which she recalls in her writings having both at her home in Savannah and at a birthday luncheon in New York, was orange halves scooped out and refilled with orange sherbet.

Caro Alston's Frozen Pudding

Beat the yolks of four eggs with 1 cup sugar. Add ½ cup wine, and then the whites, beaten stiff. Whip 1 pint cream with a pinch of salt. Mix these well, and put a layer of this in a mould [sic] you have lined with ladyfingers. Scatter macaroon crumbs over the top, then more pudding and a second layer of crumbs. Put waxed paper over the top, and close mould well. Pack in ice and salt for 4 hours.

—Family cookbook of Sophie Meldrim Shonnard, Savannah

Frozen Fruit Yogurt

Here's a good use for very ripe bananas on sale at the market.

Yield: 4 cups

1 envelope unflavored gelatin
¼ cup cold water or orange juice
½ cup sugar, or to taste
¼ teaspoon salt
1 cup mashed very ripe bananas (3 medium)
1 tablespoon lemon juice
1 8-ounce container vanilla, lemon, or orange yogurt
2 egg whites

In a small saucepan, sprinkle gelatin over water or juice. Place over low heat and stir constantly until gelatin dissolves, about 3 minutes. Remove from heat. Add sugar and salt, and stir until sugar dissolves. Stir in bananas and lemon juice. Stir in yogurt. Pour into freezer tray or 9-by-5-inch metal loaf pan. Freeze until firm.

Break up frozen mixture in a large bowl and add egg whites. Beat at high speed with an electric mixer until smooth, about 10 minutes. Return to pan and freeze. If not serving right away, store in a covered freezer container.

Café Parfait

Make one pint of sugar and 1 pint of milk into a nice custard with 2 eggs and a teaspoon of sifted flour, with 6 tablespoons of very strong coffee added when the custard is cold, and 1 pint of cream, whipped well. Freeze. Serve in glasses, with another half cup of cream nicely whipped and sweetened. Serves eight glasses.

—Mrs. T. M. Cunningham, *Some Choice Receipts of Savannah Homemakers*, Savannah, 1904

Apple Custard Sauce

Yield: about 2½ cups

⅓ cup flour
1 cup sugar
1 teaspoon ground cinnamon
¼ teaspoon ground nutmeg
2 cups apple juice or water
⅓ cup white vinegar
⅓ cup butter or margarine

Combine flour, sugar, and spices in 1-quart saucepan. Stir in juice, vinegar, and butter gradually. Cook over moderate heat, stirring constantly until thickened. Remove from heat and serve warm over apple dumplings, cobbler, apple cake, or as desired.

Cherry Sauce

Yield: about 3 cups

1 16-ounce can cherries, or
  2 cups fresh, with juice
½ cup sugar
1 teaspoon cornstarch
¼ teaspoon nutmeg or
  cinnamon
1 teaspoon lemon juice
¼ cup cherry liqueur

Drain cherries and seed if not seeded, reserving juice. Combine sugar and ¾ cup juice. Bring to a boil and boil for 5 minutes over medium heat, stirring so it will not stick. Add cherries and cook 5 minutes more. Dissolve cornstarch and spice in 1 tablespoon of the juice, and stir into fruit. Cook until clear and slightly thickened. Remove from heat, cool slightly, and then stir in lemon juice and liqueur. Serve slightly warm or cold, over ice cream, pound cake, or as desired.

Emma's Coffee-Butterscotch Sauce

Yield: about 1¾ cups

3 tablespoons instant coffee
  powder
⅓ cup water
1 tablespoon butter or
  margarine
1 12-ounce package
  butterscotch morsels
⅛ teaspoon salt
1 6-ounce can evaporated
  milk
¼ teaspoon cinnamon

Dissolve instant coffee in water in top of double boiler. Add remaining ingredients. Place over hot water. Stir until morsels are melted and mixture is well blended. Serve warm with ice cream, pound cake, or baked custard.

Note: For a chocolate sauce use chocolate morsels. If you don't have a double boiler, use a heavy pan over low heat, and stir constantly.

—Emma R. Law

Chocolate Sauce

Combine 1 cup sugar, 2 tablespoons grated chocolate, 2 tablespoons cornstarch or flour, 1 teaspoon vanilla extract, and 1 large tablespoon butter in a pan over medium heat. Add 1 cup boiling water gradually, and cook and stir until creamy. Serve hot.

—*Some Choice Receipts of Savannah Homemakers,*
Savannah, 1904

Mary Jane's Fudge Sauce

Yield: about 3 cups

¾ cup butter or margarine
2 ounces baking chocolate
1½ cups sugar
1 14-ounce can evaporated
  milk
¼ teaspoon salt

Melt butter in top of double boiler or heavy saucepan. Add chocolate and blend. Add remaining ingredients gradually, and cook over low heat about 20 minutes, stirring frequently. Serve over vanilla or chocolate ripple ice cream. Keep leftover sauce covered, and store in refrigerator.

—Ginni Rothrock

Habersham Custard Sauce

Yield: 2½ cups

2 cups milk or half and half
2 eggs
½ cup sugar
¼ teaspoon salt
½ teaspoon grated orange,
  lemon or lime peel
⅛ teaspoon nutmeg

Bring milk just to boiling point in 1-quart saucepan; do not allow to boil. Meanwhile, lightly beat eggs and stir in sugar and salt. Blend a small amount of milk into the egg mixture to warm it, and then stir eggs into hot milk. Cook over low heat, stirring constantly until mixture thickens enough to coat a metal spoon. Remove from heat and add flavoring. Serve with fruit or as desired.

Honey-Nut Sauce

Yield: 1½ cups

½ cup (1 stick) butter or
  margarine
2 teaspoons cornstarch
1⅓ cups honey
½ cup slivered toasted
  almonds or pecans

Melt butter over low heat; stir in cornstarch. Add honey and cook, stirring constantly until mixture comes to boiling point. Serve warm over ice cream, topped with nuts. Cover and refrigerate leftover sauce.

Honey Hint

Grainy honey? It will reliquefy if the jar is placed in a pan of warm water.

St. Mary's Lemon Sauce

Yield: about 1 cup

¾ cup sugar
1½ tablespoons cornstarch
1½ cups water
2 tablespoons butter or
  margarine
1 teaspoon grated lemon rind
3 tablespoons fresh lemon
  juice

In a small saucepan, combine sugar and cornstarch. Stir in water. Cook over medium heat, stirring often, until mixture begins to bubble and thicken. Cook 1 minute more, then remove from heat and add remaining ingredients. Serve warm.

Note: grate lemon rind (yellow part only) before extracting juice. For more juice from a lemon, roll it on the table, pressing down with your hand, for a minute before squeezing. For the same purpose, some heat them for a few seconds in a microwave oven before squeezing.

Rum Sauce

Yield: 1½ cups

4 tablespoons butter or
  margarine
1 14-ounce can condensed
  milk
1½ cups sugar, or to taste
¼ cup dark rum, or 1
  teaspoon rum extract
⅛ teaspoon salt
¼ cup finely chopped pecans
  (optional)

In a small saucepan, melt butter and stir in remaining ingredients. Cook and stir over low heat until mixture is warm and flavors are well-combined, about 5 minutes. Serve over gingerbread or as desired. Refrigerate leftovers, covered.

Atlanta Sherry Sauce

Yield: about 1 cup

¼ cup brown sugar
½ cup white or dark corn
  syrup, or honey
⅓ cup sherry
2 tablespoons butter

In a small saucepan, combine ingredients and simmer about five minutes. Serve with fruit.

Tapioca Topping for Fruit

Yield: about 2 cups

3 tablespoons tapioca
2 tablespoons sugar
⅛ teaspoon salt
2½ cups water, divided
1 6-ounce can frozen orange
* juice*

Stir tapioca, sugar and salt together in a small saucepan and add 1 cup water. Heat to boiling, stirring occasionally. Pour into medium size bowl and add remaining water and juice. Cover and chill at least two hours before using. Will keep at least a week in the refrigerator.

Selecting Fruit

When selecting watermelon, thump it and listen for a deep hollow sound. A smooth stem and means it's been ripened before picking.

Always smell a cantaloupe. A strong, sweet smell indicates ripeness. However, they will also ripen slightly in your refrigerator.

Bright colors in cherries, plums and strawberries indicate freshness. But with green grapes, the paler are the more recently picked!

Buttermilk Sauce for a Nice Pudding

To one cup buttermilk, add ½ cup sugar, and the yolk of one egg, beaten together. Stir in one half cup boiling water. Let all come to a boil, and flavor to taste.

—Bryan family cookbook, Savannah, circa 1885

Baked Coconut Custard

Mix ½ pound sugar with the milk of a coconut, and a pound of the grated coconut if desired. Add 2 tablespoons rose water, a pint of rich milk, whites of 8 eggs, a teaspoon of nutmeg, and one of cinnamon. Bake in cups set in a pan of hot water. When cold, grate sugar over it.

—Bryan family cookbook, Savannah, circa 1885

Cakes

Eleanor's Apple Cake

Yield: 10 to 12 servings

4 cups peeled, cored, chopped cooking apples
2 cups sugar
1 teaspoon lemon juice (optional)
3 eggs, separated
1 cup vegetable oil
3 cups flour
1 teaspoon salt
1 teaspoon baking soda
1 teaspoon vanilla extract
2 cups finely chopped nuts, or 1 cup chopped nuts and 1 cup raisins or currants, lightly floured

Brown Sugar Glaze:
1 cup brown sugar
¼ cup evaporated milk
½ cup (1 stick) butter or margarine, or ½ cup light cream

Preheat oven to 325 degrees F. Toss apples in a bowl with sugar and lemon juice. Set aside. Beat egg whites until stiff, and then gently fold into beaten egg yolks. Add oil and stir. Sift flour, salt, and baking soda together; and add to batter and stir well. Fold in apples, vanilla, nuts, and raisins.

Bake for 30 to 35 minutes in a greased 13-by-9-by-2-inch rectangular pan, or for an hour in a 9- or 10-inch tube pan. Glaze with Brown Sugar Glaze.

Shortening variation: In place of cooking oil, use 1 cup vegetable shortening. In this case, cream shortening with sugar, and add eggs one at a time, not separated, beating well after each. Fold in sifted dry ingredients and proceed as above. This is somewhat faster, and gives a fluffier batter. Toss apples with only a little of the sugar, and lemon juice.

Cook in double boiler over boiling water for about 5 minutes, and spread over cake. Wrap in foil or plastic wrap when cool, or place in covered cake box, and keep cool until time to serve. Serve at room temperature.

Note: This cake is much better 2 or 3 days after baking.

—Eleanor Blackmon, Washington

189

Rome Apple Gingerbread

Yield: 9 to 12 servings

½ cup (1 stick) butter or
    margarine, at room
    temperature
½ cup sugar
2 eggs
⅔ cup molasses
2 cups flour
1½ teaspoons baking soda
¾ teaspoon salt
1 teaspoon ground ginger
½ teaspoon ground
    cinnamon
½ teaspoon ground nutmeg
¼ teaspoon ground cloves
⅓ cup milk
1¼ cups pared, grated, or
    finely chopped apples

Preheat oven to 350 degrees F. Grease and flour a 9-inch baking pan. Cream butter and sugar together until fluffy. Beat in eggs one at a time, beating well after each. Blend in molasses. Sift dry ingredients. Add to creamed mixture alternately with milk, beginning and ending with flour mixture. Stir in grated apples. Pour into baking pan. Bake 45 to 50 minutes, or until a cake tester or toothpick inserted in the center comes out clean.

Cool in pan or a rack 10 minutes, and then turn out onto rack and cool or serve warm with whipped cream or Marie's Lemon Sauce.

Marie's Lemon Sauce

½ cup sugar
1 tablespoon cornstarch
1 cup boiling water
2 tablespoons butter or
    margarine
2 tablespoons lemon juice
⅛ teaspoon nutmeg
⅛ teaspoon salt

Mix sugar and cornstarch together in a small saucepan. Add boiling water gradually and boil for two or three minutes, stirring constantly. Remove from heat, and add remaining ingredients. Stir well and serve warm or cold.

Mrs. Spurrier's Molasses Cup Cakes

To 1 cup butter, or half lard will do, add 1 cup molasses; 4 eggs; 3 cups flour, with a teaspoon cream of tartar rubbed in; ½ teaspoon [baking] soda, dissolved in a little water; and 2 grated nutmegs, or other flavoring. Bake immediately. You could use different spices, and sugar instead of molasses.

—Bryan family cookbook, Savannah, circa 1885

Isle of Hope Banana Cake

Try this cake when your market has ripe bananas on sale!

Yield: 1 3-layer cake

⅔ cup vegetable shortening
1¾ cups sugar
3 eggs
2¼ cups flour
1 teaspoon baking soda
½ teaspoon salt
1 teaspoon baking powder
½ cup milk
1½ cups mashed very ripe bananas
⅔ cup chopped pecans
1 teaspoon vanilla extract

Preheat oven to 350 degrees F. Grease and flour 3 9-inch cake pans, or line them with circles of waxed paper.

Cream shortening and sugar together until well-blended. Beat in eggs one at a time, beating well after each. Sift dry ingredients together; add alternately with milk and mashed bananas to batter, beginning and ending with dry ingredients, and beating well after each. Fold in pecans and extract, beating another 2 minutes. Pour into pans and bake about 25 minutes, or until cake tester comes out clean. Cool 5 minutes before turning out of pan, and finish cooling on racks. Frost when completely cool with Caramel-Nut Frosting.

Note: Banana-Nut Frosting (see page 209) is also good with this cake. However, it does not keep as well as the Caramel-Nut, and is best made when you plan to use all the cake at one time.

Caramel-Nut Frosting

¼ cup brown sugar
¼ cup water
3 cups sugar
1 cup milk
½ cup (1 stick) butter
¼ teaspoon baking soda
1 teaspoon vanilla extract
⅔ cup chopped pecans

To brown sugar in a heavy skillet, gradually add water to make a thin syrup. Stir in sugar, milk, butter, and soda. Bring to a boil, and boil briskly for about 10 minutes, stirring well. Cook to soft-ball stage (234 to 240 degrees F. on candy thermometer); then place skillet in cold water and continue beating as you add vanilla and nuts. Spread between cake layers and on sides and top of cake. This is also good on spice cakes!

St. Simons scene by Barry Champion

Bluffton Blueberry Cake

Yield: 10 to 12 servings

1½ cups sifted flour
1 teaspoon baking powder
½ teaspoon salt
2 eggs, separated
½ cup (1 stick) butter or
*   margarine*
1 cup sugar
⅓ cup milk
1 teaspoon lemon juice
2 cups blueberries
Flour as needed
Sugar for topping

Preheat oven to 350 degrees F. Sift first three dry ingredients together three times, and set aside.

Beat egg whites stiff and set aside. Cream butter and beat in sugar until fluffy. Add egg yolks, beating well. Add sifted dry ingredients alternately with milk, beginning and ending with dry ingredients. Fold in egg whites and lemon juice. Toss berries with a little flour and fold into batter. Grease and flour an 8- or 9-inch square or tube pan. Pour batter into pan, and sprinkle with a little confectioners' or white sugar, as a topping. Bake for about 30 minutes, or until a nice golden brown, and when cake springs back when touched lightly with the fingers. Serve warm or cool, plain or topped with whipped cream or ice cream.

Chocolate-Beer Pound Cake

Yield: 10 to 12 servings

*1 cup (2 sticks), butter or
   margarine, at room
   temperature*
*½ cup vegetable shortening,
   at room temperature*
3 cups sugar
5 eggs
3 cups sifted flour
½ teaspoon baking powder
¼ teaspoon salt
¼ cup cocoa
1 cup beer
2 teaspoons vanilla extract

Chocolate Frosting:
4 tablespoons butter
*2 squares unsweetened
   baking chocolate*
1 teaspoon vanilla extract
*2 cups sifted confectioners'
   sugar*

Preheat oven to 325 degrees F. Cream butter and shortening together. Add sugar and beat until light and fluffy. Add eggs, one at a time, beating well after each. Remove beater. Sift dry ingredients together. Add alternately with beer and vanilla to creamed mixture, beginning and ending with dry material. Pour evenly into greased 9- or 10-inch tube pan. Bake for about an hour and 20 minutes. Cool in pan or on rack for 30 minutes. Remove from pan and finish cooling on rack. Frost when cool with Chocolate Frosting.

Melt butter and chocolate together over boiling water in a double boiler, or over very low heat in a heavy saucepan, and then cool a bit. Stir in vanilla extract. Stir in sugar until desired consistency is reached. When ready to spread, if too thick, add a very little more beer.

Note: The Chocolate Glaze, a bit lighter frosting, is also good with this cake.

—Emma R. Law

Chocolate Glaze

Yield: about 1 cup

2 teaspoons cocoa
*1 tablespoon plus 1 teaspoon
   hot water*
1 tablespoon vegetable oil
1 tablespoon light corn syrup
*1 cup confectioners' sugar,
   sifted*

Gradually combine cocoa with water in a small saucepan, and stir other ingredients except sugar in gradually. Stir over medium heat until well-blended. Remove from heat and gradually stir in sugar. Drizzle over cake.

Chocolate Chip Loaf Cake

Real chocolate addicts may wish to use a larger amount of chips in this recipe, and experiment with different flavors of chips. Smaller families will also like this quick and versatile cake.

Yield: 1 9-by-5-inch loaf cake

4 tablespoons butter or margarine, at room temperature
1 cup sugar
2 eggs
1 cup sour cream
1 6-ounce package chocolate chips
1 teaspoon vanilla extract
1 teaspoon baking soda
⅛ teaspoon salt
2 cups flour
1½ teaspoons baking powder
½ cup finely chopped pecans (optional)

Preheat oven to 350 degrees F. Cream butter or margarine and sugar. Add eggs and beat well. Add sour cream, chips, and vanilla alternately with sifted dry ingredients, beating well after each addition. Stir in nuts if desired. Grease and flour a 9-by-5-inch loaf pan. Pour batter into pan and bake for about 60 minutes, or until top springs back when touched lightly with the fingers. Cool in pan on a rack for about 20 minutes, then remove from pan and finish cooling on the rack.

Sprinkle with a little confectioners' sugar, or frost when cool with Chocolate Chip-Sour Cream Frosting or Chocolate Glaze (page 193).

Chocolate Chip-Sour Cream Frosting

Yield: about 1 cup

1 6-ounce package chocolate chips, any type
½ cup sour cream

Melt chips in top of double boiler over hot water, or in heavy saucepan over low heat. Remove from heat, add sour cream, and stir until smooth.

Note: You may of course vary this recipe with other flavors of chips, such as mint and butterscotch.

Mocha-Chip Frosting

For a mocha flavor, add ½ teaspoon instant coffee to each 1 cup or 6-ounce package chips after melting, and stir well along with other ingredients.

Ruth's Sheetcake for a Crowd

Here's a good cake for children's parties, family reunions, picnics, or other occasions when a number of servings is needed.

Yield: about 35 servings

2 cups flour
2 cups sugar
½ teaspoon salt
½ cup (1 stick) butter or margarine
½ cup vegetable shortening
1 cup water
4 tablespoons cocoa
3 eggs
1 teaspoon baking soda
½ cup buttermilk or sour cream
1 teaspoon vanilla extract

Preheat oven to 350 degrees F. Grease and flour an 11-by-17-inch cookie pan or sheet cake pan. Sift together flour, sugar, and salt; set aside. In a saucepan, combine butter or margarine, shortening, water, and cocoa; bring to a boil. Pour over flour mixture and mix well.

In another small bowl, beat eggs well. Add soda, buttermilk or sour cream, and vanilla. Stir well and add to first mixture. Mix well. Bake for about 20 to 25 minutes, or until top springs back when touched lightly with the fingers, or a cake tester comes out clean. Start Buttermilk Icing during last 5 minutes cake is baking.

Buttermilk Icing

½ cup (1 stick) butter or margarine
4 tablespoons cocoa
⅛ teaspoon salt
1 pound confectioners' sugar
1 teaspoon vanilla extract
6 tablespoons buttermilk or milk
½ cup finely chopped pecans (optional)

In a saucepan, melt margarine with cocoa and salt, but do not boil. Remove from heat, and stir in remaining ingredients. Frost cake while hot by pouring cocoa mixture over and spreading well.

—Ruth Hinely

Ebenezer Sauerkraut Cake

Yield: 1 3-layer cake

*1 cup well-drained
sauerkraut, tightly packed*
*4 squares baking chocolate
(unsweetened)*
½ cup vegetable shortening
2 cups sugar
2 eggs
2 teaspoons vanilla extract
1 cup chopped pecans
2 cups cake flour, divided
2 teaspoons baking powder
1 teaspoon salt
1½ cups milk

Preheat oven to 350 degrees F. Rinse sauerkraut well and roll in paper towels to remove excess moisture. Chop into 1- to 1½-inch pieces. Set aside.

Melt chocolate, uncovered, over hot water in a double boiler; cool. Cream shortening and gradually beat in sugar. Cream together until light and fluffy. Add eggs and vanilla; beat well. Dredge nuts in 2 tablespoons of flour in a small bowl. Set aside. Sift remaining flour with baking powder and salt. Add alternately with milk to creamed mixture, ending with flour. Beat batter well for about one minute. Fold in sauerkraut and floured nuts; mix well.

Grease and flour 3 8-inch layer pans, and pour batter into pans. Bake for about 30 minutes, or until sides of cake pull away from sides of pan. Cool 10 minutes in pans on racks, and turn out onto wire rack. Frost when cool with Chocolate-Pecan Frosting, or your favorite recipe.

Chocolate-Pecan Frosting

*2 squares unsweetened
baking chocolate*
½ cup (1 stick) butter
*2 cups sifted confectioners'
sugar, divided*
1 egg, beaten
1 tablespoon vanilla extract
1 tablespoon lemon juice
1 cup chopped pecans

Melt chocolate and butter over low heat. Add 1 cup confectioners' sugar and blend well. Remove from heat and add egg, vanilla, and juice. Gradually beat in enough remaining sugar to give the desired consistency. Add nuts and spread on a cool cake. If icing is slightly warm when it goes on the cake, it will dry to a nice shine.

Note: This icing is also good on a white cake.

Wine Cup Cakes

Take a warm cup of milk, and cut into it 1 cup of butter. Combine with 4 eggs, 3 cups sugar, 4 cups flour, 1 teaspoon soda, little salt, nutmeg and cinnamon to taste, and 1 glass wine. Bake immediately.

—Bryan family cookbook, Savannah, circa 1885

Emma's Spiced Chiffon Cake

Yield: 10 to 12 servings

2¼ cups sifted cake flour
1½ cups sugar
3 teaspoons baking powder
½ teaspoon salt
1 teaspoon ground allspice
1 teaspoon ground cardamom
½ cup vegetable oil
5 egg yolks, unbeaten
¾ cup cold water
1 cup (7 to 8) egg whites
½ teaspoon cream of tartar

Preheat oven to 325 degrees F. Sift flour, sugar, baking powder, salt, allspice, and cardamom together into large bowl. Make a well in the dry ingredients and pour in oil, egg yolks, and water. Beat until smooth. Beat egg whites with cream of tartar in a separate large bowl until mixture forms very stiff peaks. Gently fold beaten egg whites into mixture with rubber spatula just until blended. Pour into ungreased 10-inch slip-bottom tube pan (the footed kind is best.) Bake for 55 minutes. Raise heat to 350 degrees F. and bake 10 to 15 minutes longer, or until top springs back when touched lightly with the tips of fingers. Invert on funnel or bottle neck, if pan is not footed, and keep upside down to cool. Remove from pan with a thin, long sharp knife, and frost if desired with Orange Frosting or sprinkle with a little confectioners' sugar.

Orange Frosting

⅓ cup butter or margarine,
   at room temperature
3 cups sifted confectioners'
   sugar
2 tablespoons orange juice
   (approximately)
1 teaspoon finely grated
   orange peel

Cream butter and sugar together. Stir in orange juice and peel, beating to desired consistency. Swirl on sides and top of cake. Refrigerate, but bring to room temperature before serving.

Lemon Icing

The juice and grated rind of one lemon, one egg well-beaten, one cup sugar, ⅓ cup water, small lump of butter. Beat well together and boil 10 minutes, or until it thickens (Over cooking will cause it to sugar.) Good on a jelly roll, or for favorite layer cake.

—Mrs. Ann Shearouse and Mrs. Ruth Seckinger,
Ye Olde Time Salzburger Cook Book, Savannah

Coca-Cola Cake

The world-famous soft drink Coca-Cola first appeared in Atlanta in 1886, developed by Dr. John Styth Pemberton. Dr. Pemberton, who later sold his formula for $1,750, is buried in Columbus, where he worked as a pharmacist. In addition to being enjoyed as a beverage, "Coke" in Georgia today is an ingredient in punches, barbecue sauces, and a famous cake.

Yield: 1 9-by-13-inch cake

2 cups flour
2 cups sugar
1 teaspoon baking soda
1 cup (2 sticks) butter or
* margarine*
1½ cups miniature
* marshmallows*
3 tablespoons cocoa
1 cup Coca-Cola
½ cup buttermilk
2 eggs, well-beaten
1 teaspoon vanilla extract

Preheat oven to 350 degrees F. Grease and lightly flour a 9-by-13-inch flat pan. Sift flour, sugar, and soda in a mixing bowl. Heat butter, marshmallows, cocoa, and cola in double boiler over hot water to boiling. Pour over flour mixture and add buttermilk, eggs, and vanilla. Mix well. Batter will be thin. Bake about 35 minutes, or until top springs back when touched lightly with the fingers. While still hot, pour and spread Coca-Cola Frosting over cake.

Coca-Cola Frosting

6 tablespoons cocoa
6 tablespoons Coca-cola
1 cup (2 sticks) butter or
* margarine*
1 pound confectioners' sugar
1 cup chopped pecans,
* toasted if desired*

Combine cocoa and cola in a small saucepan. Bring to a boil. Add butter. Pour over sugar in a large mixing bowl. Add nuts. Blend well and spread over hot cakes.

—Mrs. J. W. Simcock, Atlanta

Frosting Hint

When frosting a cake, frost the sides before you do the top for a more finished look.

Cream Cheese Pound Cake

Yield: 10 to 12 servings

1½ cups (3 sticks) butter or margarine, at room temperature
1 8-ounce package cream cheese, at room temperature
3 cups sugar
⅛ teaspoon salt
1½ teaspoons vanilla extract (or lemon extract)
6 eggs
3 cups sifted cake flour
2 cups chopped pecans (optional)

Preheat oven to 325 degrees F. Cream butter or margarine, cream cheese, and sugar together in a large bowl until light and fluffy. Add salt and flavoring; beat well. Add eggs, one at a time, beating well after each addition. Stir in flour. Blend in nuts if desired. Spoon mixture into greased 10-inch tube pan. Bake for about 1½ hours, or until cake pulls slightly away from edges of pan and top springs back when touched lightly with the fingers. Cool in pan on a rack 10 minutes, and then remove and complete cooling on rack.

—Addie De Ferrari

Use all the Egg!

When making recipes leaving you with extra egg whites, they are perfect for meringues. Extra yolks may be added to soufflés, scrambled eggs, custards, meat loaf, and homemade mayonnaise.

Molasses Pound Cake

Stir a half pint cup of butter into a half pint of brown sugar, and mix well together with 6 beaten eggs, a half pint of milk, and a half pint of nice molasses. Seed and cut in half a pound of raisins, and dredge with flour. Add 5 half pints of sifted flour to the batter along with a small teaspoon of [baking] soda, and the raisins last. Bake in a loaf pan.

—Bryan family cookbook, Savannah, circa 1885

Sour Cream Coffee Cake

Yield: 8 to 10 servings

1 cup finely chopped pecans
½ cup brown sugar
1 teaspoon ground cinnamon
1 cup sugar
½ cup (1 stick) butter or
  margarine, at room
  temperature
2 eggs
2 cups flour
1½ teaspoons baking powder
1 teaspoon baking soda
⅛ teaspoon salt
1 teaspoon vanilla extract
1 cup sour cream

Combine nuts, brown sugar and cinnamon in a small bowl; set aside. Grease and flour a 9-inch tube or bundt pan. Preheat oven to 350 degrees F.

In a large bowl, with mixer at medium speed, a food processor, or by hand, beat sugar with butter or margarine until light and fluffy. Add eggs and combine well. Sift dry ingredients together and add to butter mixture alternately with the vanilla and sour cream, beating well until blended after each addition. Beat three minutes at medium speed, occasionally scraping bowl.

Spread half of batter in pan. Sprinkle with half of pecan mixture. Spread evenly with remaining batter, and sprinkle with remaining pecan mixture. Bake for about 60 minutes, or until cake pulls away from side of pan, and springs back when touched lightly with the fingers. Cool in pan on wire rack 10 minutes. Loosen inside edge; invert pan on rack, and remove cake to cool completely. Serve warm or cool.

Note: This cake freezes well.

Moravian Sugar Cake

Cut up ¼ pound of butter into a pint of milk, and warm it together. When soft, mix it well together. Sift in ¾ pound of flour, and stir in a large spoonful of yeast, and a little salt. Cover, and let it rise in a warm place. When light, mix it with a well-beaten egg, ¾ pound more sifted flour, and a large teaspoon of powdered cinnamon. Let it rise again.

Mix 5 ounces of brown sugar with 2 ounces of butter, and more powdered cinnamon. When the dough is light, make incisions all over the top and fill with this mixture, then closing each and pressing it together. Bake at once, in a brisk oven [375 degrees F. for 12 to 15 minutes, or until golden].

—Bryan family cookbook, Savannah, circa 1885

Laurens Orange-Carrot Cake

Yield: 10 to 12 servings

1 cup (2 sticks) butter or
  margarine, at room
  temperature
2 cups sugar
1 teaspoon ground cinnamon
½ teaspoon ground nutmeg
1 tablespoon grated orange
  peel
4 eggs
1½ cups grated or finely
  shredded carrots
⅔ cup finely chopped pecans
3 cups sifted flour
3 teaspoons baking powder
½ teaspoon salt
¼ cup orange juice

Preheat oven to 350 degrees F. Cream butter and sugar together until fluffy. Add spices and orange peel. Beat in eggs, one at a time. Add carrots and nuts. Sift together dry ingredients and add alternately with juice to the batter, beating well after each addition, and ending with flour mixture.

Grease and flour a 10-inch tube pan, and pour batter into pan. Bake for 60 to 65 minutes, or until a cake tester inserted in cake comes out clean. Cool in pan on rack 15 minutes, and then turn out of pan and cool completely on wire rack. Pour Orange Glaze over cake, if desired.

Orange Glaze

1½ cups sifted confectioners'
  sugar
1 tablespoons butter or
  margarine, at room
  temperature
½ teaspoon grated orange
  rind
2 to 3 tablespoons orange
  juice

In a small bowl, beat the sugar with the butter, rind, and enough juice to make a thin glaze.

Cake Baking Hints

Roll raisins and other fruit in a little flour before adding to batter, and they will not sink to the bottom of the pan.

Powdered sugar sprinkled on cake batter before putting it into the oven, may be better than a frosting. Easier, too!

—*Congregational Meeting House
Cookbook*, White Bluff

Eva's Japanese Fruit Cake

Since the traditional Japanese cuisine did not feature cakes, the title of this famous Southern one is a mystery. Of course, it is not even a real fruitcake, but known for its spicy middle layer, and Pineapple-Coconut Frosting!

Yield: 1 3-layer, 9-inch cake

1 cup (2 sticks) butter or
   margarine, at room
   temperature
2 cups sugar
4 eggs
3 cups flour
3 teaspoons baking powder
¼ teaspoon salt
1 cup milk
½ teaspoon lemon extract
1 teaspoon vanilla extract
½ teaspoon ground cloves
1 teaspoon ground cinnamon
1 teaspoon ground allspice
¼ teaspoon ground nutmeg

Preheat oven to 350 degrees F. Grease and flour 3 9-inch cake pans. Cream butter and sugar together until fluffy. Add eggs, one at a time, beating well after each. Sift flour, baking powder, and salt; add to batter in three parts, alternating 1 cup of flour with ⅓ cup milk, beginning and ending with flour, and beating well after each. Add lemon and vanilla extracts and beat well.

Pour ⅔ of the batter into two of the pans. Add spices to remaining batter, beat well, and pour into third pan. Bake about 25 to 30 minutes, or until cake tester comes out clean, and cake springs back when touched lightly with the fingers. Cool in pans on rack 10 minutes, and then turn out on racks to finish cooling. When cool, frost with Pineapple-Coconut Frosting, placing spice layer in the middle.

Pineapple-Coconut Frosting

2 tablespoons flour
⅛ teaspoon salt
1⅓ cups sugar
1 cup hot water
2 cups grated coconut
4 tablespoons lemon juice, or
   juice of two medium
   lemons
2 tablespoons lemon peel, or
   from one medium lemon
2 cups crushed pineapple,
   with juice

Blend flour, salt, and sugar in top of double boiler, and gradually add hot water to make a paste. Then stir in remaining ingredients and place over hot water. Bring to a boil, stirring constantly, and then lower heat and simmer about 5 minutes, or until of desired consistency. Remove from heat and frost cake.

Holiday Mince Fruitcake

An unusual cake for the holiday season, which combines the traditional appeal of fruitcake and mincemeat.

Yield: about 16 servings

2 eggs
2½ cups plus 2 tablespoons sifted flour
1 teaspoon baking soda
⅛ teaspoon salt
1 28-ounce jar prepared mincemeat
1 14-ounce can sweetened condensed milk
1 8-ounce package candied pineapple, chopped
1 8-ounce package or jar candied red cherries, chopped
1 cup pecans, coarsely chopped

Preheat oven to 300 degrees F. Oil a 9- or 10-inch tube or bundt pan. Beat eggs slightly into a large bowl. Sift flour, soda, and salt together into eggs, and beat well. Stir in remaining ingredients and beat well. Spoon into pan and bake for about 2 hours with pan on lower rack in oven and top rack removed. (Rack should be just below center of oven.) Cake is done when top springs back when touched lightly with the fingers (a more reliable test than a cake tester, for fruit cakes.) Cool in pan on a wire rack, and then remove pan. Decorate if desired with Rum Glaze.

Rum Glaze

1 cup confectioners' sugar, sifted
2 tablespoons evaporated milk or cream
1 teaspoon rum extract

Blend sugar gradually with liquid ingredients until smooth.

Black or Plum Cake

One pound of fresh butter, one of nice sugar, twelve eggs, two pounds of stoned raisins, two of currants, one pound sifted flour, one teaspoon each mace and cinnamon, two powdered nutmegs, one pound citron, glass of brandy, one of wine, and rosewater to taste. This cake will keep even longer if double the quantity of liquor and spices are used.

—Bryan family cookbook, Savnnah, circa 1885

Adel Peach Shortcake

Yield: 8 servings

Peach Topping:
*4 cups thinly sliced, peeled
    fresh peaches
1 cup light brown sugar
3 tablespoons lemon juice*

Shortcake:
*4 cups flour
1 teaspoon salt
4 teaspoons baking powder
¼ cup sugar
½ cup shortening
1 egg
1⅓ cups milk
Butter as needed*

In a large bowl, toss peaches with brown sugar and lemon juice. Refrigerate covered for 2 hours, stirring occasionally.

About 30 minutes before serving time, make shortcake.

Preheat oven to 425 degrees F. Sift and measure flour; add salt, baking powder, and sugar; sift again. Work in shortening, using 2 knives or a pastry blender. Work until mixture is crumbly. Set aside. Beat egg slightly, and add to milk. Combine wet and dry ingredients. Flour pastry board. Pat dough on board to a thickness of about ½ inch. Cut out twice as many small (2½-inch) rounds as you wish individual shortcakes, or shape dough into 2 large rounds to fit a 9-inch pie plate.

Brush top surface of these rounds generously with melted butter, out to edge of dough. Place top rounds over bottom. Bake for approximately 20 minutes. To test for doneness, remove from oven and lift a top round. If inside seems a bit doughy, put shortcakes back into oven and bake for a few more minutes. To hasten final baking, the top rounds can be turned over (inner side turned uppermost,) if desired. Set cake aside in pan on wire rack 5 minutes. Prepare Cream Topping.

Cream Topping

2 cups heavy cream
2 tablespoons confectioners'
  sugar
¼ teaspoon almond extract
1 tablespoon butter or
  margarine, at room
  temperature

Beat cream until stiff. Fold in confectioners' sugar and almond extract. Working quickly, assemble shortcake. Turn cake out of pan. Place bottom layer on serving platter; spread with butter. Spoon on ⅓ of the cream topping, 2 cups prepared peaches, and then ⅓ more cream topping. Top with other shortcake layer. Spoon on rest of peaches and cream topping. Garnish with additional fresh peach slices, if desired.

Note: Of course, this basic recipe may be used with other fruits, such as strawberries sweetened to taste with a little sugar, for a wonderful seasonal dessert.

—Georgia Peach Commission, Atlanta

Madison Peach Upside-Down Cake

Yield: 1 9-inch cake

1½ pounds (about 6
  medium) fresh peaches
2 cups sugar, divided
1 cup water
4 tablespoons melted butter
½ cup light brown sugar,
  firmly packed
½ cup (1 stick) butter, at
  room temperature
1 egg yolk
3 eggs
1 teaspoon grated lemon peel
1 teaspoon vanilla extract
1½ cups sifted flour
1½ teaspoons baking powder
¼ teaspoon salt
¾ cup milk
Whipped cream for topping

Preheat oven to 375 degrees F. Peel peaches and slice into eighths. There should be about 2 cups. Meanwhile, bring 1 cup sugar and water to boiling point. Reduce heat and simmer 5 minutes. Add peaches. Cover and cook 3 to 5 minutes, or until almost tender. Drain.

Pour the melted butter into a 9-inch layer cake pan. Sprinkle with brown sugar. Arrange peaches on top. Cream the butter. Gradually beat in remaining 1 cup sugar. Add egg yolk and whole eggs; beat well. Stir in lemon peel and vanilla.

Sift together flour, baking powder, and salt. Add to creamed mixture alternating with milk, starting and ending with flour. Blend well after each addition. Pour over peaches. Bake 1 hour, or until cake springs back when pressed gently in the center. Cool on a rack for 15 minutes. Turn upside down on serving plate. Serve topped with whipped cream.

Early print of Madison, Georgia, "The town General W. T. Sherman refused to burn," during his march to the sea in 1864. The town was spared after a plea from Senator Joshua Hill, who had not voted for secession. Today, the county seat of Morgan County is noted for its tree-lined streets and antebellum homes. Courtesy Madison-Morgan County Chamber of Commerce

Plains Peanut Butter Cake

Yield: 1 2-layer, 9-inch cake

⅓ cup butter or margarine,
    at room temperature
2¼ cups sifted cake flour
1½ cups sugar
3 teaspoons baking powder
½ teaspoon salt
½ cup chunky-style peanut
    butter
1 cup milk, divided
2 eggs
1 teaspoon vanilla extract

Preheat oven to 375 degrees F. Grease and flour 2 9-inch layer pans. Cream butter until light and fluffy. Sift in dry ingredients. Add peanut butter and half of the milk. Mix well, and then beat at low speed of electric mixer or food processor for 2 minutes, or 300 strokes by hand. Add remaining milk, eggs, and vanilla. Beat for two minutes by hand. Pour into pans and bake for about 25 minutes. Cool 5 minutes in pans on racks, and then turn out of pans and finish cooling on racks. Frost with Cocoa-Peanut Frosting.

Cocoa-Peanut Frosting

½ cup chunky-style peanut
    butter
⅓ cup cocoa
2¾ cups sifted confectioners'
    sugar
⅛ teaspoon salt
1 teaspoon vanilla extract
½ cup light cream or
    evaporated milk, undiluted

Cream peanut butter and cocoa well together. Gradually add sugar, salt, vanilla, and cream or milk as desired, until of a good spreading consistency, beating until smooth.

Mrs. Pritchard's Chocolate Roll

Take the yolks of six eggs, and beat them for three or four minutes with a spoon with one cup sugar and a teaspoon of water. Then put in four teaspoons of cocoa, and work all together about five minutes; then put in some vanilla. Beat the whites of the eggs into the whole now, all together. Grease a flat square pan with butter and wax paper, and put the batter into the pan very flat and thin. Bake it with a slow fire [375 degrees F.], 12 to 15 minutes. Put a napkin on the table, and pour the cake out on it, and roll it up. When the cake is cold, roll it out and put whipped cream (sweetened) in it, and roll it again. To serve, put more whipped cream on top. This is very good.

—Family cookbook of Sophie Meldrim Shonnard, Savannah

Americus Pumpkin-Pecan Cake

Yield: 1 2-layer, 9-inch cake

2 cups sugar
1 cup vegetable oil
4 eggs
2¼ cups self-rising flour,
  divided
2 teaspoons ground
  cinnamon
½ teaspoon ground nutmeg
1 16-ounce can strained
  pumpkin
1 teaspoon vanilla extract
½ cup seedless golden
  raisins
1 cup chopped pecans

Preheat oven to 325 degrees F. Grease and flour 2 9-inch cake pans. Cream sugar and oil until smooth, using medium speed of electric mixer or food processor, or by beating well by hand. Add eggs, one at a time, beating well after each. Sift 2 cups flour and spices together. Fold into creamed mixture and mix until smooth. Add pumpkin and vanilla; mix thoroughly. Combine the raisins and nuts with remaining flour, and add to cake batter, mixing well. Pour into pans, and bake for 30 to 35 minutes, or until cake springs back when touched lightly with the fingers in center. Cool on rack and frost with Lemon-Cream Cheese Frosting.

Note: If using regular, instead of self-rising flour, add 2 teaspoons baking soda and 1 teaspoon salt to flour before sifting with spices.

Lemon-Cream Cheese Frosting

3 cups confectioners' sugar
1 8-ounce package cream
  cheese, at room
  temperature
⅛ teaspoon salt
Juice and grated peel of one
  medium lemon (about 2
  tablespoons each, juice
  and grated peel)
2 tablespoons light cream or
  evaporated milk

Sift sugar and gradually mix in other ingredients, beating well until of spreading consistency.

—Mrs. Bertye C. Joner

Boiled Icing

Put one pound of loaf sugar into a pan with a tumbler full of water. Boil it until it ropes (forms a thread), and strain. Add the whites of six eggs, well-beaten, and season with lemon juice. Beat for an hour, and ice cake.

(Some like a pound and a half of sugar, and the whites of seven eggs).

—Bryan family cookbook, Savannah, circa 1885

Wheat Germ Spice Cake

A very nutritious cake!

Yield: 1 2-layer 9-inch cake

1 cup (2 sticks) butter or margarine, at room temperature
2 cups sugar
4 eggs, separated
2 teaspoons vanilla extract
2 cups flour
2 teaspoons baking powder
1 teaspoon salt
1 cup milk
1 cup regular wheat germ
¾ cup chopped pecans
2 teaspoons ground cinnamon
¼ teaspoon allspice
¼ teaspoon ground nutmeg
1 cup raisins or currants

Preheat oven to 350 degrees F. Grease and flour two 9-inch layer pans. Beat together butter and sugar until fluffy. Add in egg yolks and vanilla, and beat well. Sift together flour, baking powder, and salt. Stir into batter alternately with milk, beginning and ending with flour. Beat egg whites until stiff and fold into batter. Fold in wheat germ, pecans, spices, and raisins or currants and combine well. Pour into pans and bake for about 35 to 40 minutes, or until cake tester comes out clean, or cake springs back in center when touched lightly with the fingers.

Cool in pans 10 minutes on a rack and remove from pans. Finish cooling on racks. When cool, frost with favorite lemon, orange, white or coconut frosting, or Banana-Nut Frosting, below.

Banana-Nut Frosting

Yield: enough for one two- or three-layer or a 9-by-13-inch cake

⅓ cup butter, at room temperature
1 pound confectioners' sugar, sifted
½ cup mashed ripe banana
1 teaspoon lemon juice
1 cup grated coconut
⅔ cup chopped pecans

Cream butter; add sugar and bananas which have been sprinkled with juice. Blend well. Add coconut and nuts. Mix well. Spread between layers and on sides and top of cake. Serve at room temperature.

Note: Because of the ripe banana, this recipe is best made when it can be served all at one time, and should be kept chilled until serving time.

Telfair Black Bottom Cupcakes

Yield: 24

1½ cups flour
1 cup sugar
¼ cup cocoa
1 teaspoon baking soda
½ teaspoon salt
1 cup water
⅓ cup vegetable oil
1 tablespoon vinegar
1 teaspoon vanilla extract

Chocolate Chip Topping:
1 8-ounce package cream
   cheese, at room
   temperature
1 egg
⅓ cup sugar
⅛ teaspoon salt
1 6-ounce package chocolate
   chips
½ cup finely chopped pecans
¼ cup sugar

Sift dry ingredients together. Add water, oil, vinegar, and extract and beat until well blended. Grease 2½-inch muffin tins well, or use paper liners. Fill cups about ⅓ full.

Preheat oven to 350 degrees F. Combine cream cheese, egg, sugar, and salt; beat well. Stir in chips and mix well. Place about 1 tablespoon of this mixture evenly over the top of batter in each cupcake. Sprinkle with remaining combined pecans and sugar. Bake for about 30 minutes, or until cakes spring back when touched lightly with the fingers. Cool for about 5 minutes in pans. Turn out on racks to finish cooling.

Tipsy Parson

This 19th century recipe supposedly got its name from the fact that the minister ate so much of it during his Sunday rounds that he sometimes went home a bit tipsy.

Take a sponge cake several days old. Crumble it up fine. Put a layer of it in a nice glass dish and pour over it one cup of wine. Then add ½ cup finely chopped almonds; then a layer of whipped cream; and begin again the same way, ending with the cream, which you can sweeten to your taste or flavor as desired. All kinds of cake crumbs can be used, but sponge is the best. Chill before serving: store in a cool place.

—Jerry Downey

This mule-powered sugar cane mill and syrup cooking shed is one of more than 30 restored buildings which recreate life in the closing decades of the 19th Century at the Georgia Agrirama at Tifton.

Speedy White Frosting

Yield: about 1 cup

2 tablespoons light cream, evaporated milk, milk, or sour cream
2 tablespoons butter or margarine, at room temperature
1 teaspoon almond, vanilla, or other extract
1 cup confectioners' sugar, sifted

Gradually combine other ingredients with sugar, stirring well until smooth.

Chocolate Variation: Add 3 tablespoons cocoa to above ingredients along with the sugar.

Date-Pecan Cupcakes

Yield: 2 dozen

1 cup chopped dates
1 teaspoon baking soda
1 cup boiling water
¼ cup vegetable shortening
1 cup sugar
1 egg
1¾ cups sifted flour
½ teaspoon salt
½ cup chopped pecans
1 teaspoon vanilla extract

Preheat oven to 350 degrees F. Combine dates, soda, and boiling water; cool. Cream shortening and sugar; beat in egg. Sift together flour and salt; add to creamed mixture alternately with date mixture. Stir in pecans and vanilla. Fill greased and floured 2½-inch muffin cups ⅔ full. Bake 20 to 25 minutes, or until top springs back when touched lightly with the fingers. Cool slightly on racks after removing from the oven. Serve plain, sprinkle with a little confectioners' sugar, or decorate when cool with Lemon or Orange Frosting.

Lemon or Orange Frosting

1 cup confectioners' sugar
1 to 3 tablespoons orange or lemon juice
1 teaspoon grated peel (optional)

To confectioners' sugar add orange or lemon juice until of desired spreading consistency. Grated lemon or orange peel may be added if desired.

Easy Broiled Coconut Frosting

Yield: enough for 1 9-by-13-inch cake

⅔ cup light brown sugar, packed
5 tablespoons butter or margarine, at room temperature
¼ cup light cream, or evaporated milk
1½ cups grated coconut
1 teaspoon vanilla extract

Mix all ingredients. If using fresh coconut, you may wish to sweeten to taste. Spread over top of warm 13-by-9-inch cake just as it comes from the oven. Broil 3 inches from heat for 3 minutes, or until golden and bubbly. (Watch carefully to see that coconut does not burn.) Set aside a few minutes before cutting.

Pies

Crunchy Apple Pie

An all-American favorite, with a crunchy variation: this one is from the Georgia Apple Commission in Atlanta.

Yield: 1 9-inch pie

½ cup light brown sugar
½ cup sugar
½ cup flour
⅛ teaspoon allspice
⅛ teaspoon ground cloves
⅛ teaspoon nutmeg
1 teaspoon cinnamon
1 teaspoon grated lemon peel
½ cup (1 stick) butter or margarine
1 9-inch pie shell, unbaked
6 cups sliced cooking apples
2 tablespoons lemon juice

Combine sugars, flour, spices, lemon peel, and butter; cut with pastry blender until crumbly like coarse crumbs. Spread ⅓ of mixture evenly over pie shell. Peel, core and slice apples; sprinkle with lemon juice.

Preheat oven to 400 degrees F. Pour apples in pie plate over crumb mixture and sprinkle with remaining crumbs. Bake for about 15 minutes. Reduce heat to 350 degrees F., and bake for another 35 minutes, or until a nice golden brown.

Wheat Germ

For extra nutrition and crunchy flavor, add a little wheat germ, plain or honey-flavored, to pie topping in crumb pies.

213

Imperial Cream

Boil a quart of cream with the rind of a lemon, then stir it until nearly cold. Have ready in a dish the juice of three lemons, with enough sugar to sweeten the cream. Mix well, and put in a cool place. This should be made six hours before using, and eat with apple pie.

—Family cookbook of Mrs. Lucinda Williams, Milledgeville, 1857

Apple Custard Pie

To a pint of apples, peeled and cored and sliced, add ¼ pound of butter, half a pint of cream, three eggs, well-beaten, and sugar and nutmeg to taste. Mix well, and bake on pastry.

—Bryan family cookbook, Savannah, circa 1885

Fruit Variations

Substitute fresh cranberries, raisins, currants, or mincemeat for part of the apples in a favorite recipe.

Say Cheese

In making pastry for an apple pie, add ½ cup grated Cheddar to the mixture. Or, in making a crumb topping, add ½ cup cheese to the mixture.

This split-oak basket of fruit by Carol Ness has become the logo of the Georgia Folk Festival, held every Memorial Day Weekend at Rock Eagle 4-H Center near Eatonton

LaGrange Buttermilk Pie

Yield: 1 9-inch pie

1⅔ cups sugar, divided
6 tablespoons flour
2 cups buttermilk
4 eggs, separated
⅓ cup lemon juice
1 tablespoon grated lemon
  peel
2 tablespoons butter
1 9-inch pie shell, baked
¼ teaspoon salt
¼ teaspoon cream of tartar

Mix 1⅓ cups sugar and flour in the top of a double boiler and gradually stir in the buttermilk. Cook over hot water until mixture thickens, stirring constantly. Add beaten egg yolks and cook about 2 minutes longer. Remove from heat and stir in lemon juice, peel, and butter. Cool and pour into pie shell.

Preheat oven to 325 degrees F. Beat egg whites until frothy. Add salt and cream of tartar. Beat until eggs hold soft peaks. Gradually beat in last ⅓ cup sugar, beating until mixture is stiff and glossy. Swirl over pie filling, sealing well to edge of shell. Bake until golden, about 18 to 20 minutes. Cool before serving. Cut with sharp, wet knife.

—Emma R. Law

Almond-Cherry Lattice Pie

Yield: 1 9-inch pie

Pastry for 2-crust pie
¾ cup sugar, or to taste
4 tablespoons cornstarch
¼ teaspoon salt
4 cups pitted red cherries,
  fresh or canned, drained
⅓ cup cherry juice or water
½ cup chopped blanched
  almonds, or ¼ teaspoon
  almond extract
2 tablespoons butter or
  margarine

Roll out half of pastry into ⅛-inch thick pastry for 9-inch pie; fit into pan. Put rest aside for the top, rolling it into a 5-by-10-inch rectangle and cutting 10 ½-inch strips.

Preheat oven to 400 degrees F. Blend sugar with cornstarch and salt. Mix with cherries, juice, and almonds or extract. Fill pie shell and dot with butter. Add lattice crust, and bake 15 minutes. Reduce heat to 375 degrees F. and bake 30 minutes longer, or until crust is nicely browned and pie is set. Serve with ice cream, or as desired.

Cornstarch Hint

In substituting cornstarch in a recipe calling for flour as the thickening agent, use half as much cornstarch.

Dixie Chess Pie

It is said that the name of this famous Southern custard pie comes from the plantation cooks who, when asked their recipe, would murmur modestly, "Oh, it jes' pie!"

Yield: 1 9-inch pie

3 eggs
½ cups sugar
¼ teaspoon salt
2 cups scalded milk
1 teaspoon vanilla extract
1 9-inch pie shell, unbaked
1 tablespoon butter, very soft
  or melted
Nutmeg to taste

Preheat oven to 425 degrees F. Beat eggs until light and foamy. Add sugar and salt; blend well. Add the scalded milk and then vanilla extract.

Brush pie shell with the butter. Pour custard into shell. Sprinkle top lightly with nutmeg. Bake for about 10 minutes, then reduce heat to 325 degrees F. and bake about 35 to 40 minutes longer, or until filling doesn't coat a knife inserted in pie.

—Margo Caldwell

Custard Pudding

If the custard-type pie filling is too much for your crust, pour the excess into small custard cups and place in a pan of hot water. Bake at 325 degrees F. for about 40 minutes, or at 350 degrees F. for about 30, or until firm. This is also a way to cut calories when serving family members on a diet.

For variety with a small family, add a few frozen or fresh blueberries to the custard filling for pudding. Sprinkle with nutmeg before baking. Serve warm or cold, plain or with whipped cream.

Filling Hint for Custard Pies

In pouring very thin or runny pie filling into a crust, some find it easier with the crust pan on a small baking sheet, which can then be put in the oven. Others prefer mixing the filling in a large measuring cup, placing the pie shell on the oven rack, and then carefully pouring the filling into the pie.

Candy Bar Pie

For this rich, easy pie you can either use a baked pastry crust or a graham cracker or crushed wafer crust.

Yield: 1 9-inch pie

*18 marshmallows (not
    miniature)*
½ cup milk
*8 ounces crumbled chocolate
    bars, either plain or with
    nuts*
½ pint heavy cream
1 9-inch pie shell, baked
Whipped cream, for garnish
*Toasted, blanched almonds,
    for garnish*

Combine marshmallows and milk in top of double boiler over hot water. Dissolve marshmallows, stirring occasionally, and then stir broken candy bars into hot mixture. When candy is nearly melted, remove from heat and allow to cool.

Whip cream and fold into chocolate mixture. Pour into baked pie shell. Chill until set. To serve, pie may be decorated with extra whipped cream and/or toasted almonds, if desired. Serve chilled.

Note: This recipe originally called for 6 small, or 1.35 ounce bars, but since candy bar sizes change so frequently, any size bars may be used so long as the total is approximately 8 ounces.

—Mary Smith

Mill Mountain Chocolate Pie

When making chocolate pie, either from a mix or regular ingredients, add 1 to 3 tablespoons chocolate-flavored liqueur, to taste, in place of the vanilla. Be sure to reduce the amount of milk used by the liqueur added so pie will not be too runny.

—Margaret Anne DeBolt Edwards

Brandy Crust

Yield: 1 9-inch shell

1 cup flour
⅓ teaspoon salt
*6 tablespoons butter or
    vegetable oil*
3 tablespoons chilled brandy

Combine flour, salt, butter or vegetable oil, and brandy. Roll as desired.

Note: Other chilled alcoholic beverages may also be substituted for water, in making a flavored pie shell.

The Pirates' House in Savannah, formerly a seamen's tavern and now a restaurant, is located at the site of the Eighteenth Century Trustees' Garden. Printed from an original drawing by Pamela Lee. Copyright by Pamela Lee

Ice Box Lemon Pie

Crunch enough vanilla wafers to cover the bottom of a pie pan with crumbs. Place other wafers, cut in half if desired, around the edge of the tin to represent a crust.

Beat two egg yolks thoroughly, and add 1 can sweetened condensed milk, and the juice of two lemons. Mix thoroughly. Pour over crumbs. cover with a meringue made of the two egg whites, well-beaten, and 4 tablespoons sugar added to them very gradually. Brown pie in a slow oven. Then place in the icebox, and allow to chill before serving. Serves six.

—Family cookbook of Sophie Meldrim Shonnard, Savannah

Pirates' House Lemon Cream Pie

Yield: 1 9-inch pie

Vanilla Wafer Crust:
2 cups vanilla wafer crumbs
4 tablespoons melted butter

Lemon Cream Pie:
1 6-ounce can frozen lemonade, thawed
1 14-ounce can sweetened condensed milk
4 eggs, separated
¼ cup sugar
¼ teaspoon cream of tartar
6 teaspoons sugar
1 teaspoon vanilla extract

Combine vanilla wafer crumbs and melted butter or margarine. Press into pie pan and chill to set crumbs.

Preheat oven to 325 degrees F. Mix thawed lemonade, milk, beaten egg yolks, and sugar together in a bowl. Pour over wafer crust. Beat egg whites until stiff but not dry, and then gradually beat in remaining ingredients. Pour over pie and bake for about 20 minutes, or until meringue browns.

Cool thoroughly before serving. Cut with a sharp knife dipped in hot water.

Flavor Variation: Other flavors, such as limeade, may be substituted for the lemonade.

Orange Pudding

Grate the yellow rind, and squeeze the juice from two large oranges. Stir in ½ pound sugar and ½ pound butter, mixed together to a cream. Add a glass of mixed wine and brandy, and six well-beaten eggs. Bake in puff paste, and grate sugar over it when cold. Lemon pudding may be made in the same way, using lemons instead of oranges.

—Bryan family cookbook, Savannah, circa 1885

Rich Puff Pastry

Yield: 2 9-inch single pie crusts

1 cup (2 sticks) butter, at room temperature
1½ cups flour
½ cup sour cream

Cut butter into flour as for pastry, until mixture is like coarse peas. Add sour cream. Mix gently with a fork until well-blended. Divide into two balls. Chill for 8 hours or more before using.

The Tullie Smith House, circa 1840, of typical antebellum Plantation Plain architecture, is one of the few such houses remaining in the Atlanta area. Donated to the Atlanta Historical Society by Smith's descendants, it has been restored and is now open to the public as part of a living history program showing the lifestyle of a yeoman farmer in piedmont Georgia in the mid-1800s. Courtesy Tullie Smith House, Atlanta Historical Society

Molasses Custard Pie

To 1 tablespoon butter, add 3 tablespoons sifted flour, 4 well-beaten eggs, and 2 cups of molasses mixed with ½ teaspoon [baking] soda and 1 of cinnamon. Pour into pastry, and bake.

—Bryan family cookbook, Savannah, circa 1885

Peaches and Cream Pie

No wonder they call Georgia the Peach State, with so many good varieties, and in season from May through the summer!

Yield: 1 9-inch pie

¾ cup sugar
¼ cup flour
¼ teaspoon salt
½ teaspoon cinnamon
4 cups peeled, sliced peaches
1 tablespoon lemon juice
1 9-inch pie shell, unbaked
1 cup heavy cream
Nutmeg to taste

Preheat oven to 400 degrees F. Combine sugar, flour, salt, and cinnamon; set aside. Toss sliced peaches with lemon juice, and then stir in flour mixture. Arrange in pie shell. Pour cream over. Sprinkle with nutmeg. Bake for 15 minutes and reduce heat to 350 degrees F. Continue baking 30 to 35 more minutes; or until knife inserted in center comes out clean, or pie seems well set. Cool before serving.

Apple Variation: This same recipe is good with apples or blueberries, spiced to taste.

Marshallville Lattice Peach Pie

Yield: 1 9-inch pie

Pastry for 2 crust-pie
5 cups peeled, sliced fresh
  peaches
1 tablespoon lemon juice
2 tablespoons cornstarch
¾ cup sugar
¼ teaspoon salt
1 teaspoon vanilla extract
2 tablespoons butter or
  margarine

Roll out half of pastry into ⅛-inch-thick pastry for 9-inch pie; fit into pan. Put rest aside for the top, rolling it into a 5-by-10-inch rectangle and cutting 10 ½-inch strips.

Preheat oven to 400 degrees F. Combine peaches, lemon juice, cornstarch, sugar, salt, and vanilla; pour into pie shell. Dot with butter. Arrange pastry strips lattice-fashion over peach filling, trimming and fluting crust at edges. Bake 15 minutes, then reduce heat to 375 degrees F. and bake about 30 minutes longer, or until crust is a nice brown and peaches are tender. Cool. Serve plain or with ice cream as desired.

Note: You may wish to bake pie on a small cookie sheet, or circle of tinfoil, to avoid spills in your oven.

Bob's Coconut Cream Pie

Yield: 1 9-inch pie

2 cups milk
4 eggs
½ cup sugar
½ cup flour
½ teaspoon salt
About 1½ cups coconut, divided
1 teaspoon vanilla extract
1 9-inch pie shell, baked

Meringue:
⅛ teaspoon salt
½ cup sugar

Scald milk and cool to lukewarm. Separate eggs and set whites aside for Meringue. Lightly beat egg yolks and mix into lukewarm milk. Mix together sugar, flour, salt, and 1 cup coconut; stir into milk mixture. Cook over medium heat, stirring until thick. Remove from heat and add vanilla, stirring well. Cool slightly. Pour into baked pie shell.

Preheat oven to 350 degrees F. Beat reserved egg whites until stiff but not dry, and gradually add salt and sugar, beating well after each addition. Pile on top of pie, spreading all the way to edge of crust. Sprinkle with reserved ½ cup coconut, or more as desired. Bake for about 12 minutes, or until golden brown. Cool on a rack, away from drafts, before serving.

—Robert L. English

Colquitt Milk Crust

Yield: 2 9-inch pie shells

2 cups flour
1 teaspoon salt
½ cup vegetable oil
¼ cup cold milk

Mix flour with salt. Cut in vegetable oil until like coarse crumbs. Sprinkle with milk, a little at a time, and mix lightly with a fork until well-moistened. Shape into a ball and chill, covered. Roll as desired.

Note: For 1 9-inch shell, use 1⅓ cups flour, ½ teaspoon salt, ⅓ cup oil, and 3 tablespoons cold milk, or as needed.

Sumter County scene by Lois E. Theiss

Apple Pudding

Pare and core 12 large apples and put them into a saucepan with sufficient water to cover them. Stew until soft, and beat them smooth. Add ¾ pound [powdered] loaf sugar, ¼ pound of butter, the juice and grated peel of two lemons or oranges. Add the yolks of eight eggs, beaten. Bake in puff paste three-quarters of an hour in a hot oven. Grate sugar over the top when done. A tumbler of wine, with a grated nutmeg, may be substituted for the lemon or orange.

—Bryan family cookbook, Savannah, circa 1885

Peanut Butter Crumb Pie

Yield: 1 9-inch pie

1 cup confectioners' sugar
½ cup crunchy peanut
  butter
1 9-inch pie shell, baked
¼ cup cornstarch
1 cup sugar, divided
¼ teaspoon salt
2 cups milk, scalded
3 eggs, separated
2 tablespoons butter or
  margarine
1 teaspoon vanilla extract

Preheat oven to 350 degrees F. Combine confectioners' sugar and peanut butter; blend until like coarse crumbs. Sprinkle ¾ of mixture over the bottom of pie shell. Set shell and rest of mixture aside.

Combine cornstarch, ⅔ cup sugar, and salt. Add scalded milk and mix well. Beat egg yolks in a small bowl. Pour small amount of milk mixture over egg yolks. Mix well and then pour egg mixture into milk mixture. Cook in top of double boiler over medium heat until mixture thickens, stirring constantly. Add butter and vanilla. Pour over crumbs in baked pie shell. Sprinkle remaining peanut butter mixture over custard, saving a little to top meringue, if desired.

Beat reserved egg whites stiff but not dry, and fold in remaining ⅓ cup sugar. Pour meringue over pie, making sure it reaches all the way to edge of crust on all sides. Top with a little of the crumb mixture if desired. Bake for about 30 minutes, or until meringue is brown. Cool before serving.

Georgia's Pecan Industry

A state historical marker at St. Mary's states, "First pecan trees grown here about 1840 from pecan nuts found floating at sea by Captain Samuel F. Flood and planted by his wife, Rebecca Grovenstine Flood. . . . The remainder of these nuts were planted by St. Joseph Sebastian Arnow. . . . The first plantings produced large and heavy-bearing trees, as did their nuts and shoots in turn. Taken from St. Mary's to distant points throughout the southeastern states, they became famous before the Texas pecan was generally known."

Baconton in south Georgia now claims to be the "Pecan Center of the World," while nearby Albany calls itself "Pecan Capital of the World," and "Pecan Center of the World for Named Varieties," of which there are 300! Albany hosts the National Pecan Festival every September, while Baconton stages a Pecan Harvest Festival.

Georgia leads the nation in pecan production, with about half the total yield, or over 75 million pounds. That's a lot of pies and fudge—and just plain good out-of-the-shell eating!

Rum-Chocolate Pecan Pie

Yield: 1 9-inch pie

2 1-ounce squares semisweet
  chocolate
2 tablespoons butter or
  margarine
3 eggs
½ cup sugar, or to taste
½ cup dark corn syrup
⅛ teaspoon salt
2 cups thinly sliced shelled
  pecans
1 teaspoon vanilla extract
3 tablespoons dark rum or
  bourbon
1 9-inch pie crust, unbaked

Preheat oven to 425 degrees F. Melt chocolate and butter together over very low heat. Set aside. Place eggs in a large bowl and beat lightly. Add sugar, corn syrup, and salt. Beat until well-mixed. Stir in chocolate mixture until well blended. Stir in pecans, vanilla, and rum or bourbon if desired; pour into prepared pastry. Mixture will be thin.

Lightly cover edges of pastry with strips of aluminum foil to keep pastry from browning too fast. Place on middle shelf of oven and bake 15 minutes. Reduce temperature to 325 degrees F. and bake 15 more minutes. Remove foil strips and bake another 15 minutes, or until crust is browned and surface of pie is firm to the touch. Filling will rise with heat, but sink slightly as it cools.

Cool on rack for at least 25 minutes. Serve warm or at room temperature, with Angostura Topping.

Angostura Topping

½ cup heavy cream, whipped
Sugar to taste
½ teaspoon (4 dashes)
  Angostura bitters

Blend ingredients well and serve on pie slices. This is good instead of whipped cream with any recipe.

Damson Plum Pie

Mash ½ to 1 cup Damsons through a strainer. Whip the white of 1 egg stiff, and fold in ½ cup sugar (or a little less), and a pinch of salt. Mix plums in, and pour into a prepared unbaked pie crust. Bake in a moderate oven for about half a hour, or until nicely browned. Serve at once, as meringue filling droops a bit as it cools.

—Family cookbook of Sophie Meldrim Shonnard, Savannah

Pumpkin Pie with Brandy

Yield: 1 9-inch pie

1 cup canned or cooked
strained pumpkin
1 cup evaporated milk or
cream
¾ cup sugar, or to taste
3 eggs, lightly beaten
¼ cup brandy
1 teaspoon cinnamon
½ teaspoon nutmeg
½ teaspoon ginger
½ teaspoon mace
⅛ teaspoon salt
1 9-inch pie shell, unbaked
Sweetened whipped cream
for topping as desired

Preheat oven to 400 degrees F. Combine pumpkin, milk, and sugar in a bowl, stirring until well mixed. Stir in eggs, brandy, spices and salt. Mix well and pour into pie shell. Bake 15 minutes, then reduce heat to 350 degrees F. and bake about 40 minutes more, or until a knife inserted in the center comes out clean. Cool before serving.

Serve with sweetened whipped cream as desired.

Spirited variation: Bourbon or sherry may be substituted for brandy in this recipe as desired.

Cocoa

Some cooks add 1 tablespoon cocoa powder to their pumpkin pie. Others vary the flavor with 1 tablespoon dark molasses, or ¼ cup maple syrup in place of part of the sugar. With this, add 1 tablespoon maple syrup to sweetened whipped cream garnish in serving.

Crust Hint

Always add water slowly to the flour in making a pie crust, and use only as much as needed. Too much liquid makes a tough, soggy pastry that will shrink as it bakes.

Pumpkin Pudding Pie

Mix ¼ pound butter into a pint of boiled milk until soft, and stir in ¼ pound of sugar. Add 3 eggs, well-beaten, ½ pound of strained pumpkin, half a glass of wine or brandy, and 1 teaspoon mixed spices, or to taste. Bake in a pastry.

—Bryan family cookbook, Savannah, circa 1885

General Hardee's Squash Pie

Yield: 1 9-inch pie

1½ cups steamed butternut
   squash
1 cup sugar, or to taste
¾ teaspoon salt
1 teaspon cinnamon
½ teaspoon nutmeg
¾ teaspoon ginger
¼ teaspoon mace
3 eggs
1 cup heavy cream
1 9-inch pie shell, unbaked

Preheat oven to 425 degrees F. Strain squash and add sugar and flavorings; mix well and set aside. Beat eggs and add cream. Stir into squash mixture and mix well. Test seasonings. Pour into pie shell. Bake for 10 minutes, and then reduce heat to 350 degrees F. and bake about 40 minutes longer, or until pie is firm. Serve plain or with sweetened whipped cream, as desired.

Old Fashioned Sweet Potato Custard Pie

Yield: 1 9-inch pie

1½ cups strained sweet
   potatoes (6 to 8 medium
   potatoes)
1 teaspoon vanilla extract
1½ cups evaporated milk or
   cream
4 tablespoons butter, at room
   temperature
3 eggs, separated
½ cup dark brown sugar, or
   to taste
½ cup dark corn syrup
½ teaspoon salt
½ teaspoon ginger
1 teaspoon cinnamon
½ teaspoon nutmeg
1 9-inch pastry shell,
   unbaked

Preheat oven to 375 degrees F. If using fresh potatoes, boil with jackets until tender when pierced with a fork, about 20 to 30 minutes. Peel and mash; strain and measure.

Mix potatoes with vanilla, milk, and butter; set aside. Blend beaten egg yolks, brown sugar, syrup, salt, and spices together in a large bowl. Add potato mixture and beat until well mixed. Whip egg whites until stiff and fold into potato mixture. Pour into pie shell. Bake for about 45 minutes, or until knife inserted in center comes out clean.

—Jean Young (Mrs. Andrew), Atlanta

Sweet Potato Pie

Mix one pound grated sweet potatoes with ½ cup sugar or to taste, 4 beaten eggs, 2 lemons, both juice and grated rind, 1 cup milk, and ¼ pound melted butter. Bake between crusts.

—Bryan family cookbook, Savannah, circa 1885

Dad's Raisin Pie

Yield: 1 9-inch pie

3 cups raisins
2¼ cups hot water
¾ cup sugar
3 tablespoons corn starch
1½ teaspoons grated lemon
   rind
3 tablespoons lemon juice
2 tablespoons margarine
½ teaspoon salt
Pastry for a 2-crust 9-inch
   pie

In a saucepan, stir raisins and hot water. Let stand for 5 minutes. Mix sugar and corn starch; add to raisins. Bring to a boil over low heat, stirring constantly. Boil 1 minute. Remove from heat and add remaining ingredients. Pour into pastry-lined pie plate. Cover with remaining dough. Cut several slits to permit escape of steam. Seal and flute edges of pastry. Bake in a preheated 425 degree F. oven 20 to 25 minutes, or until golden.

Marietta Strawberry Pie

Yield: 1 9-inch pie

4 cups (1 quart)
   strawberries, divided
¾ cup sugar
¼ cup cornstarch
¼ teaspoon salt
½ cup water
1 tablespoon lemon juice
1 9-inch pie shell, baked
Sweetened whipped cream

Wash and hull berries. Slice 2 cups, leaving the rest whole. Set aside.

Blend sugar, cornstarch, and salt in top of double boiler. Gradually add water and mix until smooth. Add sliced berries. Place over boiling water and cook, stirring constantly until mixture thickens. Remove from heat and cool. Fold in remaining two cups of berries, reserving a few nice ones for garnish, and add lemon juice. Pour mixture into baked pie shell. Chill and serve with sweetened whipped cream and whole berries, as desired.

Rice Pudding

Mix ¼ pound rice flour with cold milk to the consistency of cream. Stir this into a quart of boiling milk, and let boil until it thickens. Remove from the fire and stir in ¼ pound of butter, and a little salt. After cooling, add 5 eggs well-beaten, a cup of sugar, and a wine glass of brandy. Flavor with vanilla and nutmeg. Bake in a rich crust.

—Bryan family cookbook, Savannah, circa 1885

Wine Chiffon Pie

A light and delightful pie which can be made ahead of time for a dinner party.

Yield: 1 9-inch pie

1 envelope unflavored gelatin
⅔ cup sugar, divided
4 eggs, divided
⅔ cup dry white wine
¼ teaspoon salt
½ cup heavy cream
1 teaspoon vanilla extract
1 9-inch pie shell, baked
Sweetened whipped cream,
    for garnish

Mix gelatin with ⅓ cup sugar. In the top of a double boiler, beat the egg yolks. Stir in the wine and then the gelatin mixture. Cook and stir over boiling water about 5 minutes, or until thickened. Remove from heat.

Beat egg whites with salt until fairly stiff. Beat remaining ⅓ cup sugar in gradually, beating until stiff peaks form. Set aside. With the same beater, then beat the ½ cup cream with the vanilla until stiff. Fold beaten egg whites into wine mixture, and then fold in whipped cream. Pour into pie shell. Chill until set. If desired, serve with additional sweetened whipped cream.

Note: This pie is best served the same day it is made.

—Emma R. Law

Decatur Meringue Crust

Yield: 1 9-inch crust

3 egg whites
½ teaspoon baking powder
¾ cup sugar
⅔ cup shortbread or vanilla
    wafer crumbs
½ teaspoon salt
1 teaspoon vanilla extract
½ cup finely chopped pecans

Preheat oven to 300 degrees F. Beat egg whites with baking powder until foamy. Gradually add sugar, beating until stiff and glossy. Gently fold in crumbs, salt, vanilla, and nuts. Spread in lightly greased 9-inch pie pan. Bake until lightly browned, about 30 minutes. Cool on wire rack. Fill as desired with a cooked pudding or custard, or sweetened whipped cream and fresh sliced fruit, garnished with fruit.

Frozen Yogurt Pie

Yield: 1 9-inch pie

2 8-ounce packages cream
   cheese, at room
   temperature
½ cup honey
2 8-ounce cartons vanilla-,
   lemon-, or coffee-flavored
   yogurt
1 9-inch graham cracker
   crust (see index)

Beat cream cheese until smooth in a large mixing bowl. Gradually add honey, mixing well. Add yogurt a little at a time, beating well after each addition. Pour into crust and freeze until firm, about 5 hours. Leave out of freezer at room temperature about 20 minutes before serving. Serve plain, with a sprinkling of wheat germ (honey-sweetened type preferred), or graham crumbs, or with Blueberry Glaze, below.

Blueberry Glaze

Yield: 1¼ cups

1 cup blueberries, fresh or
   whole frozen, unsweetened
½ cup sugar or honey
⅛ teaspoon salt
½ cup water, divided
1½ tablespoons cornstarch
1 tablespoon lemon juice

Place berries in a large saucepan with sugar, salt, and ¼ cup water. Bring to a boil, and cook three minutes. Mix cornstarch and remaining water together. Stir into berries and cook, stirring until thick. Add lemon juice. This is also a good glaze for cheesecake, pound cake, or over ice cream.

Georgia Pecan Crust

If you can find pecan meal—finely ground pecans, at a store specializing in pecan products, it makes an excellent unbaked pie crust.

Yield: 1 9-inch pie

1¼ cups pecan meal
¼ cup sugar
¼ cup finely chopped pecans
   (optional)
¼ cup melted butter or
   margarine

Mix ingredients and press into the sides and bottom of a pie pan to form a shell. Chill until firm and use as you would a baked pie shell.

Ambrosia Tarts

This recipe features a cooked, coconut-topped meringue which you may also wish to use with other fruit recipes.

Yield: 6 tarts

¾ cup sugar
¼ cup cornstarch
¼ teaspoon salt
1¼ cups cold water
½ cup orange juice
2 tablespoons lemon juice
1 tablespoon grated orange peel
1 teaspoon grated lemon peel
2 eggs, separated
1 teaspoon vanilla extract (optional)
6 individual-serving baked pastry shells for tarts

Meringue:
½ cup sugar
½ teaspoon salt
2 tablespoons water
1 cup orange slices
1 cup grated coconut

Combine sugar, cornstarch, and salt in saucepan or top of double boiler. Gradually add water, stirring constantly. Cook over boiling water in double boiler or over medium heat, stirring constantly, until thick and clear and thoroughly cooked, about 10 minutes. Add fruit juices and peel and cook 2 minutes more. Slowly add a little of this mixture to beaten egg yolks, and then stir back into custard mixture. Cook until thick. Add vanilla and cool. Pour into tart shells. Top with Meringue.

Note: Strawberries or other fruits may also be used for baked tarts!

To make meringue, combine the two unbeaten egg whites from Ambrosia recipe with sugar, salt, and water in the top of a double boiler. Beat until well blended. Cook one minute over boiling water, beating all the time. Remove from hot water. Beat two minutes longer, or until mixture stands in peaks. Pile meringue on tarts, and arrange orange slices over top. Sprinkle with coconut.

Note: If making your own tart shells, try adding 1 tablespoon concentrated orange juice along with the ice water and/or 1 teaspoon grated orange or lemon rind, for more flavor. This is true of all fruit pies.

Mandarin oranges may be used here, well drained, as garnish, with the juice used in recipe both where it calls for orange juice, and as part of the cold water in making tarts. Tangerine slices in season are also attractive. Freshly-grated coconut is good here, but the packaged sweetened kind may also be used.

—Helena Crutcher DeBolt

Treutlen Egg Crust

*Yield: 3 single 8- or 9-inch
  pie shells*

*1¼ cups vegetable
  shortening
3⅓ cups flour
1 teaspoon salt
1 chilled egg, well-beaten
5 tablespoons ice water
1 tablespoon vinegar or
  lemon juice*

Cut shortening into flour and salt in a large mixing bowl until coarse, like crumbs. Combine egg, water, and vinegar or lemon juice. Pour into center of flour mixture. Mix until moist and well-blended. Set aside, covered, to chill well before rolling out. Divide into 3 parts, and keep the rest of the pastry chilled while you begin rolling out dough.

For baked pie shells, bake in a preheated 425 degrees F. oven until nicely browned, about 12 minutes.

Golden Crust: For beautiful, golden brown crusts, brush unbaked pastry lightly with cream, melted butter or margarine, beaten egg, or undiluted evaporated milk before baking.

Light Crust: One cook we know adds about ⅛ teaspoon baking powder per cup of flour, in making pie pastry.

Sweeter Crust: Add 1 teaspoon sugar per cup of flour.

Water Hint: Always add water slowly in making pie crust, and use only what is needed. Too much liquid makes a tough, soggy pastry that will shrink as it bakes.

Rolling Pastry: Pastry is easiest to work with if well-chilled, and rolled out on a well-floured surface, or between 2 pieces of waxed or kitchen parchment paper.

No-Roll Pie Crust

Some cooks feel this is an easier pie crust to make, though the crust may be a little thicker and less uniform.

Yield: 1 9-inch pie shell

*1½ cups flour
⅛ teaspoon salt
¾ teaspoon sugar
½ cup vegetable oil
2 tablespoons cold milk*

Mix dry ingredients together in a mixing bowl. Mix oil and milk together and pour in a well in center of flour mixture. Mix with fork until well-moistened. Dump into pie pan and press with fingers to line bottom and sides of pan. Crimp top edges.

Cookies

Spicy Apple-Oatmeal Bars

Yield: 36 1½-inch squares

¾ cup sifted flour
¾ teaspoon baking powder
½ teaspoon baking soda
½ teaspoon salt
1 tablespoon cocoa
1 teaspoon cinnamon
½ teaspoon ground nutmeg
¼ teaspoon ground cloves
⅓ cup vegetable shortening
¾ cup sugar
2 eggs
1 cup raw rolled oats
1½ cups peeled, diced raw
  apples
1 tablespoon lemon juice
½ cup chopped pecans or
  walnuts
Confectioners' sugar as
  needed

Preheat oven to 375 degrees F. Grease and flour a 9-by-9-inch pan. Sift dry ingredients. Set aside. Cream shortening with sugar and add eggs, well-beaten. Stir in dry ingredients and mix well. Mix in oats, apples tossed with lemon juice, and nuts; blend well. Bake for 25 minutes, or until top springs back when touched lightly in the middle. Sprinkle with confectioners' sugar. Cool on wire rack and cut into squares.

—Claire Lowell Crosby

Sugar Cookies

One cup butter, 2 cups sugar, 2 eggs, 1 cup milk, teaspoon of soda, and flour enough to form a dough; nutmeg. Roll, and cut into cakes. Bake a light brown.

—Bryan family cookbook, Savannah, circa 1885

Benne Seed Tarts

Yield: about 3 dozen

2 cups flour
¼ teaspoon salt
½ teaspoon nutmeg or mace
*1 cup (2 sticks) butter, at
    room temperature*
¼ cup sugar
1 teaspoon vanilla extract
⅔ cup benne (sesame) seeds
Jam or jelly as needed

Preheat oven to 350 degrees F. Sift together flour, salt, and nutmeg; set aside. Cream butter and sugar together. Beat in vanilla. Work dry material into this mixture, blending well. Roll about a tablespoon of dough into a ball and roll it in a saucer of benne seed. Press down on ungreased cookie sheet. Make an indentation with your thumb in the middle of each cookie. Fill this with jam or jelly, any flavor, or mix them for more color on the plate. Bake for 10 to 12 minutes. Cool on racks and store in airtight container.

Note: This dough has more flavor than most tarts because of the spice. You may wish to vary it with more spice, or almond extract to taste, in place of the vanilla.

—Claire Lowell Crosby

Chocolate-Pistachio Cookies

Yield: about 6 dozen

2 cups sifted flour
1½ teaspoons baking powder
½ teaspoon salt
*⅔ cup butter, at room
    temperature*
1 cup sugar
1 egg
1 teaspoon vanilla extract
½ teaspoon almond extract
*1 cup finely chopped
    pistachio nuts or almonds,
    divided*
*Green food coloring
    (optional)*
*1 6-ounce package chocolate
    chips, melted*

Sift flour with baking powder and salt and set aside. In a large bowl, beat butter, sugar, egg, and extracts until fluffy. Slowly add flour mixture. Take out ¾ cup of the batter, and combine with ¼ cup chopped nuts and 2 or 3 drops green food color, if desired. Mix well. Fold into two long, thin rolls. Wrap in plastic and refrigerate.

Form remaining dough into two rectangles. Unwrap first rolls from refrigerator and place on top of these. Roll lengthwise and wrap. Refrigerate 8 hours, or freeze.

Preheat oven to 375 degrees F. Cut dough with a sharp knife into slices ⅛- to ¼-inch wide. Place on ungreased cookie sheets and bake 8 to 10 minutes. When cool, roll edges first in melted chocolate chips and then in remaining nuts. Let set well before serving or storing. Store in airtight box in cool place.

—Helen Glenn

Chocolate Surprise Bars

Yield: about 4 dozen

First layer:
½ cup (1 stick) butter, at
   room temperature
1 egg yolk
2 tablespoons water
1¼ cups flour
1 teaspoon sugar
1 teaspoon baking powder
⅛ teaspoon salt

Second layer:
1 12-ounce package
   chocolate chips

Last layer:
2 eggs
¾ cup sugar
6 tablespoons melted butter
2 cups finely chopped pecans
   or walnuts
1¼ teaspoons vanilla extract
Confectioners' sugar
   (optional)

Preheat oven to 350 degrees F., and grease a 13-by-9-by-2-inch pan. Cream ½ cup butter and beat in egg yolk and water. Mix well. Sift in dry ingredients; mix well. Press mixture into baking pan and bake about 10 minutes.

Remove pan from oven and sprinkle chips evenly over dough. Return pan to oven for about 2 minutes, or until chips melt. Take from oven and spread chocolate evenly over crust.

While the first layer is baking, beat 2 eggs thick in the same mixing bowl you used for the first layer. Beat in sugar and blend well. Stir in butter, nuts, and extract. Mix well and pour evenly over chocolate layer.

Return pan to oven and bake about 30 to 35 minutes more, or until a light golden brown, and dough springs back when touched lightly in the center with the fingers. Cool on a rack and cut into bars. Sprinkle with confectioners' sugar if desired.

—Helen Glenn

Mrs. Scott's Brownies

1 cup sugar, ¼ cup butter, 1 egg, 2 squares melted baking chocolate, 1½ cups flour, ¼ teaspoon salt, 1 teaspoon baking powder, ⅓ cup milk, ½ cup walnut meats, 1 teaspoon vanilla. Mix well, and bake in a greased pan [at 350 degrees F. for about 25 minutes]. Cut in squares, and remove from pan immediately.

—Recipe collection of Mary Howell Scott, Milledgeville, circa 1918

The historic Eagle Tavern in Watkinsville dates to 1787, when the oldest part was supposedly built as a block house against Indian attack. It was later a stagecoach and wagon stop, tavern, and hotel. Restored in 1965, it is now owned by Oconee County, and operated as a Georgia Welcome Center and Museum by the Georgia Department of Industry and Trade and the Oconee County Commissioners.

Forgotten Cookies

These easy meringues bake while you sleep!

Yield: about 3 dozen

3 egg whites
¾ cup sugar
1 cup finely chopped pecans
1 6-ounce package chocolate chips (or other flavor)

Preheat oven to 350 degrees F. Beat egg whites stiff. Add sugar and continue beating until very stiff. Fold in pecans and chips. Cover cookie sheet with waxed or baking paper and drop dough by spoonfuls on cookie sheet. Place in oven and turn heat off immediately. Leave overnight, without opening door. Store in airtight containers.

—Clarice Ashmore

Peanut Butter-Chocolate Refrigerator Cookies

Yield: about 4 dozen

¾ cup vegetable shortening
½ cup sugar
½ cup light brown sugar
1 egg
1 cup crunchy peanut butter
3 cups flour
¼ teaspoon baking soda
⅓ cup cocoa
1 teaspoon vanilla extract

Cream shortening and stir in sugars. Beat well. Beat in egg and peanut butter. Sift dry ingredients into batter and mix well. Stir in vanilla. Shape mixture into two rolls, about 2 inches in diameter. Wrap and chill, overnight if desired.

Preheat oven to 350 degrees F. Cut cookie dough into thin (about ⅛ inch) slices. Bake on cookie sheets for 10 to 12 minutes. Cool on rack and store in airtight containers in a cool place.

—Georgia Peanut Commission

Mrs. Meldrim's Chocolate Nut Cakes

½ cup butter; 1 cup sugar; 2 eggs; 2 squares of baking chocolate, melted; 1 cup chopped walnuts or pecans; ¼ teaspoon salt; ¼ teaspoon vanilla; ⅔ cup flour.

Cream butter, and then beat in sugar, eggs, (well-beaten), melted chocolate, nuts, salt, vanilla, and flour. Drop from a spoon on [greased] paper, one inch apart. Bake in a moderate oven [350 degrees F. for 12 minutes, or until golden].

—Family cookbook of Sophie Meldrim Shonnard, Savannah

Coconut Refrigerator Cookies

Yield: about 5 dozen

1 cup (2 sticks) butter or
* margarine, at room*
* temperature*
¾ cup sugar
1 teaspoon vanilla extract
2 cups sifted self-rising flour
1½ cups freshly grated or
* semi-sweet shredded*
* coconut*

Cream butter and sugar until light; add vanilla. Blend flour and coconut well into butter mixture. Shape dough into a roll about two inches in diameter. Wrap and chill, at least overnight.

Preheat oven to 325 degrees F. and lightly grease cookie sheets. Slice dough into ¼-inch slices. Bake for about 20 minutes, or until very lightly browned. Cool on racks and store in airtight containers in a cool place. These are excellent to make ahead and have fresh with fruit for a luncheon.

Mrs. Berrien's Filled Cookies

A very old recipe.

Yield: about 36

¾ *cup sugar*
½ *cup (1 stick) butter,*
   margarine or vegetable
   shortening or mix them
1 egg
½ *cup milk*
3½ *cups flour*
1 teaspoon baking soda
2 teaspoons baking powder
½ *teaspoon salt*
1 teaspoon vanilla extract

Filling:
1 tablespoon flour
½ *cup brown sugar*
1 tablespoon lemon juice
½ *cup water*
½ *cup finely chopped pecans*
1 cup chopped raisins, or
   half raisins and half
   currants

Cream sugar and butter together in a large bowl until fluffy. Beat in egg and mix well. Add milk and mix well. Sift in dry ingredients and mix well. Stir in vanilla and mix well. Chill dough, covered, in refrigerator or freezer.

Mix flour and brown sugar together in a small saucepan. Add lemon juice, and then water very gradually, stirring to make a paste. Add pecans and raisins, stirring well. Cook over medium heat, stirring, until thick. Remove from heat and cool.

Preheat oven to 375 degrees F. Grease and flour cookie tins. Roll cookie dough on floured surface rather thinly, about ¼-inch thick. Cut with floured round cookie tin, and place on cookie sheet. Place a tablespoon of the filling on each cookie, with a second cookie on top. Press edges together as you would a pie crust. Continue until all the filling is used. If any cookies are left over, bake them plain, with a little sugar on top and a raisin in the center. Bake cookies about 15 minutes, or until nicely browned. Cool on racks, and store covered in very cool place.

Note: If you should have any filling left over, combine with mincemeat filling in a pie.

The filling could be made one day, and the cookies made the next, if convenient.

Noel Gingerbread Cookies

A stiff batter cookie, ideal for holiday decorations.

Yield: about 6 dozen,
depending on shapes

1 cup vegetable shortening,
butter, or margarine
1 cup brown sugar
1 cup molasses
1 egg, well-beaten
1 teaspoon baking soda
½ cup warm water
5 cups sifted flour
½ teaspoon ground cloves
1 teaspoon ground cinnamon
1 teaspoon ground ginger
½ teaspoon salt

Cream shortening and blend in sugar, beating well. Add molasses and egg, and beat well. Combine soda with warm water and stir in. Sift in dry ingredients and blend well. Chill dough, covered, for at least two hours, or overnight.

Preheat oven to 325 to 350 degrees F. Grease cookie sheets. Roll out dough on floured board rather thinly, about ¼-inch thick. Cut as desired with floured cutters. Bake for about 15 minutes, depending on size of cookies; do not get too brown. Cool on rack before decorating.

Note: If you don't want to ice the cookies, decorate with raisins or currants, or decorative candies available in the gourmet or baking section of the supermarket.

Decorative Icing

1 pound box confectioners'
sugar
½ teaspoon cream of tartar
3 egg whites
1 teaspoon vanilla extract
Food coloring as desired

Combine ingredients, beating together until stiff but of spreading consistency. Divide into small quantities and add food coloring for desired colors. Store in containers with tight-fitting lids when not in use and store in refrigerator. Add a little more water if icing is too thick.

Turning Cookie Pans

If your oven browns cookies unevenly, hotter in one part of the oven than another, it helps to set your kitchen timer, and turn the pans around in the oven, halfway through the baking process. Or, line pans with greased aluminum foil for easier clean-up and better baking.

Ginger Snap Cookies

Finely chopped, crystalized ginger gives these cookies an unforgettable flavor:

Yield: 3½ to 4 dozen

2 cups flour
1 teaspoon baking soda
1 teaspoon cinnamon
1 teaspoon ground cloves
1 teaspoon ground ginger
¾ cup (1½ sticks) butter or margarine, at room temperature
1 cup sugar
1 egg
¼ cup molasses
1½ tablespoons finely chopped crystalized ginger
1 cup raisins or dried black currants
¾ to 1 cup finely chopped pecans or walnuts, (optional)
A little extra sugar

Preheat oven to 350 degrees F. Sift flour, soda, cinnamon, cloves, and 1 teaspoon ginger together; set aside. Cream butter and sugar together until light and fluffy. Beat in egg and molasses. Fold sifted dry ingredients into sugar mixture. Fold in chopped ginger, raisins or currants, and nuts if desired.

Take about 1 teaspoon dough and roll into a ball; place in a flat plate of sugar, to coat; then, mashing down a bit, about 1 inch apart, on greased or non-stick cookie sheet.

Bake for about 15 to 16 minutes; do not let them get too brown. (You will want to time the first panful, as oven temperatures vary.) Cool on racks. Store in an airtight container, in a cool, dry place.

—Claire Lowell Crosby

Salzburger Ginger Snaps

1 cup molasses or Georgia corn syrup; 2 tablespoons butter or hogs' lard; 1 tablespoon ginger; 1 teaspoon baking soda; plain flour, as much as needed to make a good dough. Boil the molasses and stir in the butter, ginger and soda while it is hot. Add flour, and roll out very thin on floured surface. Cut with a cookie cutter, and bake, at 375 degrees F. in a hot oven until light brown.

—Mrs. Ann Shearouse and Mrs. Ruth Seckinger,
Ye Olde Time Salzburger Cook Book, Savannah

Molasses Hint

To substitute molasses for sugar in a recipe, use 1⅓ cups molasses instead of one cup sugar, and reduce other liquid called for in the recipe by ⅓ cup.

The 1818 Wayne-Gordon House in Savannah, where Juliette Gordon was born in 1860, is now the Juliette Gordon Low Girl Scout National Center. Mrs. Low founded the Girl Scouts of America in Savannah in 1912. Drawing by her great-niece, Peggy Dockery

Confederate Jumbles

Also called "Jeff Davis Jumbles" in some Southern family cookbooks.

Two pounds flour, one pound butter, one pound sugar, five eggs, two ounces ginger (or one teaspoon ginger, one of nutmeg, and the rind and juice of a lemon). Mix well, and roll as thin as possible; cut like a doughnut with a hole in the middle. Bake on sheets quickly, (about eight minutes), in a hot oven (375 degrees F.).

—*Centennial Receipt Book,* Juliette Gordon Low,
Hostess and Homemaker, Girl Scouts, Savannah
featuring Gordon family recipes

Emma's Lace Cookies

Yield: about 50

½ cup (1 stick) butter or margarine, at room temperature
½ cup light brown sugar
½ cup sugar
1 egg
½ cup sifted flour
1 cup very finely chopped pecans

Preheat oven to 350 degrees F. Cream butter and sugars together until light and fluffy. Beat egg in well. Fold in flour and pecans. (Pecans may be chopped in a blender or food processor.) Drop by teaspoons on aluminum foil on cookie sheet. Do not grease foil. Bake for 8 to 10 minutes. Remove from foil and cool on racks. Store in airtight container.

—Emma R. Law

Eatonton Lemon Ice Cookies

Yield: about 4 dozen

4 cups sifted flour
2 teaspoons baking powder
½ teaspoon salt
½ teaspoon ground nutmeg
1 cup vegetable shortening
2 cups sugar
2 eggs
2 tablespoons lemon juice
1 tablespoon grated lemon peel

Sift dry ingredients together; set aside. Cream shortening and sugar together until fluffy. Add eggs and beat well. Add lemon juice and peel. Stir in dry ingredients and mix well. Form into two or three rolls, about 1½-inches in diameter. Cover and refrigerate overnight, or freeze for later use.

Preheat oven to 350 degrees F. Grease cookie pans. Slice cookies about ¼-inch thick and bake until golden brown, about 10-12 minutes. Cool on rack, and store in air-tight containers.

Note: This recipe may be varied with orange or lime flavor instead of lemon.

—Mrs. Floyd M. Allen

Emma's Decorative Icing

A good recipe from a professional cook.

Yield: about ½ cup

1¼ cups sifted confectioners' sugar
¼ teaspoon cream of tartar
1 unbeaten egg white
¼ teaspoon lemon extract

Sift sugar with cream of tartar. Stir gradually into egg white and extract. Beat until mixture holds soft peaks. Pipe onto cookies or cake with writing tip of pastry tube or as desired.

—Emma R. Law

Emma's Pecan Meringues

Yield: about 30

1 egg white
¾ cup light brown sugar
⅛ teaspoon salt
¼ teaspoon vanilla extract
1 cup ground pecans

Preheat oven to 300 degrees F. Grease cookie sheet. Beat egg white until stiff but not dry. Gradually beat in brown sugar. When mixture is quite stiff, fold in salt, extract, and pecans. Mix well. Drop by scant teaspoons onto cookie sheet. Bake for about 25 minutes. Cool on a rack and store in airtight container in a cool place.

Note: Unless you are using the packaged ground pecans, a blender or mouli grater is good to grind the pecans.

You can vary this recipe by using walnuts and rum extract in place of vanilla, or ground almonds and almond extract. If you need a lot of cookies, why not make up one batch of each?

—Emma R. Law

Pecan Shortbreads

Yield: about 24

4 tablespoons butter, at room
*   temperature*
2 tablespoons sugar
⅛ teaspoon salt
¼ teaspoon vanilla extarct
½ cup sifted flour
½ cup ground pecans

Cream butter and sugar together until light. Stir in salt and vanilla. Fold in flour and pecans, blending well. Shape into a roll about an inch in diameter. Chill.

Preheat oven to 325 degrees F. Slice cookies into ¼-inch slices with a sharp knife. Transfer to ungreased cookie sheet. Bake for about 20 minutes. Cool on racks and store in an airtight container.

Note: If you have one, a blender, food processor, or mouli grater is good for grinding the pecans, unless you buy the ground variety.

Recipe may be varied by using almond extract and ground almonds, or by using ground English walnuts.

—Emma R. Law

Praline Cookies

A traditional Georgia cookie.

Yield: about 3½ dozen

¾ cup brown sugar
¾ cup vegetable shortening
½ cup molasses
1 egg, beaten
2½ cups sifted flour
1½ teaspoons baking soda
1 teaspoon cinnamon
½ teaspoon ground ginger
½ teaspoon salt
1 teaspoon vanilla extract
1 cup finely chopped pecans

Cream brown sugar and shortening until light and fluffy. Add molasses and egg; beat well. Sift in dry ingredients; mix thoroughly. Stir in extract and nuts. Chill batter for about 2 hours.

Preheat oven to 350 degrees F. Grease cookie tins. Drop dough by small spoonfuls onto tins and bake for about 10 minutes. Cool on rack and store in airtight container.

Note: Some prefer to put a pecan half on each cookie as it is ready for baking instead of chopped nuts in the dough.

Wheat Germ-Date Cookies

A very wholesome cookie!

Yield: about 4 dozen

¾ cup shortening
1 cup brown sugar
2 eggs
1 cup wheat germ
1¼ cups flour
¾ teaspoon salt
½ teaspoon baking soda
1 teaspoon ground cinnamon
½ teaspoon ground cloves
¼ teaspoon ground nutmeg
¼ cup buttermilk
1 teaspoon vanilla extract
1 8-ounce package pitted
  dates, snipped
½ cup chopped pecans

Preheat oven to 350 degrees F. Grease baking sheets. Beat together shortening and brown sugar until fluffy. Beat in eggs and beat well. Mix wheat germ with sifted dry ingredients, and add to batter alternately with buttermilk and vanilla, beating well after each addition. Stir in dates and pecans.

Drop by teaspoons onto greased baking sheets. Bake for about 10 to 12 minutes, or until light brown. Remove from baking sheet and cool on racks. Store in air-tight container in a cool place.

Columbus Pumpkin Squares

Yield: about 4 dozen

Bottom layer:
1 cup sifted flour
½ cup dry rolled oats
½ cup brown sugar
½ cup (1 stick) butter

Filling:
1 16-ounce can pumpkin
(2 cups strained cooked
pumpkin)
1 13-ounce can evaporated
milk
2 eggs
¾ cup sugar
½ teaspoon salt
1 teaspoon pumpkin pie
spice
(or mixed cinnamon,
nutmeg and ground ginger)
1 teaspoon vanilla extract

Topping:
½ cup chopped pecans
½ cup brown sugar
Dash nutmeg
2 tablespoons butter or
margarine

Preheat oven to 350 degrees F. Grease a 9-by-13-by-2-inch pan. Combine bottom layer ingredients in a mixing bowl. Mix until crumbly, using an electric mixer on low speed or food processor, or by hand, until well mixed. Press into pan, and bake for 15 minutes.

Combine filling ingredients in mixing bowl, beating well. Pour into pan over bottom layer and bake for 20 more minutes.

Combine topping ingredients. At the end of the 20 minute baking time, remove pan from oven and sprinkle nut mixture over filling. Return to oven and bake 20 minutes longer, or until filling is set. Cool in pan. Cut into squares and serve with whipped cream. Refrigerate leftovers, covered.

—Darla Sparks

A Butter Idea

When you use the last of the butter or margarine in baking cookies, there will probably still be enough left on its waxed wrapper to grease your cookie tins!

Sand Tarts

Mrs. Torrey's grandson called this update of a very old recipe, "Santa Tarts."

Yield: about 6 dozen thin
  2½-inch cookies

½ cup (1 stick) butter, at
  room temperature
1 cup sugar
1 egg, beaten
1¾ cups flour
⅛ teaspoon salt
2 teaspoons baking powder
1 egg white for the top
Cinnamon to taste
Sugar to taste
Almond halves (optional)

Cream butter and sugar. Add egg, beaten with a fork, and mix well. Sift flour, salt, and baking powder together and add to mixture. If it is difficult to mix dough with a spoon, use your hands. Chill at least overnight.

Roll out as thinly as possible on a floured surface, with more flour on the rolling pin, and on the dough as desired. Take only a small amount of dough to work with from the refrigerator at a time, keeping the rest chilled.

Preheat oven to 325 degrees F. Cut out cookies as desired and place on ungreased cookie sheets. Decorate with the whipped froth of an egg white, beaten with a fork, and then mixed with cinnamon and sugar, and spread on the cookies. Top with almond halves. Bake until lightly browned, about 10 minutes. Watch that they do not get too brown. Remove from pans immediately. Store in a cool place.

—Helen Baker Torrey

Santa's Gumdrop Cookies

Yield: about 36

1 cup butter or margarine, at
  room temperature
1 teaspoon vanilla
½ cup brown sugar, packed
½ cup sugar
1 egg
2½ cups sifted flour
¾ teaspoon cream of tartar
¾ teaspoon salt
1 tablespoon grated orange
  rind
½ cup chopped gumdrops

Preheat oven to 375 degrees F. Blend softened butter, vanilla and sugars until fluffy. Add egg and beat well. Add sifted dry ingredients, rind and gumdrops. Mix well. Drop by teaspoons on greased cookie sheets about 2 inches apart. Bake 10 to 12 minutes, or until light brown. These are pretty and somewhat different.

Snowflake Cookies

A delicate, pretty cookie to decorate as desired.

Yield: 4 dozen

⅓ cup butter, margarine, or
vegetable shortening
½ cup sugar
1 egg
½ teaspoon lemon or vanilla
extract
1¼ cups flour
½ teaspoon baking powder
½ teaspoon salt

Blend butter or shortening well with sugar in a large bowl until fluffy. Stir in egg and lemon or vanilla extract; beat well. Sift in dry ingredients, and blend well. Chill, covered.

Preheat oven to 400 degrees F. Roll cookies about ⅛-inch thick, on a floured surface, and cut as desired, with floured cutters. Keep dough chilled, working with a little at a time for easier handling. Bake on ungreased tins for 6 to 8 minutes, or until very light brown; do not overbake. Cool on racks and decorate with Shiny Glaze.

Shiny Glaze

3 cups confectioners' sugar
4 teaspoons light corn syrup
¼ cup hot water
⅛ teaspoon salt
½ teaspoon lemon or vanilla
extract
Food coloring if desired

Mix ingredients until smooth and shiny. Pour ½ to 1 teaspoon on each cookie, and decorate while glaze is still warm, before it dries. Colored decorative candies are very good here. You may wish to stack some cookies sandwich-style, and decorate, for a different effect.

—Gladys Ballard Wayt

Holiday Snowballs

Yield: about 6 dozen

1½ cups (3 sticks) butter or
margarine, at room
temperature
1 cup confectioners' sugar
¼ teaspoon salt
3½ cups flour
1 cup finely chopped pecans
1 teaspoon vanilla extract
Confectioners' sugar for
coating

Preheat oven to 325 degrees F. Grease cookie tins. Cream butter or margarine and sugar together. Add salt to flour and then fold flour into creamed mixture gradually, beating well. Stir in nuts and vanilla, mixing well. Shape into small balls. Place on cookie sheets and bake for about 15 minutes. Shake warm cookies in a bag of confectioners' sugar. Cool on racks and store in airtight containers in a cool place.

—Wanda Dugger

One-Minute Chocolate Frosting

Yield: about 2 cups

2 cups sugar
½ cup milk
½ cup (1 stick) butter
½ cup cocoa
1 teaspoon vanilla extract

Mix first four ingredients in a small saucepan. Boil one minute, stirring constantly. Remove from heat and stir in vanilla. Cool and beat until creamy and of spreading consistency.

—Gladys Ballard Wayt

Mocha Cream Frosting

Yield: about ½ cup

2 tablespoons butter
1 teaspoon instant coffee, or to taste
½ teaspoon ground cinnamon
⅛ teaspoon salt
1 tablespoon milk
1 cup confectioners' sugar

Melt butter. Dissolve coffee, cinnamon, and salt in milk, and then add to butter. Beat well, beating in confectioners' sugar to desired consistency.

Tipsy Frosting

Yield: about 1 cup

2 tablespoons butter
1 tablespoon coffee-flavored liqueur
2 teaspoons cream or milk
1⅓ cups sifted confectioners' sugar

Melt butter in a saucepan and stir in other ingredients. Beat smooth. Excellent for brownies.

Candy

Savannah Cream Caramels

Yield: about 3 pounds

2 cups sugar
½ cup (1 stick) butter or margarine
2 cups light corn syrup
¼ teaspoon salt
1 13-ounce can evaporated milk
1 teaspoon vanilla extract
1½ cups chopped walnuts or pecans

Grease a 9-by-13-inch pan. Combine the sugar, butter or margarine, syrup, and salt together in a heavy 2-quart saucepan. Stir until sugar is melted, over moderate heat, scraping down the sides of the pan often to be sure sugar is dissolved. When it comes to a boil, add very slowly, so as not to stop the boiling, the evaporated milk. Stir constantly with a wooden spoon and cook until it forms a very firm ball (see page 264) or 242 degrees F. on the candy thermometer.

Remove from heat and add vanilla and nuts. Pour into pan. When it cools a little, cut into strips, and then as desired with the kitchen scissors. Wrap in small pieces of waxed paper, and keep in a cool place, in an airtight container.

Chocolate Caramels

For chocolate caramels, add two ounces melted baking chocolate with first ingredients in the saucepan. May also be made without the nuts, in an 8-inch square pan.

Cranberry Caramels

Yield: about 4 pounds

1 pound cranberries (4 cups)
6 cups sugar
⅛ teaspoon salt
½ cup water
1 cup (2 sticks) butter, at
* room temperature*
2 cups heavy cream, at room
* temperature*

Coarsely grind cranberries directly into a large stainless steel or enamelware Dutch oven. (Use a large pan, as stirring room is badly needed in this recipe). Stir in sugar, salt, and water. Stir over medium heat, scraping down the sides of pan often to prevent a grainy texture from uncooked sugar. Cook, stirring often, until the mixture is at a little more than soft crack stage (see page 264) or about 270 degrees F. on the candy thermometer.

Stir in butter and cream slowly, in order not to stop mixture from boiling. Continue cooking over moderate heat, stirring almost constantly, especially at the end, until the thermometer comes back to 270 degrees F.

Remove from heat, let bubbling stop, and pour into a well-greased 13-by-9-by-2-inch pan. Let stand on a rack until almost hard. Then turn candy out on a wooden chopping block, and "saw" with a heavy knife into strips about 1 inch wide. Snip these into bite-size pieces with the kitchen shears, dipping shears in warm water frequently so they won't get too sticky. Wrap each piece in heavy waxed paper, twisting the ends. Store in airtight container in a cool place. If necessary to refrigerate, bring to room temperature before serving.

—Emma R. Law

Evelyn's Chocolate Caramels

Take one pound chocolate, and if not sweet, add to it two cups of sugar. Put in a kettle with two cups of molasses, and begin to cook. Meanwhile, rub well together two tablespoons of butter and two of flour with a cup of milk. Add half of this to the chocolate when it looks about half done, and when nearly done, add the rest. Boil until a little is crisp when dropped into cold water. It usually takes about an hour for this. Pour on a greased plate, and cut into little cakes.

—Bryan family cookbook, Savannah, circa 1885

Chocolate Bourbon Balls

A special favorite at holiday time.

Yield: about 3 dozen

2 sticks butter, at room temperature
1 pound confectioners' sugar
¼ cup bourbon
1½ to 2 cups finely chopped pecans
½ pound semi-sweet baking chocolate
1 inch (1 square) paraffin wax

Cream butter and sugar. Add bourbon. Blend in nuts. Place in freezer for at least 20 minutes to chill. Then roll dough into balls and return to refrigerator for 20 minutes more. Heat chocolate and wax in a double boiler over hot water. When melted, dip balls in chocolate. Set balls on waxed paper, not touching, to dry. Store, covered, in a cool place.

—Debra Rogalski

Chocolate-Coconut Clusters

Yield: about 3 dozen

1 12-ounce package chocolate chips
2 cups finely grated coconut
1 cup finely chopped pecans

Melt chips over low heat, stirring constantly, or over hot water in a double boiler. Stir in coconut and nuts. Drop on waxed paper by teaspoons. Chill. Store covered in a cool place.

Note: For variety, top clusters with pecan halves, or use butterscotch chips instead of chocolate.

Plain Chocolate Fudge

Boil together 3 cups light brown sugar, ¼ pound baking chocolate, and 1 cup cream or evaporated milk, until it forms a soft ball when dropped into cold water. Add 1 tablespoon butter. Take from the fire, and add one teaspoon vanilla. Beat until thick and creamy, and pour into a [greased] pan or drop from spoon onto waxed paper.

For nut fudge, add pecans or toasted almonds or any nuts desired, along with vanilla.

—Family cookbook of Sophie Shonnard, Savannah

Fudge in a Hurry

A simple recipe, requiring no testing or thermometers.

Yield: 2 dozen pieces

1 pound confectioners' sugar
½ cup cocoa
¼ teaspoon salt
6 tablespoons butter or
  margarine
4 tablespoons milk
1 teaspoon vanilla extract
1 cup chopped pecans

Combine first five ingredients in the top of a double boiler or heavy pan over medium heat, stirring constantly. Place over hot water and stir until smooth. Remove from heat and stir in vanilla and nuts. Spread in greased 9-by-5-inch baking pan. Cool and cut into squares. Store in covered container in cool place.

Chocolate-Covered Peanuts

Yield: about 1 pound

1 6-ounce package semi-
  sweet chocolate chips
2½ cups roasted shelled
  peanuts

Melt chocolate pieces in top of double boiler over hot (not boiling) water. Add peanuts to melted chocolate and coat well. Turn out on waxed paper or a greased surface, spreading so that peanuts are separated as much as possible. Cool and cut as desired. Store covered in a cool place.

—Georgia Peanut Commission

Peanut-Mallow Fudge

An easy recipe for young cooks.

Yield: 64 1-inch pieces

1 12-ounce package semi-
  sweet chocolate or
  butterscotch chips
¾ cup peanut butter,
  chunky-style
3 cups miniature
  marshmallows

Melt chocolate over low heat or hot water in double boiler, stirring in peanut butter until well-blended. Cool slightly and fold in marshmallows. Press into a greased 8-inch pan. Chill until firm and cut into squares. Store in an airtight container in a cool place.

Drawing by Georgia artist Barry Champion

Welsh Candy

Mix 2 pounds brown sugar with ½ pound butter and nearly ½ pint water. Put in a small kettle, and let it boil about 20 minutes. Do not stir it while it is cooking. To tell when it is done, put a little in a tumbler of cold water. If it is brittle enough to snap between your teeth, take it off and add some lemon juice and peeled grated nutmeg for seasonings. Pour into a [greased] pan to cool.

—Bryan family cookbook, Savannah, circa 1885

Emma's Sour Cream Fudge

Yield: nearly 2 pounds

1½ cups sugar
1½ cups light brown sugar, firmly packed
1 cup sour cream, at room temperature
6 tablespoons butter
1½ teaspoons vanilla extract
1½ cups chopped pecans or walnuts

Mix sugars and cream into a 3-quart saucepan and cook and stir gently until sugar dissolves. Add butter. Cover and cook over very low heat for about 3 minutes. (This will dissolve any crystals on the side of the pot, and help prevent "grainy" fudge). Remove cover and boil gently to soft ball stage (see Candy Stages, page 264) or 234 to 240 degrees F. on a candy thermometer. Stir very gently to keep from burning toward the end of cooking time.

Remove to a rack and cool until pan can be comfortably held in palm of hand. (Lukewarm, or below 150 degrees F. on the candy thermometer). Add vanilla and beat until mixture turns creamy and thick. Stir in pecans.

Pour into a greased 9-inch square pan. (To prevent graining, do not scrape saucepan.) Set aside until firm. Cut into squares and store in airtight container.

—Emma R. Law

Mocha-Nut Fudge

Yield: 36 1¼-inch pieces

½ cup very strong coffee
3 cups sugar
2 tablespoons light corn syrup
1 cup light cream or evaporated milk
¼ teaspoon cream of tartar
3 tablespoons butter or margarine
1 teaspoon vanilla extract
1 cup chopped pecans

Grease an 8-inch square baking dish. In a heavy 2-quart saucepan, combine coffee, sugar, syrup, cream, and cream of tartar. Stir over medium heat until sugar is dissolved and mixture comes to a boil. Boil without stirring until soft ball stage (page 264) or 238 degrees F. on candy thermometer.

Remove from heat, and for faster cooling set saucepan on a trivet. Add butter and vanilla, but do not stir. Cool until lukewarm, or 110 degrees F.

Beat with a wooden spoon until mixture begins to lose its glossy appearance. Beat in nuts. Pour into prepared pan and cool completely. For easier cutting, refrigerate pan, covered, before cutting candy into squares. Store covered in a cool place.

Surprise Mints

An easy, non-cooking fondant, with several variations.

Yield: about 1 pound

1 egg white
1 tablespoon water
⅛ teaspoon almond extract
1 teaspoon vanilla extract
¼ teaspoon salt
1 pound sifted confectioners' sugar, divided
2 tablespoons butter or margarine, melted
Food coloring (optional)

Combine egg white, water, extracts, and salt in a large bowl. Stir in half the sugar and mix well. Add melted butter, and several drops food coloring if desired. Blend well. Add remaining sugar, and food coloring as desired. Mix well. Shape as desired.

Peppermint: Following the basic recipe, substitute 1 teaspoon peppermint or wintergreen flavoring for the vanilla. Tint with green food coloring.

Chocolate mints: Add about ¼ cup cocoa to sugar when sifting.

Mints may also be rolled in flaked coconut, finely chopped nuts, or grated chocolate. Store in aluminum foil in the refrigerator.

—Claire Lowell Crosby

Eggnog Fudge

Yield: about 1½ pounds

4 cups sugar
1 cup eggnog, canned or fresh
½ cup light corn syrup
½ cup butter or margarine
½ teaspoon salt
1 tablespoon brandy or 1 teaspoon vanilla: more to taste

In a heavy 3-quart saucepan, stir all ingredients except flavoring together. Stirring constantly, bring to boil over medium heat. Cook without stirring to 238 degrees F. on candy thermometer, or to soft ball stage (page 264.) Remove from heat; add flavoring. Do not stir. Cool to lukewarm (110 degrees F.) Beat with a wooden spoon for about 8 minutes, or until mixture is creamy and begins to lose its gloss. Turn into a prepared buttered pan. Cool; cut into squares. Store covered in a cool place.

Benne Divinity

An original recipe using the South's favorite benne seeds.

Yield: about 1¾ pounds

2½ cups sugar
½ cup white corn syrup
½ cup water
⅛ teaspoon salt
3 egg whites, whipped until stiff but not dry
1 teaspoon almond extract
1 cup toasted benne seed (see page 10)

Simmer sugar, syrup, water and salt over moderate heat, without stirring, to 275 degrees F. on the candy thermometer, or until syrup is at soft crack stage when a bit of it is dropped into very cold water (see page 264).

Remove from heat. When it no longer bubbles, start beating it gradually into the whipped egg whites. Whip mixture until it begins to hold a shape. Fold in almond extract and benne seed.

Pour onto a lightly greased 9-by-9-by-1-inch layer pan. When cool and set, cut into squares. Remove from pan, turn over, and let them dry on the bottom, so they will not be sticky. (Or, drop by teaspoons onto a lightly greased marble slab or large platter, and allow to cool). Store in airtight container.

—Louise Helmey

If you want a bit of chocolate flavor, drizzle or brush 1-ounce melted and cooled semi-sweet baking chocolate over divinity or fudge in the pan, before cutting. This is true of many candy recipes.

Divinity

2½ cups sugar (granulated); ¼ cup water; ¼ cup light corn syrup; 1 teaspoon vanilla; 2 egg whites, stiffly beaten; ½ pound white raisins; ¼ pound candied cherries or any variety nuts and fruit.

Boil the sugar, water, and syrup together until it spins a thread when dropped into a little cold water. Add vanilla, and pour candy into stiffly beaten whites of the eggs, beating constantly. Add the fruit, and beat until thick and creamy. Drop on waxed paper, or pour into [greased] pan.

—Family cookbook of Sophie Meldrim Shonnard, Savannah

Richmond Marshmallows

Easy to make, and as good as the commercial kind!

Yield: 3 dozen
1-inch squares

2 cups sugar
3 envelopes unflavored
  gelatin
⅛ teaspoon salt
1 cup water
1 teaspoon vanilla extract
Confectioners' sugar as
  needed

In a heavy 2-quart saucepan, combine sugar, gelatin, and salt. Stir in water, and heat until sugar is dissolved. Bring just to boiling, then remove from heat and cool slightly, about 5 minutes. Transfer the mixture to a large bowl, and stir in vanilla. Beat with electric mixer at high speed for 10 minutes, or until mixture resembles thick marshmallow cream.

Pour into greased 9-by-13-inch pan, that has been generously dusted with confectioners' sugar. Cut into squares with kitchen shears or a pizza cutter, and roll pieces in confectioners' sugar. Store covered in a cool place.

Coconut Variation: Candy may also be poured into a pan lined with a mixture of confectioners' sugar and finely grated coconut, and rolled in finely grated coconut after being cut into squares.

Mrs. Betty Hilton's Candied Grapefruit Rind

Take the rind, and scrape out all pithy matter, as well as any dark spots. Soak in cold water overnight. Cut in thin slices, and parboil through two waters, until it is tender. Take out and place in a sieve or on a piece of cheese cloth to drain well. Make a syrup of 1½ cups of sugar to ¼ cup of water for the rind of 2 grapefruit. Boil the rind in this until it absorbs nearly all the syrup. Have a dish ready with granulated sugar, and roll the slices in it one at a time, until each is covered.

—Family cookbook of Sophie Meldrim Shonnard, Savannah

Bull Street Pulled Mints

A very old recipe and favorite of yesterday's "candy parties."

Yield: about 4 dozen

2 cups sugar
4 tablespoons butter
1 cup water
¼ teaspoon salt
4 or 5 drops of oil of peppermint
Green food coloring if desired

Combine sugar, butter, water, and salt in heavy 2-quart saucepan. Stir over medium heat until sugar is dissolved. Bring to a boil and cook until candy registers 262 degrees F. on candy thermometer, or very hard ball stage (see page 264.)

Remove from heat and pour onto large greased platter, or a greased cold marble slab, if you have one. Do not scrape pan.

Cool until you can handle it (should still be quite warm). Drop on flavoring and color. Fold outer edges in as they cool, and pull and pull until light-colored and glossy. Stretch in a long rope, about ½ inch in diameter. Cut with kitchen scissors into 1-inch pieces. When cool, store in airtight tin box. Flavor will be better the next day, and they will be creamier.

Note: For red candy, use oil of spearmint rather than peppermint and red food coloring. If more than one color is desired, make recipes up twice, or half of it in each of two batches, as each batch must be pulled all at once and you can only make it one color.

Mable's Vanilla Taffy

Boil together ½ cup butter, 2 cups sugar, 1 cup good molasses until done, then stir in a teaspoon of vanilla. Cook over low heat, stirring frequently till sugar has dissolved. Increase heat until syrup forms a thread when dropped into very cold water (see page 264). Pour syrup onto a greased platter and cool slightly. As edges cool, fold them toward the center. When cool enough to handle, press it into a ball with lightly-greased fingers. Pull and stretch from 5 to 20 minutes, until candy turns light and holds a shape. Place on a board dusted with confectioners' sugar and cut into desired pieces. Wrap each piece separately.

—Bryan family cookbook, Savannah, circa 1885

Bull Street, Savannah. Scene from an 1855 print

Hampton Pound Candy

Tastes just like a certain famous candy!

Yield: about 3 pounds

*3 cups chopped pecans or
  walnuts, divided*
*1 pound butter or margarine
  (2 cups)*
2¼ cups sugar
1 tablespoon corn syrup
*1 6-ounce package milk
  chocolate chips*

Grease a jelly-roll pan. Sprinkle 2 cups of chopped nuts evenly over bottom of pan. Combine butter, sugar and syrup in a heavy 2-quart saucepan, stirring to keep from sticking, and cook to soft crack stage (see page 264) or 270 to 290 degrees F. on a candy thermometer. Pour over nuts.

Meanwhile, melt chips over hot water in the uncovered top of a double boiler or over very low heat. Top hot candy with melted chocolate. Sprinkle remaining cup of nuts on top. Cool and cut into squares. Store covered in a cool place.

—Anne Gordon

Buckhead Stuffed Dates

Easy to make, and a conversation piece!

Open each pitted date and stuff with one half of a marshmallow and one half a pecan. Press closed. Place in a shallow bowl of bourbon or rum to absorb flavor. Set on foil to dry slightly, then store in a covered tin in a cool place. Keeps well. Especially nice at the holiday season.

Marzipan

Mix one pound finely ground almonds with 1 pound of [confectioners'] sugar and two beaten egg whites. Flavor with 3 teaspoons rose water, and roll in cinnamon. [Work ingredients into a paste. If mixture becomes too thick, add lemon juice a drop at a time till it becomes manageable. If it becomes too oily, knead it in a dish over ice. Mold it into desired shapes. Wrap each piece separately.]

—Family cookbook of Sophie Meldrim Shonnard, Savannah

Plains Peanut Brittle

A favorite recipe from the first Georgian to become president of the United States.

Yield: 3 pounds

3 cups sugar
1½ cups water
1 cup light corn syrup
3 cups raw, unblanched
   peanuts
1 teaspoon baking soda
4 tablespoons butter
1 teaspoon vanilla extract

In a heavy 3-quart saucepan, stir together sugar, water, and corn syrup. Cook, stirring constantly, until mixture comes to a boil. Continue cooking until mixture reaches 232 degrees F. on a candy thermometer, or spins a two-inch thread when spoon is raised (see Candy Stages, page 264). Stir in peanuts; continue boiling, stirring occasionally, until mixture reaches 300 degrees F. or hard crack thread stage (see Candy Stages).

Remove from heat; stir in baking soda, butter, and vanilla. Quickly pour the candy into 2 15½-by-10½-by-1-inch greased jelly-roll pans. As mixture begins to harden, pull until thin. Break into pieces, and store in tightly-closed containers.

—Jimmy Carter

Rebel Pralines

Yet another version of an old Southern favorite!

Yield: about 18

2 cups sugar
1 cup buttermilk
1 teaspoon baking soda
2 tablespoons butter
1 teaspoon vanilla
1 cup pecan halves

Mix together in a heavy 2-quart saucepan sugar, buttermilk, and soda. Cook over medium heat, stirring as little as possible, until it reaches soft ball stage (page 264) or 236 degrees F. on the candy thermometer.

Remove from heat, and add butter, vanilla, and pecans. Beat with a wooden spoon until glossy. When it begins to harden on bottom of pan, spoon on greased foil in small patties. Cool and store covered in a cool place.

—Jack Eyler

Sherried Pecans

Yield: 2 cups

1½ cups light brown sugar
1 teaspoon light corn syrup
1 teaspoon cinnamon
½ cup sherry
¼ teaspoon salt
2 cups pecan or walnut
   halves

Combine all ingredients except nuts in a heavy 2-quart saucepan. Gently cook to soft ball stage (see page 264) or 236 degrees F. on the candy thermometer. Remove from heat and beat until mixture is ready to set. Add pecans and stir gently. Turn out on waxed paper or a greased, shallow pan. Separate at once, using two forks. Store covered in a cool place.

Garden City Apricot Balls

This wholesome candy requires no cooking and is versatile to make. It may also be made with other dried fruits.

Yield: 3 dozen

1 cup dried apricots
⅓ cup grated coconut,
   unsweetened if possible
¼ cup wheat germ
½ cup chopped almonds or
   other nuts
1 or 2 tablespoons honey
Extra coconut or nuts
   (optional)

Run apricots through food grinder once. Then mix with coconut, wheat germ, and almonds and run through grinder twice more. Mix with honey and shape by hand into balls the size of walnuts. Roll in extra coconut or finely chopped nuts as desired. These can also be made up into logs, and chilled and sliced.

Note: These may also be rolled in confectioners' sugar.

—Alma Halsford

Access to the Kitchen

We often hear excellent housekeepers remark that their failures were the cost of their triumphs. It is a mistaken economy to deny young girls access to the kitchen on account of the loss of material it incurs. It is not a high price to pay for the accumulated wisdom which renders its owner a blessing in the household ever afterwards.

—*House-Keeping in the Sunny South,* Atlanta, 1885

The 1840 Chapman-Green-Poe-Ragan House, Poplar Stret, Macon. Drawing by Sterling Everett

Peach Leather

Stew as many peaches as you choose, allowing a quarter of a pound of sugar to one of fruit; mash it up smooth as it cooks, and when it is dry enough to spread in a thin sheet on a board greased with butter, set it out in the sun to dry. When dry, it can be rolled up like leather, wrapped in a cloth, and will keep perfectly from season to season. School children regard it as a delightful addition to their lunch of biscuit or cold bread. Apple and quince leather are made in the same fashion, only a little spice or flavoring is added to them.

—*White House Cook-Book,* 1887

Strawberry Treats

The kids will love making these!

Yield: about 36

1 14- or 16-ounce package finely flaked sweetened coconut
2 6-ounce packages strawberry-flavored gelatin, divided
⅛ teaspoon almond extract, or to taste
Red food coloring as needed
1 14-ounce can Eagle Brand sweetened condensed milk
½ cup pecans or almonds, finely chopped

Combine coconut, 1 package gelatin, almond extract, and food coloring until all are well mixed. Add condensed milk and pecans. Mix very well.

Store overnight in the refrigerator in an air-tight container, to chill dough for easy handling. Next day, roll by small balls into strawberry shapes. Roll these in a mixture of gelatin and a little more food coloring. Store in refrigerator, covered.

Candy Stages

The art of making candy is far older than candy thermometers. For those who do not own the latter, and for help in deciphering recipes still written in this manner, the following chart is included.

Thread Stage (230 to 234 degrees F.); hot candy syrup spins a 2-inch thread when dropped from a fork or spoon into very cold water.

Soft Ball (234 to 240 degrees F.); syrup forms a soft ball when dropped into very cold water, which flattens on removal from water.

Firm Ball (244 to 248 degrees F.); syrup, when dropped into very cold water, forms a firm ball which does not flatten on removal from water.

Hard Ball (250 to 266 degrees F.); syrup forms a hard ball when dropped into very cold water, one which holds its shape and yet is plastic.

Soft Crack (270 to 290 degrees F.); syrup, when dropped into very cold water, separates into threads which are hard but not brittle.

Hard Crack (300 to 310 degrees F.); syrup, when dropped into very cold water, separates into threads which are brittle and hard.

Pickles and Relishes

In a Pickle

In pickling, do not use iodized table salt; it darkens pickles. Hollow pickles usually result from poorly developed cucumbers, holding cucumbers too long before pickling, too rapid fermentation, or too strong or too weak a brine solution.

ૐ

If you can, buy unwaxed cucumbers direct from the farmer for your pickling efforts, or raise your own.

ૐ

Although old pickle and relish recipes simply say to pour the boiled pickle mixture in hot sterile jars and seal, many economists now believe that all home-canned foods should be processed in a boiling-water bath in the canner after the jars are filled. If you choose to do this, you can still follow the old recipes as to amounts and methods of preparation, and then process to finish according to the directions with your canning equipment.

To Make Good Vinegar

Mix together 7½ gallons of rain water or boiled water, 3 quarts molasses, 3 quarts whiskey, and ¾ pint yeast. Put it all in a stout cask with thick brown paper over it. Nail a double piece of cloth over the bung, and sit it in the sun for 6 weeks.

—Cookbook of Mrs. Lucinda Williams, Milledgeville, 1857

Emma's Apple Chutney

Like many apartment dwellers with limited storage space, Emma Law preferred relish and chutney recipes which did not require canning. Also, she liked to make a smaller amount of some recipes, enough to store in her refrigerator or share with friends. This one has a hint of curry.

Yield: 3 cups

3 medium cooking apples, peeled, cored and coarsely chopped
1 tablespoon lemon juice
½ cup dark molasses
½ cup currants
¼ cup red wine vinegar
2 tablespoons finely chopped or instant minced onion
½ teaspoon ground ginger
½ teaspoon dry mustard
1 tablespoon curry powder
Dash cayenne pepper (optional)
½ teaspoon salt
1 cup apple juice or water

In a medium saucepan, bring all ingredients to a boil. Simmer, stirring often, about 20 to 25 minutes, until thick and apples very tender. Cool and store tightly covered in the refrigerator. Serve with both pork and chicken dishes. You could also use canned apples. May be frozen.

—Emma R. Law

Drawing by Barry Champion

Lime-Tomato Chutney

Yield: 12 pints

12 limes, quartered and
    seeded
10 pounds green tomatoes,
    quartered
8 pounds (18 cups) sugar
3 tablespoons salt

Coarsely grind the limes and tomatoes. Add remaining ingredients and bring to a boil. Simmer for one hour and remove from heat. Cover and let set overnight refrigerated, or in a cool place. Reheat and bring again to a boil. Pour into hot, sterile jars and seal.

Note: For some reason, the overnight setting and reheating makes all the difference in flavor here, so don't omit this step!

—Betty W. Rauers

Ogeechee Peach Chutney

Yield: 5 pints

2 cups vinegar
1½ to 2 cups brown sugar,
    or to taste
4 cups peeled, pitted,
    chopped peaches
1½ cups currants
1 3-ounce package
    crystalized ginger, snipped
    into small pieces
1 tablespoon mustard seed
¼ cup chopped onion
1 garlic clove, finely chopped
    or pressed
Dash red pepper

Bring vinegar and sugar to boil in a large saucepan. Add remaining ingredients and stir well. Cook over medium heat until as thick as desired, stirring frequently. Pour into sterile jars and seal.

Pepper Ketchup

Gather 50 large red peppers. Cut them and take out the seeds with a spoon, avoiding the use of the hands. Put them in a kettle with ½ gallon vinegar and a tablespoonful of salt. Boil until they are well done, and strain, getting as much of the peppers through as possible. Handle carefully.

—Cookbook of Mrs. Lucinda Williams, Milledgeville, 1857

Rosy Chutney

A dish as delicious as it is beautiful in color, by a noted grower of roses in Savannah.

Yield: 1 quart

1 3-inch cinnamon stick, broken into pieces
2 tablespoons mustard seed
10 whole cloves
1½ cups plain red wine vinegar
2¾ cups sugar
2 teaspoons salt
2 cups minced, peeled, and seeded ripe tomatoes
2 cups minced, unpeeled, seeded tart red apples
1 cup minced, peeled onion
1 cup minced, ribbed, and seeded sweet bell peppers
1 cup minced celery (no leaves)

Tie spices in a cheesecloth bag. Place in a large, at least 6 quart, saucepot. Add vinegar, sugar, and salt. Bring to a rolling boil. Lower heat and simmer while preparing remaining ingredients. Remove spice bag. Add minced ingredients all at once to spice mixture. Bring to a boil, lower heat, and simmer, stirring occasionally, until thick and clear— about 30 minutes. Do not allow to scorch. Cool. Refrigerate covered. Will keep indefinitely.

—Millie Fischer

Chutney Hints

When chopping ingredients for chutney, chop the onions and garlic first, and then the milder vegetables such as celery and green pepper, ending with the candied ginger, to remove the scent of onion and garlic from your cutting board and hands.

Chopping parsley, or rubbing it on your hands, will also help remove the scent of onion; so will fresh lemon.

Sweet Pickled Peaches

Take 7 pounds peaches, and either peel them or rub the down off with a coarse cloth. Now to 1 quart of good vinegar, add 1 teaspoon powdered cloves, and some powdered cinnamon, along with three pounds of nice brown sugar. Boil these together, and then pour over the peaches. Boil all together until the peaches are soft, but not broken. Put all covered in a cool place. Once a week for three weeks, pour off the vinegar, and scald the fruit with it. This makes them keep better.

—Bryan family cookbook, Savannah, circa 1885

Dilled Carrots

Yield: about 4 cups

4 medium carrots
1 garlic clove, peeled and
  thinly sliced
½ cup white wine vinegar
1 teaspoon dried dill weed

Peel carrots and cut into medium thin strips. Cook in boiling salted water just until tender, 5 to 7 minutes. Drain and place in a shallow container. Add remaining ingredients. Cover and refrigerate overnight. Drain before serving.

Note: The same recipe may be used with green beans.

Cordele Pickled Peaches

Also known in the Peach State as Peach Pickles.

Yield: about 8 pints

8 cups sugar (2 quarts)
4 cups cider vinegar
1 cup water
1 ounce stick cinnamon
1 teaspoon allspice, or to
  taste (optional)
4 quarts (8 pounds) small
  peaches
½ ounce whole cloves

Boil sugar, vinegar, water, stick cinnamon, and allspice uncovered in a large, heavy kettle for 10 minutes. Peel peaches, but leave whole. Stick 2 whole cloves in each peach. Add peaches to syrup and simmer until tender, about 8 minutes. Remove from heat and cover. Let stand in syrup about 12 hours, or overnight.

Remove peaches and strain syrup to remove cinnamon. Bring to a boil and boil syrup rapidly, uncovered, for 5 minutes. Pack peaches in hot sterile jars and cover completely with hot syrup. Seal. Store in a cool, dry place for several weeks before using.

Note: If peaches are very juicy, omit or cut down on water.

Peaches will peel easily if dropped for a minute in a pan of boiling water, as will tomatoes.

Spiced Currants

Five pounds of currants, four pounds of brown sugar, two tablespoons of cloves, the same of cinnamon, one pint of good vinegar. Boil all together until quite thick.

—*House-Keeping in the Sunny South*,
Atlanta, 1885

Mansfield Dilled Okra

Brought to the South by Africans, okra is often associated with the thick gumbos of the region. It is best when young and tender, two or four inches. Here it is a dilled pickle.

Yield: 6 pints

3 pounds whole young okra
Celery leaves
Garlic cloves to taste
Dill heads, with stems
1 quart water
1 pint vinegar
½ cup salt

Wash okra and celery leaves. Pack okra in hot, sterile pint jars with a few celery leaves, garlic cloves to taste, and dill heads in each jar. Combine water, vinegar, and salt in a large kettle and heat to boiling. Pour over okra. Seal jars. Let stand 3 to 4 weeks before using, to develop flavor.

—Betty Mullins

Pickled Black-Eyed Peas

Known as Southern Caviar, black-eyed peas are popular the year around, but especially on New Year's Day, when they are supposed to bring good luck for the coming year.

Yield: about 6 cups

5 cups cooked, drained
   black-eyed peas
1 cup vegetable oil
¼ cup wine vinegar (may be
   part lemon juice)
1 garlic clove, or garlic
   powder to taste
⅓ cup thinly sliced onion
½ teaspoon salt
1 teaspoon celery seed
⅛ teaspoon black pepper, or
   to taste

Mix ingredients and store covered in refrigerator. If a whole garlic clove was used, check seasoning after 24 hours, and remove garlic if desired. Make at least 2 days before serving. Drain well before serving. Will keep in refrigerator about two weeks.

Note: This can also be done with garbanzos.

The 1853 Green-Meldrim House in Savannah was the home of English cotton merchant Charles Green at the time General W. T. Sherman made his headquarters there in 1864. Later the residence of Judge Peter Meldrim, it was the childhood home of the late Mrs. Sophie Meldrim Shonnard, who generously made her family cookbook available for this book. The elegant mansion is now the Parish House of St. John's Episcopal Church. Drawing by Mark Lindsay. Copyright 1973 by the Lady Print Shop

Mrs. Edward Anderson's Sweet Pickles

1 gallon of the best vinegar; 2 gallons mixed pickles, cutting cucumbers if used; 4 pounds brown sugar; 1 ounce alspice [*sic*]; 1 ounce cloves; 2 ounces celery seed; 1 ounce white mustard seed; one-fourth pound English mustard. [Note: English mustard was a hot, highly seasoned prepared mustard.]

Mix all together, and let come to a boil, keeping covered.

—Family cookbook of Sophie Meldrim Shonnard, Savannah

Emma's Cucumber Relish

Yield: about 4 cups

*1½ teaspoons instant
  chicken bouillon
½ cup water
1 cup vinegar
2 tablespoons dried dill
  weed
1 medium to large cucumber,
  pared and thinly sliced
1 small rib celery, thinly
  sliced
1 small onion, peeled, thinly
  sliced and separated into
  rings
1 small carrot, pared and
  thinly sliced*

In a small saucepan, stir together instant bouillon, water, vinegar, and dill; bring to a boil. In a warm glass jar, layer cucumbers, celery, onion, and carrot; pour the hot marinade over the vegetables. Cover and chill overnight. At serving time, remove vegetables with a slotted spoon.

—Emma R. Law

St. John's Onion Relish

A best-selling recipe from one of the state's famous autumn fund-raisers—cut down for at-home cooks.

Yield: about 3 pints

*14 medium onions (3½
  pounds), peeled and
  quartered
6 sweet bell peppers, ribbed,
  seeded, and quartered
6 fresh red hot peppers, or 3
  dried hot peppers, ribbed,
  seeded, and quartered (see
  note)
1 quart cider vinegar
3 cups sugar
2 tablespoons salt*

Blender-chop prepared vegetables, a few at a time, in water, or use a food processor. Strain into a large bowl. Repeat process until all are chopped. Heat remaining ingredients in a large kettle to boiling. Add vegetables, stirring well, and bring to a boil again. Simmer 15 minutes. Pour into sterilized jars and seal.

Note: In chopping red hot peppers, always wear rubber gloves to protect your hands.

—Annual Bazaar Committee, St. John's
Episcopal Church, Savannah

Golden Isles Pear Relish

Yield: about 8 to 10 half-pint jars

6 pounds pears
6 sweet bell peppers, mixed red and green for color
6 medium onions
4 cups sugar
5 cups vinegar
1 tablespoon allspice
1 teaspoon turmeric
⅛ teaspoon cayenne pepper
2 tablespoons salt, or to taste

Peel about half the pears; leave the rest unpeeled. Core and chop all pears. Take stems, "ribs," and seeds from peppers and finely chop. Peel and chop onions. Combine all ingredients in a large kettle and boil together about 30 minutes, stirring often. Check seasonings. When thick as desired, pour into hot sterile jars and seal.

Cranberry-Prune Relish

Yield: about 1 quart

4 cups fresh cranberries
1 orange, quartered and seeded
1 lemon, quartered and seeded
1 cup plumped pitted prunes, chopped
1½ cups sugar
⅛ teaspoon allspice
1 cup chopped walnuts

Put cranberries, orange and lemon through a food chopper, using coarse blade. Stir in prunes, sugar and spice. Chill several hours, covered. Before serving, mix in chopped nuts.

Note: to plump dry prunes, soak overnight in water, 1 quart to 1 pound prunes. Drain if necessary.

—Barbara Olive

Pickled Eggs

Save the sweet juice from pickled canned beets. Leave shelled hard-cooked eggs in it for at least a day, and serve whole on picnics, or use in salads.

Fish Fry Chow-Chow

A great relish for fish and meats!

Yield: about 1 quart

3 large cucumbers
⅛ cup salt
3 medium onions
1 small sweet bell pepper
1⅛ cups white vinegar
1 cup light brown sugar
1 tablespoon prepared mustard
2 teaspoons ground turmeric
2 teaspoons cornstarch
1 2-ounce jar pimentos, with liquid

Peel and slice cucumbers, about ¼ inch thick. Place in a bowl and sprinkle with salt. Cover and refrigerate overnight. Drain off any liquid. Chop the cucumbers, onions, bell pepper (ribbed and seeded), and set aside.

Combine vinegar and sugar in a large, heavy kettle. Blend together the mustard, turmeric, and cornstarch. Add a little of the vinegar mixture to the dry mixture to make a thin paste. Stir well, and then stir cornstarch paste into vinegar mixture. Bring to a boil, stirring frequently. Add chopped vegetables and bring to a full rolling boil; then add the pimentos and liquid. Cook, stirring constantly, until as thick as desired. Cool. Ladle into a tightly covered container and store in the refrigerator.

Note: If desired, recipe may be doubled, made as above, and ladled into pint jars. Process in a boiling water bath five minutes, according to the directions with your canning equipment.

—Lou Dobbs

Mrs. Winburn's Chow Chow Pickles

½ pint green tomatoes; ½ pint ripe tomatoes; 3 hard cabbages; 2 dozen onions; 6 hot green peppers; 6 hot red peppers. Chop through a meat chopper, and press out until perfectly dry. Then add: 1 teaspoon grated horseradish; two pounds sugar; three tablespoons celery salt; 3 tablespoons plain salt, more if needed; and 1 tablespoon each white mustard seed, ground mustard; ground ginger, and turmeric; mixed dry pickling spices as desired. Cover all with vinegar, and cook one hour.

—Family cookbook of Sophie Meldrim Shonnard, Savannah

Guyton Squash Pickles

Also caled "bread and butter pickles," these are best if chilled before serving.

Yield: 2 quarts

2 quarts small yellow squash, sliced thinly
2 cups thin onion rings
Uniodized salt
2 cups cider vinegar
4 sweet bell peppers, chopped, with ribs and seeds removed
2 teaspoons celery seed
2 teaspoons mustard seed
3 cups sugar

Combine squash and onions, and sprinkle heavily with salt. Let stand one hour. Drain and rinse slightly.

Combine remaining ingredients in a large, heavy saucepan. Bring to a hard boil. Add squash mixture and bring to a hard boil again. Pour hot into hot sterilized jars and seal. Store in a dark, cool place.

—Miriam Conner

Refrigerator Pickles

A crisp cucumber pickle that requires no cooking.

Yield: about 3 quarts

1 cup white wine vinegar
2 cups sugar
1 tablespoon salt
2 teaspoons celery salt
7 cups sliced cucumbers, unpeeled if desired
1 cup chopped onions
1 cup chopped sweet bell peppers, mix red and green for color

Combine first four ingredients well. Pour over mixed vegetables. Refrigerate covered for a few hours. Will keep up to 3 months in the refrigerator.

Note: If you don't want to peel the cucumbers, the unwaxed kind are best to use.

—Jean Baker

Save that Pickle Juice!

Drain and save the liquid from your favorite sweet pickles. Bring to a hard boil over high heat. Pour over small, drained cooked beets to cover. Refrigerate at least 24 hours, covered, before serving, for best results.

—Frank E. Harris, *The Pirates' House Cook Book*

Mrs. Lowe's Pickled Zucchini

Yield: 4 pints

2 pounds zucchini
2 small onions
¼ cup salt
2 cups sugar
2 cups vinegar
1 teaspoon celery seed
2 teaspoons mustard seed
½ teaspoon prepared mustard
1 teaspoon ground turmeric
¼ cup dill weed (optional)

Wash and cut zucchini into thin slices. Peel onions and slice thinly also. Add salt and cover with cold water. Let stand two hours and drain.

Bring remaining ingredients to a boil in a large saucepan. Add zucchini and onions. Remove from heat and let stand two hours. Bring all to a boil again and boil 5 minutes. Remove from heat, pack into hot sterile jars, and seal.

Mrs. Whitehead's Pickles

1 gallon cider vinegar; ½ ounce cloves; ½ ounce nutmeg; ½ ounce celery seed; ½ ounce fine pepper; ¼ pound ginger; ½ pound whole mustard seed; ¼ pound dry mustard; 1 ounce turmeric; handful of alspice [sic]; horseradish, onion and garlic to taste. Mix this all together and store for one month before using. For your vegetables to pickle, put them in water salty enough to bear an egg, for three days. Take them out, and heat salt water to boiling. Pour over them, and leave again until cold. Drain them and put them in this vinegar.

—Family cookbook of Sophie Meldrim Shonnard, Savannah

Fine Tomato Ketchup

Gather ripe sound tomatoes. Cut them in half. Place them in a large vessel, and sprinkle salt over each layer. Let them remain overnight, and in the morning pour off the salt pickle. Boil the tomatoes until they can be mashed through a sieve. Then put them in the preserving kettle. Add to every gallon of tomato juice, one pint of good vinegar; 2 tablespoons of black pepper, ground fine; 3 of mustard; 1 of allspice; 1 onion, chopped fine; and 8 or 10 pods red peppers. Boil slowly for 2 or 3 hours, stirring occasionally. Cork the bottles tightly and seal.

—Bryan family cookbook, Savannah, circa 1885

The Old Governor's Mansion at Milledgeville, Baldwin County, constructed in 1838. One of the few cities in the U.S. designed as a capital, Milledgeville has many elegant homes built between 1803 and 1825 that remain as outstanding examples of Federal period architecture. Although the Union forces under General W. T. Sherman on his infamous "March To The Sea" performed many acts of vandalism in the area in 1864, it was spared the wholesale destruction of cities such as Atlanta. The capital of Georgia was moved to Atlanta in 1868. The elegant stucco and granite mansion was restored in 1967 and is now the home of the president of Georgia College, with portions of it open to the public. Drawing from the Historic Milledgeville series of Sterling Everett

Tomato Mash

Slice a peck of green tomatoes and 12 onions, and let them remain in salt 2 days. Then drain from the juice, and put in a kettle with 1 ounce allspice, 1 of cloves, and one of black pepper. Cover with good vinegar, and boil until quite clear. You may also add if you like, 2 ounces of turmeric, ½ ounce of mustard seed, and some dried mustard to taste.

—Bryan family cookbook, Savannah, circa 1885

Tomali

A favorite old Wanamaker family recipe.

Yield: 12 pints

½ gallon peeled, quartered ripe tomatoes or 4 16-ounce cans, including juice)

4 sweet bell peppers, quartered, with ribs and seeds removed

3 hot peppers, quartered, with ribs and seeds removed (see note)

3 cups sugar

2 teaspoons salt

1½ cups vinegar

Chop tomatoes and peppers coarsely, in a food grinder or processor. Do not use a blender; it chops too fine. Put all ingredients in a large pot and cook until mixture comes to a boil. Turn heat down and simmer, stirring frequently, uncovered, until mixture becomes as thick as desired. Pour into warm, sterile jars and seal.

Note: Be sure to wear rubber gloves when working with the hot peppers, or they will blister your hands.

—Betty W. Rauers

Mamma's Chili Sauce

Take 6 sweet bell peppers; 2 red hot peppers; 24 ripe tomatoes; and 8 onions; 4 cups vinegar; 8 teaspoons salt; 2 teaspoons cinnamon; 2 teaspoons allspice; 2 teaspoons ground cloves; 1 tablespoon celery seed; and ½ heaping cup brown sugar. Remove seeds and ribs from peppers. Chop all vegetables coarsely, and put through a food grinder. Put in a large kettle with vinegar and other ingredients. Boil slowly one hour, or to desired thickness, stirring often. Taste occasionally and add more salt or spices as needed. Makes about 2 quarts.

Note: In working with red peppers, be sure to wear rubber gloves to protect your hands.

—Family cookbook of Sophie Meldrim Shonnard, Savannah

Sweet Tomato Sauce

To two pounds of peeled tomatoes, add one pound of sugar, vinegar to taste, and season with cloves and mace as desired. Cook until well done.

—Bryan Family Cookbook, Savannah, circa 1885

Candler Tomato Ketchup

Yield: about 1 quart

36 medium, ripe tomatoes
  (9 pounds)
1 cup chopped onion
½ cup chopped sweet bell
  pepper
3 tablespoons salt
1 cup sugar
1⅓ cups vinegar
2 sticks cinnamon
½ teaspoon whole cloves
2 teaspoons whole allspice
1½ teaspoons mustard seed
1 teaspoon celery seed

Wash tomatoes, remove the stem end, and cut into pieces. Combine tomatoes with onion and pepper; cook 20 minutes over medium heat, adding a little water if necessary. Press pulp through a fine sieve. Pour liquid into a large kettle along with the salt, sugar, and vinegar. Tie spices loosely in a cheesecloth bag. Add spices to mixture. Boil until thickened, about one hour, stirring to prevent sticking. Remove spice bag. Pour into hot sterile jars and seal immediately.

Tomato Barbecue Sauce

A great way to use up the extra tomatoes in the garden!

Yield: about 1 quart

4 pounds fresh tomatoes
  (about 12 medium), or 4
  16-ounce cans
1 cup chopped onion
2 garlic cloves, finely minced
1 cup brown sugar
4 tablespoons butter or
  margarine
1 cup chili sauce
¼ cup Worcestershire sauce
¼ cup lemon juice
2 teaspoons salt (for fresh
  tomatoes, to taste if you
  use canned)
1 teaspoon dry mustard
Dash nutmeg (optional)

Combine all ingredients in a large saucepan. Bring to a boil. Reduce heat and simmer, uncovered, stirring frequently for about 1½ to 2 hours, or until thickened. Check seasonings. Serve with meats and poultry. Store covered in the refrigerator.

—Chatham County Extension Service

Cut-Up Artichoke Pickles

Cut up 3 quarts artichokes, 3 pounds white cabbage, 1 quart onions, and six green peppers. Soak in a brine of 1 gallon water to two cups of salt, overnight.

In the morning, mix ½ gallon vinegar with 3 pounds sugar, 1 tablespoon black pepper, red pepper to taste, 1 tablespoon turmeric, and 3 tablespoons white mustard seed.

Squeeze vegetables out of brine, and put in sugar-spice mixture after it has come to a boil. Boil for 20 minutes.

Make a paste of ¾ cup flour, one ounce prepared mustard or to taste, and a little of the vinegar, and stir it in. Let boil for 5 minutes.

Take off heat, and put in jars.

—Miss Mary Lou Phinizy, Family cookbook of
Sophie Meldrim Shonnard, Savannah

The Ross-Ellis-McCreary House, built about 1858 in Macon. Drawing by Sterling Everett

Jellies and Preserves

Speaking of Preserves

The word preserve is sometimes used to describe any food processed for future use. Generally, however, it applies to a fruit cooked whole or in large pieces, with sugar to help it hold its shape.

The term fruit butter means a thick, smooth product which spreads easily, but with more fruit in proportion to sugar than in jam.

Jams are crushed fruits and sugar boiled to a thick consistency, while jellies are lighter, generally made of the fruit juice, strained, plus sugar and flavorings.

Marmalade is a mixture—a jelly with pieces of fruit plus rind in it.

Conserves today are generally the richest of all, a jam-like mixture of more than one fruit, and often with nuts or raisins as well.

Whatever the term, a pantry of homemade preserves, pickles, and jellies is the pride of a good cook, whether competing for blue ribbons at the county fair, putting up a few extra jars for the autumn church bazaar, or just to share with family and friends.

Processing Information

For the past few years, some food experts have been urging cooks to process fruit butters, jams, marmalades, preserves, and conserves, so that there will be no danger of spoilage. If you elect to do this, follow the recipe for preparing the food prior to filling the jars, as usual. Then process according to instructions with your canning equipment. This will generally consist of immersing jars on a rack in a canner in boiling water for about 10 minutes.

281

General Directions for Making Jelly and Jam

Prepare fruits as recipe directs. Measure the proper amount of sugar and set aside. Measure the directed amount of prepared fruit into a large pot. Add the pectin and mix in. While mixing, bring to a hard boil and immediately add the sugar. Bring to a hard rolling boil that cannot be stirred down. Boil for 1 minute, stirring constantly.

Remove from heat and skim off foam. Stir again and skim off foam. If making jam, stir and skim for about 5 minutes to cool some, so fruit will stay suspended. Fill hot glasses or jars, leaving about ½ inch space at top. If glasses are being used cover the jam or jelly immediately with about ⅛ inch hot paraffin. If two-piece lids are being used, place lid tightly on jar and invert jar. After all the jars have been filled, stand upright, and cool. Store in a cool place, marking with date and contents.

—Judy Phillips

Mint-Apple Jelly

Yield: about 4 8-ounce jelly glasses

1½ cups packed mint leaves, washed
3¼ cups apple juice
1 1¾-ounce box dry fruit pectin
4 cups sugar
Green food coloring, if desired

Crush the fresh mint leaves (with stems), and combine with juice in a heavy saucepan. Bring to a boil and remove from heat. Cover and allow to stand for about 10 minutes. Strain and return to saucepan. Add dry pectin and bring to a hard boil, stirring constantly. Add sugar. Bring again to a hard rolling boil and boil for 1 minute, stirring constantly. Remove from heat and skim off foam; add food coloring if desired. Continue to stir and skim off foam for a minute or so. Pour into hot, sterile jars, leaving at least ½-inch space at the top.

Apple Jelly

Quarter and boil some sour apples, without peeling the fruit, until it is soft. Pour it into a flannel bag, and hang it to drip. Take to each quart of juice one pound of sugar, and the juice of a lemon. For every two pounds of sugar, add a little rose water if desired. Boil until it turns to a jelly. If it should turn to candy, a small amount more of apple water should be added, and boil a short time longer.

—Cookbook of Mrs. Lucinda Williams, Milledgeville, 1857

Oven Apple Butter

Yield: about 1 quart

3 pounds cooking apples
3½ cups water
1 cup apple cider
2 cups brown sugar
1 small lemon, juice and peel
1 teaspoon ground cloves
1 teaspoon ground allspice
1 tablespoon cinnamon
½ teaspoon nutmeg

Wash and quarter apples. Place in a large pot with the water and cook for about 15 minutes, or until soft. Press through a sieve or purée. Add remaining ingredients and bring to a boil in a large, heavy saucepan. Cook gently for 30 minutes, stirring often. Check flavorings. Pour into an oven-proof dish or casserole, and preheat oven to 300 degrees F.

Bake uncovered for about 2 hours, stirring occasionally. Cool and store in refrigerator: will keep for several weeks. Or pour into hot, sterile jars as soon as you take it from the stove and seal at once. Recipe may be doubled, adjusting seasonings to taste.

Note: You may also peel the apples, and purée after cooking in a blender or food processor.

Pepper-Cranberry Jelly

A beautiful jelly which is especially nice at the holiday season with a buffet of cold meats, or with cream cheese on crackers. A pretty color without food coloring!

Yield: about 4 pints

1 cup red or green hot
peppers, seeded and
chopped
3 cups cranberry juice
cocktail
7 cups sugar
1 cup red wine vinegar
1 6-ounce bottle liquid fruit
pectin

In a blender or food processor, process peppers and juice until peppers are finely chopped. Drain liquid into a large saucepan. Add sugar and bring to a boil. Boil hard while stirring constantly for one minute. Remove from heat and stir in wine vinegar and pectin. Skim. Pour into hot, sterile jars, leaving at least ½ inch headspace. Seal. Let stand several days before serving.

Note: You may use either red or green hot peppers, but do not mix colors or jelly will not be as pretty a color. Pickled red-hot banana peppers may also be used. If jelly is too hot for your taste, next time use part sweet bell peppers. Be sure to wear rubber gloves while working with the peppers!

Atlanta Blackberry Jelly

Boil and strain the juice from your berries. To a quart of juice, put a pound of sugar, and boil until jellied.

—Mrs. H. N. Starnes, *House-Keeping in the Sunny South*, Atlanta, 1885

Miss Julia McCall's Fig Preserves

Gather some nice figs without bruising them, and wash them well. To every pound of figs, add a pound of sugar in a vessel, putting first a layer of figs, then one of sugar, and so forth until vessel is filled. Let stand until morning, then cook like peach preserves.

—Bryan family cookbook, Savannah, circa 1885

Claire's Fig Preserves

Yield: about 1 quart

1½ quarts figs, whole or cut in half and seeds removed
1 cup water
1 lemon, very thinly sliced, seeded; use peel and all
Peel from one orange, finely chopped or grated
1 cup raisins or currants
1 teaspoon ground cinnamon
1 teaspoon ground nutmeg
1 teaspoon ground dried cloves
1 or 2 cups sugar, to taste (see note)
½ cup finely chopped pecans (optional)

Place all ingredients in a large, heavy saucepan. Bring to a boil and turn down heat. Cook until thickened over low heat, stirring occasionally to keep from sticking. This will thicken in approximately 45 minutes, depending on temperature and humidity. Take off heat when it is thick as desired; it will thicken more as it cools.

Allow to cool. Pour into sterile jars, pour melted paraffin over the top, and seal.

Note: Use a few pellets saccharin with the sugar, in order to use less sugar: taste while cooking and add more flavoring as needed.

—Claire Lowell Crosby

The Midway Museum in Liberty County's historic "Children of Pride" country, is a replica of the 1827 Riceboro Inn. (Courtesy Liberty County Historical Society)

Peach County, Georgia

Georgia is not only the Peach State, renowned in song and recipe, but even has a Peach County, created in 1924 in the central part of the state. According to a state highway marker at Fort Valley, "The Georgia Peach is known throughout the nation and beyond. The famous Elberta Peach was developed in Georgia by Samuel B. Rumph, and is widely grown in this area."

Mincemeat with Brandy

If you make this brandied mincemeat before the holiday season, you will have a good supply for pies, tarts, and cookies for yourself and for gifts. It keeps in the refrigerator for a month to six weeks, or for several months in the freezer.

Yield: about 9 pints

3 pounds cooking apples, peeled, cored, and chopped
4 pounds ripe pears, peeled, cored, and chopped
Grated peel and juice of one orange (prefer one without color added)
Grated peel and juice of one lemon
1½ cups seedless raisins
1½ cups currants
1 pound pitted dates, chopped
½ pound dried figs, chopped and stems removed
6 cups brown sugar
1 cup wine vinegar
1 tablespoon ground cloves
1 tablespoon ground nutmeg
1 tablespoon ground allspice
1 tablespoon ground cinnamon
1 teaspoon ground ginger, or finely chopped crystalized ginger, to taste
Brandy as needed

Blend all ingredients except brandy in a large, heavy pot. Cook over medium heat, stirring occasionally, until mixture comes to a good boil. Simmer, stirring occasionally, for about an hour, or until thick as desired. Pour into freezer containers and add about 3 tablespoons brandy to each 2 cups of mincemeat. Stir well. May also be sealed hot in warm sterilized jars. This is better if made at least a month before using.

Note: Rum or whiskey may be used instead of brandy if desired, or ½ dry sherry to ½ brandy, or to taste.

Mince Meat for Pies

Take two large beef tongues, and rub them over with a mixture of equal proportions of salt and brown sugar, with a little powdered cloves mixed in. Let them lie in this in a very cool place until the mixture soaks in, about two days. Boil and skin them. When cold, mince very fine.

Then, mince three pounds of beef suet very fine, and 1½ pounds of citron. Add to this four pounds of washed currants, 1½ pounds [finest] sugar, three pints of Madeira wine, one teaspoon of cinnamon, and one of cloves. Pack all together in a jar, placing a piece of white paper over the top, and pour 1½ pints brandy over the paper and contents. When ready to use, mix minced apples with it, one finely minced apple to each pie. Bake in puff pastry.

—Bryan family cookbook, Savannah, circa 1885

Wrens Nectarine Butter

Nectarines, actually a smaller, smooth-skinned peach, do not appear in many cooked recipes because they do not seem to hold their flavor as well as peaches do if heated. This spicy oven recipe may also be used with peaches, seasoned to taste.

Yield: about 3 pints

4 pounds ripe nectarines
Water as needed
2 cups sugar
¼ cup lemon juice
2 teaspoons grated lemon peel
2 teaspoons ground cinnamon
½ teaspoon ground cloves
½ teaspoon ground nutmeg

Wash, pit, and quarter nectarines. Place in a large, heavy pan and add enough water to half cover fruit. Cover and bring to a boil; then simmer until tender. Preheat oven to 300 degrees F. Purée and strain fruit through a sieve or collander if not smooth enough for your taste. Combine with remaining ingredients, well blended, in a 2-quart baking pan. Bake, stirring every 20 minutes or so, until thick. (Or return to stove and simmer until thick as desired). Spoon into hot sterile jars and seal.

Note: In addition to a good taste, nectarines are a fine source of vitamins A and C.

Drawing and copyright by Barry Champion

Seminole Orange Marmalade

Yield: about 8 6-ounce glasses

6 large oranges (prefer without color added)
Water as needed
Sugar as needed
2 tablespoons lemon juice
2 teaspoons grated lemon peel (optional)

Wash oranges and cut into halves. Remove seeds and stem part. Slice very thin. Add 2 cups water for each cup of cut fruit, and let stand overnight, covered, in a cool place and then simmer until tender. Bring to a full boil in a large, heavy kettle. Add 1 cup sugar for each cup of the cooked mixture. Add lemon juice, and peel if desired, and cook about 20 minutes, or until thick, stirring frequently. Remove from heat and cool 5 minutes, stirring often to prevent larger pieces of fruit from floating on surface. Pour into warm, sterile glasses and seal.

Note: This same recipe may be used with mandarin oranges at Christmas time.

Orange Jelly

Take the peel of sweet oranges, and soak them in salt water 12 hours. Then soak in alum water six hours, and then in clear water until the alum and salt are extracted, changing the water frequently. Make a weak green tea, and spoon over the peel, washing it nicely. To one pound of the peel, allow 1½ pounds sugar. Boil the sugar with some water to make a syrup, and add the peel. Cook slowly until clear, skimming all impurities from the top. When it is done, if the syrup is not thick enough, continue boiling until it is done.

—Bryan family cookbook, Savannah, circa 1885

Gunn Farm Peach Conserve

Yield: 6 8-ounce jars

*4 cups peeled, chopped
    cantaloupe*
*5 cups peeled, chopped
    peaches*
¼ cup lemon juice
1 teaspoon grated lemon rind
6 cups sugar
¼ teaspoon salt
1 teaspoon grated nutmeg
½ cup finely chopped pecans

Combine ingredients in a large, heavy kettle and boil gently about 30 minutes, stirring frequently, until of desired consistency. Ladle into hot, sterile jars and seal.

—Jeanette Gunn

Healthful Peaches

Peaches are not only delicious, but are a good source of Vitamin A. They also contain some Vitamin C, iron and calcium. One medium peach, plain, contains only about 38 calories.

Georgia Peach Jam

Peel and slice peaches. Add ¾ cup sugar for every pound (about 4 medium) of peaches. Also add 2 tablespoons lemon juice and a little grated lemon peel, if desired, for each pound fruit. Place covered in the refrigerator overnight. The next day, pour into a heavy kettle and bring to a boil. Simmer, stirring frequently, until of desired consistency. Pour into hot, sterile glasses and seal, or store covered in the refrigerator.

Auburn Peach-Plum Jam

Yield: about 8 6-ounce jars

*2 pounds peeled, seeded
   sliced peaches*
*1½ pounds seeded, chopped
   ripe plums*
1 tablespoon lemon juice
*2 teaspoons grated lemon
   peel (optional)*
*1 1¾-ounce box dry fruit
   pectin*
6 cups sugar

Chop or grind fruit. Mix with lemon juice, peel, and pectin and bring to a hard rolling boil. Stir in sugar, stirring constantly, and bring again to a hard rolling boil. Boil one minute. Remove from heat. Skim and ladle into hot, sterile, glasses. Cover and seal.

Warm Springs Plum Preserves

Yield: 3 pints

3 pounds small purple plums
4½ cups sugar
½ cup water

Select plums which are ripe and sound, but not too ripe. Remove stems, wash fruit, and pierce each with a fork several times. Place in a glass, china, or pottery bowl or jar, not a metal one. Cover with sugar and add water. Cover and set in a cool place overnight.

In the morning, drain the plums and boil juice for 5 minutes. Add plums and cook until tender. This will only take a few minutes, as syrup thickens on standing. Pour into hot sterile jars and seal.

Plums in the Sun

Many persons find it very difficult to seed Damsons or Blue Plums. With a sharp knife, cut a slit length-wise in each Damson, and set them in the sun for an hour or two. Then the seed slips out without trouble.

—*House-Keeping in the Sunny South*, Atlanta, 1885

Nellie H. Bradham's Pear Preserves

Peel your pears, and slice thinly. Layer in a large pan with sugar between each layer, and leave overnight, covered, in the refrigerator. In the morning, drain, and combine juice with an equal amount of sugar. Bring to a boil, add the pears, and cook thoroughly. Season with nutmeg, cinnamon, ground cloves, and ginger to taste. These will crystalize in the pan as they cook, and be very sweet, spicy, and delicious. You can do the same thing with apples.

—Family cookbook of Stephen Bohlin-Davis, Savannah

Sparta Raspberry-Currant Jam

Yield: about 5 cups

1 pint box red currants
¾ cup water
8 cups raspberries
3½ cups sugar

Wash and stem currants. Crush slightly and add to water in a heavy saucepan. Cook, covered, until currants are soft, about 10 minutes. Drain through a collander or cloth jelly bag to remove seeds and get as much of the pulp as possible. Combine currant juice with raspberries. Bring fruit mixture to a boil and boil uncovered for 10 minutes. Add sugar, bring to a boil again, and boil uncovered for 10 minutes more. Pour into hot, sterile jars. Cool a little and seal.

Lorna's Rhubarb Preserves

Yield: 4 pints

5 cups diced rhubarb
5 cups sugar
1 20-ounce can crushed pineapple, undrained
1 6-ounce box strawberry-flavored gelatin mix

Boil rhubarb, sugar and pineapple together for 20 minutes. Stir in gelatin powder. Cook one minute more, stirring, to dissolve gelatin.

Remove from heat and seal in hot sterile jars, or process as desired.

—Lorna Williams

Strawberry Preserves

Pick the stems off the berries very carefully. The berries are best of the large kind. To every quart of berries, add a quart of sugar. Put the fruit into a preserving kettle, mixed well with sugar. After letting stand 15 minutes, place the kettle on a very slow fire, until the syrup begins to foam. Then add more fire under it, and let it boil quickly, for 15 to 20 minutes, carefully removing the skim as it rises. Put mixture boiling into hot, clean jars until quite full. Cork and seal them tightly, covering each with a piece of linen next to the preserves. Put the jars into a box of sand, and keep very dry. These are quite fine if properly preserved.

—Bryan family Cookbook, Savannah, circa 1885

Freezer Strawberry Jam

Little cooking! A good recipe for the small family who wants just a little fresh jam in berry season.

Yield: 5 cups

4 cups fresh strawberries
4 cups sugar
¾ cup water
1 1¾-ounce box dry fruit pectin

Rinse and hull berries. Crush with a fork or in food processor. Stir in sugar and set aside 10 minutes. Mix water and pectin together in a large, heavy saucepan and bring to a full boil. Boil for one minute, stirring constantly. Pour in fruit and continue cooking and stirring for 3 minutes. Ladle into sterile containers. Cover and let stand at room temperature for 24 hours. Freeze. Will also keep in the refrigerator for several weeks.

Tomato-Sherry Marmalade

Yield: about 3 cups

3 cups tomatoes, skinned and coarsely chopped
3 tablespoons lemon juice
2 teaspoons grated lemon peel
2 cups sugar
6 tablespoons sweet sherry, divided

Combine tomatoes, lemon juice, peel, sugar, and 4 tablespoons sherry and let stand 2 hours. Bring to a boil; cook, stirring frequently, until syrup is thickened. Remove from heat and add remaining sherry. Pour into hot sterile jars. Seal or refrigerate.

Note: Canned tomatoes may also be used. If desired, tomatoes may be put through a colander to remove seeds.

Green Tomato Marmalade

A good use for those end-of-the-season green tomatoes.

Yield: 6 to 7 pints

4 pounds green tomatoes
3 cups sugar
3 lemons, thinly sliced
1 teaspoon Chinese Happy
spices or ½ teaspoon each,
cinnamon and allspice

Peel tomatoes and thinly slice. Cover with sugar and let stand for about 2 hours, using an enamel or stainless steel pot. Stir in lemons and spices. Cook mixture until it thickens, about 25 minutes, stirring frequently, or until 220 degrees F. on the candy thermometer. Strain. Put about a cup of the solid part and a little of the syrup into container of electric blender, or use your food processor. Blend for about 30 seconds; repeat until all solids are blended. Return all blended mixture to remaining syrup. Stir well. Bring to a boil and pour into hot, sterilized jars. Seal.

—Edith Cohen Burr

Tomato Jelly

Peel and weigh the fruit and take an equal amount of sugar. Boil the sugar and some water together, allowing a pint of water to two pounds of sugar, and the white of one egg. Skim syrup well and strain it. Mash the fruit, and remove the seed by straining it through a sieve. Place the pulp and juice, free of seed, into the syrup, and boil until perfectly clear, and the syrup is thick. Season with cloves and cinnamon or with ginger, or with lemon, one to every two pounds. Grate the lemon peel and add. You may also put a little grated ginger in with the lemon.

—Bryan family cookbook, Savannah, circa 1885

Butter Your Jelly Kettle

A little butter on the bottom of your jelly kettle will prevent sticking, and also make the jam clearer. Also, some butter rubbed around the top of the kettle will prevent the mixture boiling over.

The 1818 Williams-Ferguson House, Milledgeville, where Lucinda Park Williams (Mrs. Peter) was living at the time she copied her favorite recipes for her children in 1857. Drawing by Sterling Everett

Ogeechee Limes

Let them stand 24 hours in salt water. Parboil them in two waters, each time changing in cold water, to remove salt. Cook them in a syrup of two pounds of sugar to one of limes, until thick as desired.

—Cookbook of Mrs. Lucinda Williams, Milledgeville, 1857

Watermelon Rind Preserves

Cut the rind, which must be a good thick one, into shapes, as desired. Soak these in salt water for two days, then in alum water one day. Then soak it in cold water all night, and boil in a weak sugar syrup until the salt is all extracted. To every pound of fruit, put two pounds of sugar, and bits of orange peel, along with some ground ginger. Boil together until sufficiently thick.

—Bryan family cookbook, Savannah, circa 1885

Potpourri

Yesterday's Potpourris

Potpourri—A mixture of flower petals and spices, which can be easily made at home. It was particularly popular in Victorian and Edwardian times, when bowls of potpourri (silver ones, preferably), stood in all the best drawing rooms, giving the air a lovely, haunting fragrance.

—Women's Day Encyclopedia of Cookery

Baldwin County Potpourri

Yield: about 6 cups

6 cups dried rose petals
¼ cup fresh mint leaves
½ teaspoon each ground cloves, cinnamon, allspice, rosemary, and nutmeg
1½ tablespoons orrisroot, available at pharmacies

Pick the freshest blossoms of as many varieties of roses as possible. Separate the petals, and lay them in single layers on paper towels or cloths in the bottom of cardboard boxes. Place in a dry, shady spot for 3 to 4 days (a covered porch is perfect), or until very dry. Do the same with the mint leaves. Mix in a large container with the spices and orrisroot. Pack into a large jar, and cover tightly. Let stand for 4 to 6 weeks, stirring every 2 to 3 days. (Don't forget it!)

At the end of that time, potpourri may be tied in little cloth bags, decorated with a pretty ribbon, and used to scent drawers. It may also be placed in attractive little jars: when the lid is removed, it scents the room. These make nice and personal gifts.

Benne Granola

Better than the commercial variety, and not as sweet, this is also excellent in cookies!

Yield: about 5 cups

2 cups quick-cooking rolled
    oats
1 cup wheat germ
3 tablespoons benne
    (sesame) seeds
1 cup grated coconut
½ cup slivered almonds
¾ cup raisins or currants
½ cup dates, chopped and
    seeded
¼ teaspoon ground
    cinnamon
⅛ teaspoon ground cloves
⅛ teaspoon ground ginger
½ teaspoon salt
¾ cup molasses
⅓ cup vegetable oil
1 teaspoon vanilla extract

Preheat oven to 300 degrees F. Mix all dry ingredients in a large bowl, stirring well, and then add molasses, oil, and vanilla. Mix well. Spread on lightly greased shallow baking pans and bake for about 30 minutes, stirring often. Cool and store in an airtight container in a very cool place.

—Dr. Dottie Tate, University of Georgia
Extension Service

Versatile Wheat Germ

Rich in vitamins and protein, wheat germ can add flavor and nutrition when used with flour or bread crumbs in breading meat or fish; as a crumb topping on casseroles; on cereals; sprinkled on chef's salads; mixed with meatball and meatloaf dishes; blended in sandwich spreads; as a pudding or ice cream topping; or added to the batter of pancakes, hot breads, and cookies, at the ratio of 2 tablespoons per cup of flour. Plain wheat germ is preferred for main dish recipes. If you use honey-flavored wheat germ, subtract a little sugar from the recipe.

Toasted Pecans

When a recipe calls for toasted pecans, pour shelled halves into a shallow pan. Add enough vegetable oil, 1 or 2 tablespoons, to coat well. Salt to taste. Preheat oven to 325 degrees F. Toast until brown, watching carefully after the first 8 minutes, as pecans scorch easily.

Blender Peanut Butter

Yield: about 1 cup

1 cup roasted shelled
  peanuts, without skins,
  crushed or chopped
2 tablespoons peanut oil, or
  to taste
½ teaspoon salt, if nuts are
  unsalted, or to taste
1 or more teaspoons honey
  (optional)
1 tablespoon wheat germ, or
  to taste (optional)

Place nuts and 1 tablespoon oil in the blender or food processor. Blend until smooth, gradually adding more oil to reach desired consistency. Add salt, honey, and wheat germ to taste. Store covered, and stir well before using.

Boiled Peanuts

Wash shelled raw peanuts thoroughly. Place in a saucepan and cover with water. Add about ¼ box salt, or to taste, for 5 pounds peanuts.

Cook until firm but tender, at least one hour. Taste. Add more salt if needed. Leave in salted water for another 10 minutes or so, to absorb salt. When salty enough, drain well. They may be eaten warm, at room temperature, or chilled. May be frozen and reheated in boiling water as needed.

It ain't Peanuts!

Georgia is the nation's number one peanut-producing state, with about one-third of the country's peanut acreage. Georgia produces nearly half the nation's peanuts, and peanuts are Georgia's leading cash row crop. They are grown commercially in 80 of its 159 counties. Georgia is also the leading source of peanuts for peanut butter and is the home of the world's largest such plant.

Peanuts are not really a nut, but a pea derived from a tender annual vine of the legume family. They were first grown in South America, taken to Africa by missionaries, and then brought to the New World on the slave ships. Peanuts were given a boost nationally in popularity by the Civil War, and the spread of baseball. The first peanut butter appeared in the 1890s.

Roasted Peanuts, Southern Style

Spread shelled or unshelled peanuts in a shallow pan. Preheat oven to 300 degrees F. and roast 30 to 45 minutes. Stir several times for even baking, and start checking for doneness after 30 to 35 minutes.

They will still look pale but will turn browner as cooled. Peanuts with the shells on will take a little longer to roast.

Breakfast Treat

Start the day right, no matter how hurried you are, with a glass of milk blended with an egg and peanut butter, and a little sugar and salt added to taste.

Peanutty Oatmeal

For a new taste, stir chopped dried apples into hot oatmeal, with some peanut butter and raisins. Serve with brown sugar and a dash of cinnamon.

Peanutty Touches

Add a dash of peanut butter to potato pancakes, hot broccoli, baked sweet potatoes, and salad dressings.

Mix it in baked or cooked custards.

Combine it with raisins or currants in a sandwich spread, or mix with vanilla flavored or plain yogurt, and raisins, for a lunch break.

Peanut butter rubbed in a child's hair will help remove chewing gum.

Grunch

A wholesome snack!

Yield: about 5 cups

1 cup dark raisins
1 cup golden raisins
2 cups assorted dry roasted nuts
1 cup dried apricots, cut into quarters

Combine, tossing lightly. Keep in an airtight container. May be varied with different nuts and other dried fruits, or even some M&Ms.

The handsome Federal style Davenport House in Savannah was built about 1815-1820, and is now a house museum operated by Historic Savannah Foundation. This drawing by Pamela Lee shows it decorated for the annual Christmas tours

Low Country Christmas

Down in the low country of the Georgia coast, when I was a boy, we never had a white Christmas, but this didn't bother us. We liked our Decembers the way they were, camellias glowing like rubies in their glossy foliage, sunlight like a golden rug on the amber pine needles. Spanish moss stirring faintly in the soft air. If we had stopped to think about it, we'd probably have considered all this snow-and-sleigh-bells stuff some kind of Yankee hoax. After all, there hadn't been any snow at Bethlehem, had there?

—Arthur Gordon, "Low Country Christmas,"
Woman's Day Encyclopedia of Cookery, 1967

Christmas Wreaths

Yield: 24 3-inch wreaths, or
   1 large one

½ cup (1 stick) butter or
   margaine
36 large marshmallows
1 teaspoon vanilla extract
2 teaspoons green food
   coloring, or as needed
4 cups (1 quart) cornflakes
Red cinnamon or gumdrop
   candies

Melt margarine and marshmallows in a double boiler over warm water, or in a heavy 2-quart saucepan over very low heat. Add vanilla and food coloring. Stir into cornflakes in a large mixing bowl, and toss until cereal has a green color. With greased hands, either shape one large wreath or several small ones, working on a large piece of waxed paper, kitchen parchment paper, or tinfoil, taped down at the ends so it won't slide. Decorate as desired with candy "berries." Allow to harden before eating. (To speed the process, place wreath on a cookie sheet in the refrigerator.) This makes an attractive centerpiece or place card holder for a child's party at the holiday season, or table decoration.

Popcorn Cake

Popcorn is an inexpensive treat, and fun to make in an electric popper or the old-fashioned way over the open fire. One cup unpopped corn equals 5 cups popcorn.

Yield: 1 9- or 10-inch tube
   cake

1 cup sugar
½ cup cold water
¼ cup white corn syrup
1½ tablespoons butter or
   margarine
4 quarts popped popcorn
Nuts, chocolate bits, and
   gumdrops as desired

Combine first four ingredients in a heavy 1-quart saucepan, and cook over medium heat to 240 degrees F. on the candy thermometer, or soft ball stage (see Candy Stages, page 264). Pour over popped corn and mix completely.

Pack into a well-greased angel food tube pan, using greased hands if desired. (The 2-part pans are easier to unmold). Place chopped nuts, chocolate or butterscotch bits, and candies as desired between layers. Decorate with cut-up gumdrops. Chill until solid. Remove from pan and allow guests to break off pieces with a fork. Use varied colors to carry out a theme for a holiday.

Caramel Popcorn Balls

Yield: about 15 balls

1 14-ounce package caramels
3 tablespoons water
1 tablespoon butter or
  margarine
Dash cinnamon or nutmeg
2½ quarts popped popcorn

Combine caramels, water, and butter in a heavy saucepan. Heat over medium heat, stirring occasionally, until melted. Add spice to taste. Pour over popcorn, tossing lightly to coat evenly. Shape into balls with lightly greased hands. When cool, store in airtight container in a cool place.

Cheesy Popcorn

Yield: 2 quarts

2 quarts popped popcorn
3 tablespoons melted butter
  or margarine
¼ teaspoon celery salt
¼ teaspoon garlic salt
½ teaspoon onion powder
2 cups grated Cheddar
  cheese

Preheat oven to 300 degrees F. Pour popcorn into a shallow casserole or large pan. Toss well with remaining ingredients. Place in oven about 10 minutes, or long enough to melt cheese, stirring occasionally.

Pizza Variation: Follow above directions, tossing corn with ¼ cup melted butter or margarine; ¼ cup grated Parmesan cheese; and ½ teaspoon each garlic salt, onion powder, celery salt, crushed oregano, and crushed basil, or to taste. When cool, store in airtight cans in a cool place.

Nutty Corn

Yield: 6 cups

1 cup pecans
1 cup almonds
1 to 2 tablespoons vegetable
  oil
Salt to taste
4 cups popped popcorn
½ cup brown sugar
½ cup butter

Preheat oven to 325 degrees F. Spread nuts in a shallow roasting pan with oil to coat well. Add salt. Toast until golden brown, about 10 minutes. (Pecans burn easily, so check after 8 minutes). Mix with popped corn.

Meanwhile, in a small saucepan over medium heat, combine and melt sugar and butter. Stir into popcorn, with more salt if desired. When cool, store covered in a cool place.

Popcorn Decorations

For Christmas garlands, keep popped corn warm in a 200-degrees F. oven so it will be easier to work with, take out a little at a time, and separate into two or three kernel clusters on foil or waxed paper. Cool until firm. String on coarse white thread or double waxed thread, using a strong needle.

To make a star, take a portion of the warm popcorn mixture out of the oven and form into a flat star shape on a foil-covered cardboard pattern about 8 inches across. Insert a 10-to-12-inch long wooden dowel halfway up the star pattern to use to secure the star to the top of the tree. Press gently to star shape; cool until firm. If you only want a table centerpiece, you don't have to use a dowel. Decorate as desired with food coloring or gum candies.

Christmas Dough Decorations

Fun to make for that "country Christmas" look!

Yield: over 3 cups dough

1 cup salt
2 cups flour (not self-rising)
1 cup water

Preheat oven to 325 degrees F. Combine salt and flour; mix well. Add water a little at a time, mixing as added, to form a ball of dough. Knead about 10 minutes on a floured surface, or until dough is smooth and firm. Place dough that won't be used right away in a plastic bag to keep it from drying out.

Roll dough, a little at a time, about ¼-inch thick. Cut with cookie cutters into desired shapes. Punch a tiny hole in each for the string later on.

Bake for about 30 minutes on a greased cookie sheet. Cool on a rack and decorate as desired. If you want a natural flour look, use whole-wheat flour and brush with egg or milk during baking for a golden, shiny look.

When shapes are dry, paint with acrylic paints as desired. Dry well. Spray with a clear spray or varnish to seal. Hang on the tree with gold or other metallic cord, ribbon, or yarn. To store, wrap each in plastic, and tie in an air-tight plastic bag. Stored in a cool place, they should be ready for next year. These also make nice before-Christmas gifts.

—Susan Grant and Debra Rogalski

Candy Ornaments

Another homemade specialty: the stained glass look!

Yield: about 15 large or 25
small ornaments

2 cups sugar
1 cup honey or corn syrup
½ cup water
1 teaspoon vanilla extract
Food coloring as desired

Butter or oil cookie cutters that are open at both top and bottom, or metal candy molds. Place on a well-greased baking sheet. Place a nylon string loop under each cutter or mold, to hang from the tree.

Combine sugar, honey, and water in a heavy 2-quart saucepan. Cook, stirring constantly, until sugar dissolves, scraping down the sides of the pan to get all the sugar crystals. Cook at that point without stirring again until 300 degrees F. on the candy thermometer, or hard crack stage (see Candy Stages, page 264).

Remove from heat and stir in extract and coloring. Using a large wooden spoon and, working quickly, spoon candy into cookie cutters about ¼-inch deep, or fill molds with mixture. If candy cools too fast to pour, stir over low heat again just enough to melt.

Allow candy to harden thoroughly before removing from molds.

Note: In place of vanilla extract, you may want to use lemon for yellow candy, lime or peppermint for green, spearmint for red, etc. For red candy, cranberry juice may be used in place of water, or fruit juice for other colors and flavors.

The "Jingle Bells" City

A marker in Savannah's Troup Square celebrates the fact that James Lord Pierpont (1822—1893,) was living in the city at the time his popular winter song, first titled "One Horse Open Sleigh," was copyrighted in 1857. Pierpont, a native of Boston, served with a Confederate cavalry regiment during the War Between The States, and is buried in Savannah. Though he wrote sentimental ballads, minstrel music and Confederate tunes, only his immortal "Jingle Bells" (retitled in 1859) has survived him. He was also the uncle of financier J. P. Morgan.

Useful Flowers

You may some day have a garden of your own—if you do not already—and then you will be able to grow all your own herbs for cooking and for medicines . . . such as rosemary, which is good for the hair. . . . Carnations were formerly steeped in casks of wine to flavor the wine. Sunflower seeds roasted and ground make a sort of coffee, and uncooked are food for fowls. They are also a cure in whooping-cough. . . . Dandelion tea is a tonic, and good for one's liver.

"How Girls Can Help Their Country,"
Handbook For Girl Scouts by W. J. Hoxie, 1913

Thyme On Your Hands

If you don't already know the joy of growing and using fresh herbs, now is the time to plant some in your garden, in pots on your kitchen sill, and in hanging baskets. Make those greens useful as well as ornamental! Pots of basil on outdoor dining tables repel insects. Parsley is a biennial that stays green all winter and lasts for two seasons. Eating parsley also seems to sweeten the breath!

Hanging baskets of thyme, rosemary, sweet marjoram, parsley, pennyroyal, and some mints are especially attractive—and so handy!

Basil seems to enhance the flavor of almost everything—try some in your next omelet! It is excellent with tomatoes, essential for spaghetti sauce, and good with fish, salads, and vinegar combinations.

Chervil is also good in omelets. Try about one teaspoon mixed basil and chervil per egg, along with a little minced fresh parsley or chives. If you must use dried, use ¼ teaspoon total, along with the fresh chopped parsley or chives.

Cool Lunch

For a quick, cool summer lunch, combine a can of cream of celery soup, an equal amount of milk, a sprig of fresh thyme, and a slice of onion in the blender, along with 3 crushed ice cubes.

For summer sandwiches, add a few leaves of mint marigold. It is also excellent in cottage cheese, along with fresh parsley.

Bay is for Winners

Herbs add flavor to meals with few calories and less dependence on salt. Their worth has been recognized since ancient times. Rosemary was worn by brides for good fortune, sage was thought to prevent aging, dill was depended on to avert the evil eye, basil meant good wishes, and of course—bay was for winners.

Herb Butters

Soften a stick of butter. Stir in 1½ tablespoons of minced fresh herb, or dried herbs to taste. Lemon juice (1 teaspoon or to taste), may also be added. Some herbs to try are French tarragon, marjoram, parsley, rosemary, sage, dill, chives, basil, and thyme. Try them one at a time or in combination, labeling each, so you'll know your favorites. They are better a day or so after making, and will keep refrigerated for two weeks, or indefinitely in the freezer.

Herb butters are wonderful for seasoning poultry, fish, and meats. They may also be used in hot vegetables, including mashed potatoes, and for toasted breads.

For biscuits, dip each in a little melted herb butter before baking. Or after baking, split each, spread with herb butter, and toast—great for left-overs.

Before heating French bread, spread slices with herb butter, and then wrap in foil and heat. If you bake bread, add a favorite herb or two, 1 tablespoon per cup of flour, and proceed with the recipe.

—Lane Furneaux

Cooking with Spirits

The nice thing about cooking with alcoholic beverages is that much of the alcohol evaporates during the cooking process, leaving behind a distinctive flavor and a few of its calories.

However, do not use "cooking sherry." Cook only with a wine or liquor that you would want to drink. So-called "cooking sherries" are much too salty, allegedly from the time when extra salt was added to keep the kitchen help from drinking them.

Here are a few recipe hints from Savannah hostess Betty W. Rauers, who says she got them from a liquor store owner:

Rub the inside of your roasting bird with lemon juice and brandy—the outside, too!

Near the end of the cooking time, baste fried chicken with bourbon.

Rub a steak with vermouth before you broil it.

Whip a stick of soft butter with 3 tablespoons water and 3 tablespoons cream sherry to make a super spread for raisin bread.

Beat softened cream cheese together with some dry white wine and serve over fresh strawberries or peaches for an easy and delicious dessert.

Plant Tonic

This mixture, created by the Dow Company, gives strength and color to house plants.

Yield: 1 gallon

1 teaspoon Epsom salts
1 teaspoon baking powder
1 teaspoon saltpeter
½ teaspoon household
  ammonia
1 gallon water

Combine, and use weekly as desired. Store in a covered container, such as an old milk jug.

Saving Roses

Tests show that long-stemmed roses last up to four times longer in the home if placed in vases containing equal parts warm tap water and Sprite or 7-Up (not diet variety). It's the combination of sugar, citric acid, and carbonation that does it.

As soon as you receive roses, cut the stems on an angle while holding them under water. It helps the ends take up more water.

Plant Hints

Don't throw out that half can of stale soda. Your plants will enjoy it.

Weak tea is occasionally good for plants; so is the water in which eggs have been boiled.

African Violets will flourish with the tea from tea bags, and crushed egg shells, rubbed into their soil.

Some like to plant a bud or clove of garlic in the same pot as a houseplant, to keep pests away.

Candle Time

If candles are chilled in the refrigerator for several hours before using, they will drip less.

Hose Hints

A little vinegar added to the water in which hose are washed, will increase elasticity and make them wear longer.

Pantyhose with runs may still be worn under slacks. Mark the tops with an "X" with marking pencil, so you won't mix them with good ones.

The Uncle Remus Museum in Turner Park, Eatonton, is a log cabin made of two early Putnam County buildings moved to the site. It houses mementoes of the plantation childhood of Joel Chandler Harris, (1848—1908) who was born nearby. Harris was the creator of the Uncle Remus stories which, it is said, "made the lowly cabin fires light the far windows of the world." Drawing by Julia Jenkins

Play Clay

Yield: about 3 cups

½ cup salt
1½ cups water
2 tablespoons powdered alum
1 tablespoon vegetable oil
2½ cups flour
Food coloring (optional)

Heat salt and water in a 2-quart pan until salt is dissolved. Remove from heat and stir in remaining ingredients in order listed. Knead well to make a soft dough, adding a little more oil as necessary. Add color as desired. Store in an airtight container.

Recipe for Making Soft Soap

Take 6 pounds of potash, 4 pounds lard or pure grease, and ½ pound hard rosin. Beat up the rosin. Mix all well together, and set aside for 5 days. Then put the whole in a 10 gallon cask of warm water, and skim twice a day for 10 days. At the expiration of that time, you will have 100 pounds of excellent soap.

Mrs. Matthew's Recipe for Colored Clothes

Take half a pound of turpentine soap, half a pound of sal soda [baking soda], five pints of water, and mix and boil for 20 minutes. This will yield you five pounds of fine soap.

—Family cookbook of Mrs. Lucinda Williams, Milledgeville, 1857

Mildew Removal Mix

Yield: about a gallon

1 quart bleach
1 cup Tide or Spic'n Span
⅔ cup soilax (TSP)
3 quarts water

Mix well and use on walls and woodwork, inside and out. Be sure to rinse surfaces well with clear water immediately after using. Wear rubber gloves.

Spring Cleaning Time

A mixture of sour milk or buttermilk and baking soda, rubbed on as a paste, will polish copper or brass pots and pans.

Give your jewelry an occasional bath in a solution of 1 quart warm water to 1 tablespoon ammonia. Use in a well-ventilated place.

The paste type of silver polish will also clean formica tops and take tea stains out of plastic containers and china. Rinse well.

Camphorated oil rubbed into furniture will often remove water marks.

—*Congregational Meeting House of White Bluff
Cookbook,* Savannah

Index